CW01649532

ESSENTIAL HOME MAINTENANCE

tasks, tools & techniques

ESSENTIAL HOME MAINTENANCE

tasks, tools & techniques

• Over 100 common household jobs expertly explained and illustrated with step-by-step instructions • Authoritative and practical advice on general do-it-yourself techniques, with more than 1000 photographs • Detailed guidance on tools and equipment and how to use them

Consultant Editor: John McGowan

HERMES HOUSE

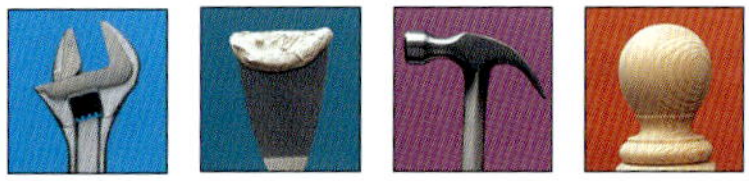

This edition is published by Hermes House

Hermes House is an imprint of Anness Publishing Ltd
Hermes House, 88–89 Blackfriars Road, London SE1 8HA
tel. 020 7401 2077; fax 020 7633 9499
www.hermeshouse.com; www.annesspublishing.com

A CIP catalogue record for this book is available from the British Library.

Publisher: Joanna Lorenz
Editorial Director: Judith Simons
Project Editor: Felicity Forster
Text: Diane Carr, Sacha Cohen, Mike Collins, David Holloway and Mike Lawrence
Illustrators: Peter Bull and Andrew Green
Photographers: Peter Anderson, Colin Bowling, Jonathan Buckley, Sarah Cuttle, Rodney Forte, John Freeman, Andrea Jones, Debbie Patterson, Lucinda Symons and Jo Whitworth
Editor: Ian Penberthy
Designer: Bill Mason
Production Controller: Wendy Lawson

Previously published as part of a larger volume, *Complete Do-It-Yourself*

1 3 5 7 9 10 8 6 4 2

CONTENTS

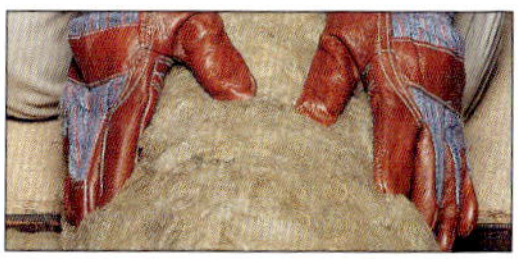

INTRODUCTION

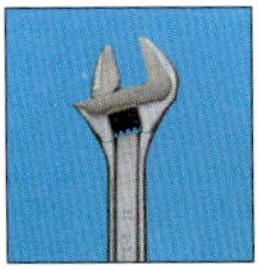

In recent years, the advent of the do-it-yourself superstore, the development of tools and materials aimed specifically at the amateur, and the proliferation of TV makeover shows have meant that when a job needs doing in or around the home, we no longer automatically reach for the telephone to call in a professional. We ask if we can do it ourselves, and more often than not, the answer is "yes". Today there are many home maintenance, repair and improvement tasks that can be done by anyone with a practical frame of mind. The major advantage is a saving in money, but that's not always the prime reason for tackling a job. There is an immense amount of satisfaction to be gained from learning a new skill and, most of all, being able to stamp your own personality on your home.

SAFETY AND TOOLS

The most important requirements for any do-it-yourself job, even the simplest, are an understanding of the potential dangers involved and to take steps to protect not only yourself, but others around you. Many tasks involve the use of sharp tools, electrical equipment or ladders, but there are other less obvious risks, such as injuries caused by lifting or dropping heavy objects, or work on areas that are difficult to reach. Always keep safety uppermost in your mind whatever you do.

ABOVE: Having the right tools will make any job go smoothly. As you learn new do-it-yourself skills, you can obtain the relevant special tools; look after them and they'll last a lifetime.

Ensuring you have the right tools for the job will be a big help in carrying out the task safely. Never scrimp when buying tools; get the best you can afford and look after them. They'll pay you back with a lifetime's service.

WOODWORK IN THE HOME

One of the commonest and most versatile materials found in the home is wood, which has many structural and decorative uses; in some cases, the entire house may be built on a wooden framework. Certainly, the doors and windows are likely to have wooden frames, and the rooms will have wooden skirtings (baseboards), architraves (trims) surrounding door openings and possibly wooden dado (chair) and picture rails. Then, of course, there is the furniture.

Wood has so many uses that most do-it-yourselfers will regularly encounter woodworking tasks. Fortunately, many jobs can be carried out with the minimum of specialist skills and tools, and wood is a forgiving material to work with. As experience is gained, quite complex woodworking projects may be tackled with confidence.

SHELVES AND STORAGE

Without a variety of storage facilities, our homes would soon become cluttered with our belongings, but it is also true that no two homes will have the same requirements for storage; it depends on individual circumstances. Consequently, tailoring storage to suit specific needs is essential to achieve the most efficient solution to the problem. Shelves, cupboards and drawers all have a role to play, and the combination of these elements must be determined in the light of what items have to be stored.

In addition, storage can take the form of freestanding pieces of furniture or built-in structures that make the most of available space within the home. The latter can be made successfully by the do-it-yourselfer, as can pieces of furniture – normally purchased ready-made or in self-assembly form – provided care is taken.

HOME REPAIRS

It makes sense to look after your home; it's likely to be the biggest investment you ever make. Regular maintenance will do much to keep it in good condition, but from time to time

BELOW: Building your own storage allows you to tailor it exactly to your needs.

ABOVE: Doors can be rehung to change the way they open, requiring the furniture to be repositioned.

more ambitious repair work may be required. This may be necessary for a variety of reasons: you may need to make good walls after removing old fittings, or cracks may have developed, internal woodwork may have become damaged, or floorboards or stairs may have become worn and loose. Moving items, such as doors and windows, also can suffer from wear and tear. All can be repaired effectively provided you have the correct tools and knowledge.

HOME INSULATION

These days, few can be unaware of the importance of keeping energy consumption in our homes to a minimum. Not only does this have a positive effect on our pockets, but also it prevents the wastage of fossil fuels, the burning of which contributes so much to global warming.

The efficient insulation of our homes is essential to prevent loss of heat, and a variety of techniques can be used to achieve this. The roof, walls, windows, doors and floors can all be protected. Fortunately, the methods are well within the scope of the do-it-yourselfer, providing even more savings.

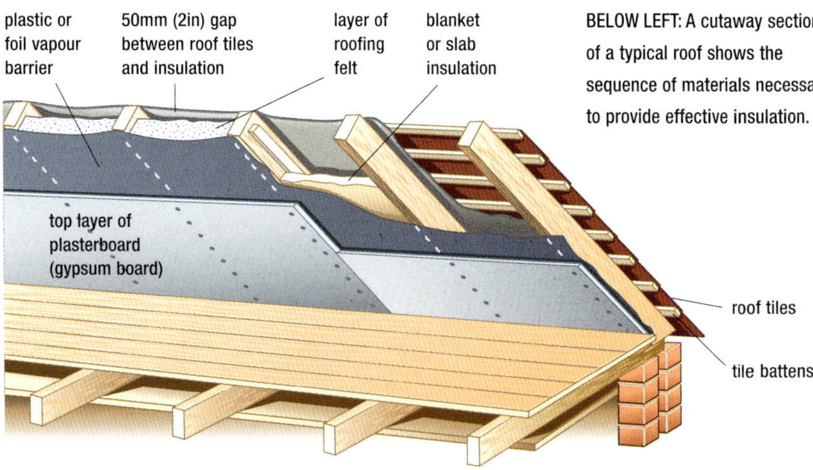

BELOW LEFT: A cutaway section of a typical roof shows the sequence of materials necessary to provide effective insulation.

Draughtproofing is essential as well, to prevent cold air from entering the house, but must be teamed with ventilation to allow moist air to escape, otherwise damage may be caused by condensation.

ABOVE: Freezing water that has seeped into walls can cause damage to brickwork. Repointing the joints with fresh mortar minimizes this damage. A hosepipe will give a concave profile.

OUTDOOR REPAIRS

The biggest cause of maintenance and repair work around your home is the weather. Sun, rain, frost, snow and wind all combine to carry out a relentless attack on the exposed exterior structures. And once they begin to break down protective finishes or get into the raw materials, the rate of decay accelerates. Where the maintenance of your home's exterior is concerned, there is no room for complacency; immediate action is essential as soon as you notice a problem. Fortunately, much outdoor maintenance and repair work is well within the abilities of most do-it-yourselfers, although particular care is needed to ensure that the weather is kept at bay.

IN THIS BOOK

In the following pages you'll find a comprehensive collection of do-it-yourself techniques that will allow you to tackle just about any job you come across in and around the home. If you study the step-by-step photographs and follow the simple text, you'll soon learn the skills you need to give your home a personality that matches your own at a fraction of the cost of employing the professionals.

RIGHT: Crazy paving repair jobs may require re-laying quite large areas, using new slabs. The joints should always be well mortared. Once finished, the paving looks best when cleaned with a pressure washer.

DEWALT

SAFETY & TOOLS

- Safety & preparation
- Measuring, shaping & cutting tools
- Assembling & finishing tools

INTRODUCTION

Most people have a few basic tools in their home: a hammer, a screwdriver or two, perhaps a saw of some sort and a couple of paintbrushes – just about enough to tackle the occasional simple job or essential temporary repair. The more competent are likely to have a more comprehensive basic toolkit containing such items as a retractable tape measure, a craft knife, adjustable spanner (wrench), hand and tenon saws, a spirit (carpenter's) level, screwdrivers for different types of screw head, perhaps a chisel or two, pliers, pincers, an electric drill and a variety of decorating tools.

ABOVE: A power drill makes drilling easy. Buy one that offers a choice of speeds, has a chuck capacity of at least 12mm (½in), and a hammer facility if you intend drilling masonry.

ABOVE: Mounting your tools on a perforated tool board is a good idea. You will be able to find what you need quickly, and it will be obvious when a tool is missing. Buy one or make your own.

Some people, of course, are determined do-it-yourselfers who gain much pleasure and satisfaction from doing as many jobs as they can around the home. Others may even have a practical hobby, such as woodwork or model-making, that requires a dedicated home workshop containing a variety of complex and versatile machinery together with a range of specialized hand tools.

Whatever your level of interest in do-it-yourself, choosing the right tools for each job you tackle is essential. Attempting any task without the proper tools is a recipe for disaster.

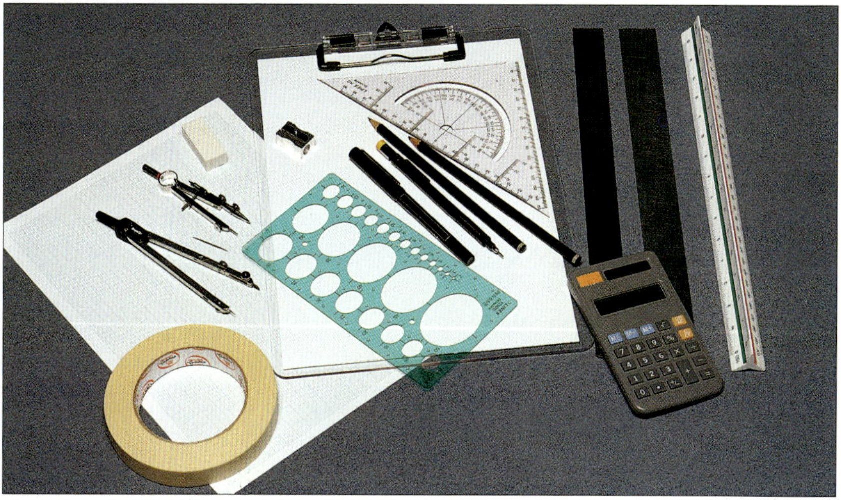

ABOVE: Graph paper, masking tape, pairs of compasses, set squares, pencils and rulers will prove invaluable when planning your projects, and a calculator is useful for converting measurements.

LEFT: A belt sander is useful for heavy-duty shaping and sanding. As well as being hand-held, it can be inverted and secured in a woodworking vice.

Most toolkits grow organically as specific tools are added when the need arises. The tools featured in this chapter show a useful selection for starting your own projects.

When buying tools, always go for the best you can afford; the adage, "You get what you pay for," is particularly appropriate. Cheap tools may bend or break and are unlikely to last long; good-quality tools will last you a lifetime. If your budget is tight, it is best to buy several hand tools rather than one power tool. This has the benefit of improving your manual skills at an early stage, which will give encouraging results as well as increase the range of jobs you can undertake.

USING PROFESSIONALS

As a do-it-yourself enthusiast, you have to be familiar with several trades, but it is often well worth employing a professional for structural work to save time and possibly money. There are many jobs, especially in plumbing and electrics, where professional help is welcome and indeed necessary. Professionals can also advise you in advance if your project is likely to fail for a reason you may not even have considered.

SAFETY & PREPARATION

Even the simplest of do-it-yourself jobs carries with it some degree of risk, if only the chance of losing your balance on a chair. Some tasks, however, have the potential to cause serious injury, so safety should be uppermost in your mind at all times. You must use the proper tools in the correct manner, wear appropriate clothing, ensure you have safe access to the job and take steps to protect others. Storing your tools correctly is important, too. Not only will they be ready for use when you need them, but they will also be protected from damage and from damaging other tools. Completing any do-it-yourself task can be immensely satisfying; the following pages show you how to do so in the safest possible way.

AWARENESS AND CLOTHING

A complete book could be devoted to the subject of safety in the home, and there is a wide range of equipment designed to minimize our capacity for hurting ourselves. Nevertheless, there is one requirement that we cannot buy, without which all that equipment is virtually useless, namely concentration. This is particularly important when working alone.

ABOVE: Wear overalls to protect your clothes when painting, decorating or carrying out any dirty or dusty job. Disposable types are available for one-off jobs.

AWARENESS

Concentration is essential when using any form of power tool, especially a saw, where one slip can mean the loss of a finger, or worse. The dangers of accidents involving electricity are well documented, as are those involving falls from ladders, spillages of toxic materials, and burns and injuries caused by contact with fire or abrasive surfaces. In almost every case, there is a loss of concentration, coupled with poor work practices and inadequate protective clothing or equipment. So, although the items shown here are all useful, concentrating on what you are doing is the best advice to prevent accidents from occurring.

CLOTHING

Overalls are a good investment because they not only protect clothing, but are also designed to be close-fitting to prevent accidental contact with moving machinery. Industrial gloves provide protection against cuts and bruises when doing rough jobs, such as fencing and garden work. Safety boots should be worn when lifting heavy objects or when the use of machinery is involved.

Knee pads are necessary for comfort when carrying out any job that requires a lot of kneeling. They will also protect the wearer from injury if a nail or similar projection is knelt on accidentally. Finally, a bump cap will protect the head from minor injuries, but is not so cumbersome as the hard hat required on building sites.

ABOVE: A pair of thick gloves will be essential when handling rough materials such as sawn wood or sharp objects such as broken glass. Make sure they fit well.

ABOVE: If you have to do a job that involves a lot of kneeling, rubber knee pads will be invaluable. They provide comfort and protection from sharp projections such as nail heads.

ABOVE: Safety boots with steel toe caps will protect your feet from injury when working with heavy items such as large sections of wood, bricks and concrete blocks.

ABOVE: When working in situations where you may hit your head accidentally, the bump cap will provide protection without being as cumbersome as a conventional hard hat.

SAFETY EQUIPMENT

Make sure you have the appropriate safety equipment to hand when carrying out do-it-yourself tasks, and always use it. Doing so can prevent nasty accidents and serious injury.

KEEPING IN TOUCH

Perhaps the most basic advice is never to work alone with machinery and, if it is possible, always have a friend or colleague nearby to help. If there is no telephone, having a mobile (cell) phone in the workshop is useful.

AIRBORNE DANGERS

When you are working with wood, the most common airborne danger is dust, mainly from sawing and sanding. This can do long-term damage to the lungs. Many do-it-yourself enthusiasts do not do enough work to warrant a workshop dust extractor, but it would be worth considering if funds allowed. Such a device can be wall-mounted or portable. In the latter case, it can be moved around the house or workshop to suit any tool in use.

A simple face mask, however, will offer adequate protection for occasional jobs. These can also be purchased for protection against fumes, such as from solvents, which can be very harmful. Dust, of course,

BELOW: Typical personal safety equipment – first aid kit, impact-resistant safety spectacles, ear protectors, two types of dust mask and sturdy industrial-type gloves.

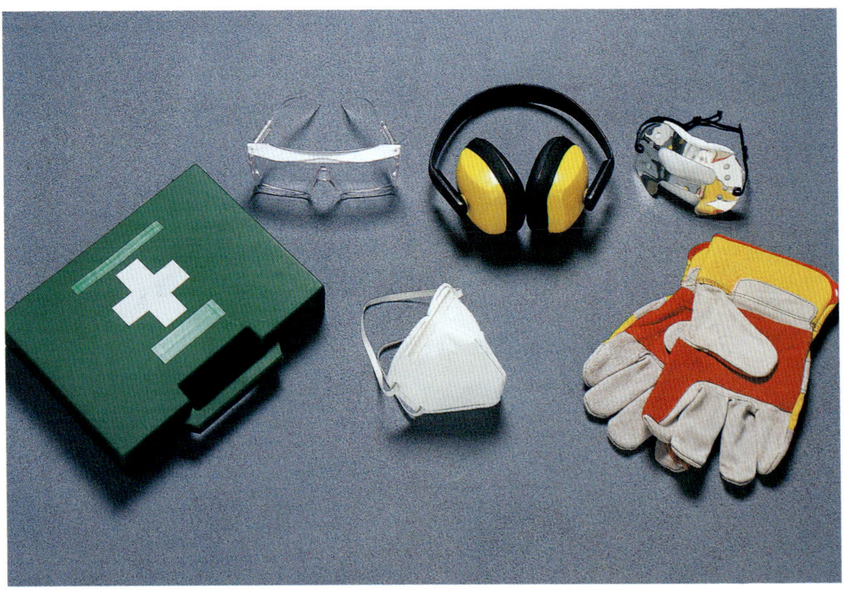

also affects the eyes, so it is worth investing in a pair of impact-resistant goggles, which will protect the wearer from both fine dust and flying debris. Full facial protection is available as a powered respirator for those working in dusty conditions over long periods.

Excessive noise is another airborne pollutant that can be dangerous over a long period. Power tools, particularly woodworking machinery such as planers and circular saws, are major culprits. Earplugs are the simplest solution and can be left in the ears over a long period. If you need to be able to hear between short bouts of working, ear protectors are the answer. These can be worn in conjunction with other facial protection quite easily.

FIRST AID

Keeping a basic first aid kit is a common and wise precaution even before any do-it-yourself work is envisaged. It should always be prominently displayed for people unfamiliar with your workshop.

You can buy a home first aid kit that will contain all the necessary items to cope with minor injuries, or you can assemble your own, keeping it in a plastic sandwich box with an airtight lid, which should be clearly marked. You should include items such as bandages, plasters, wound dressings, antiseptic cream, eye pads, scissors, tweezers and safety pins. If you have cause to use the kit, replace the items you have removed as soon as possible.

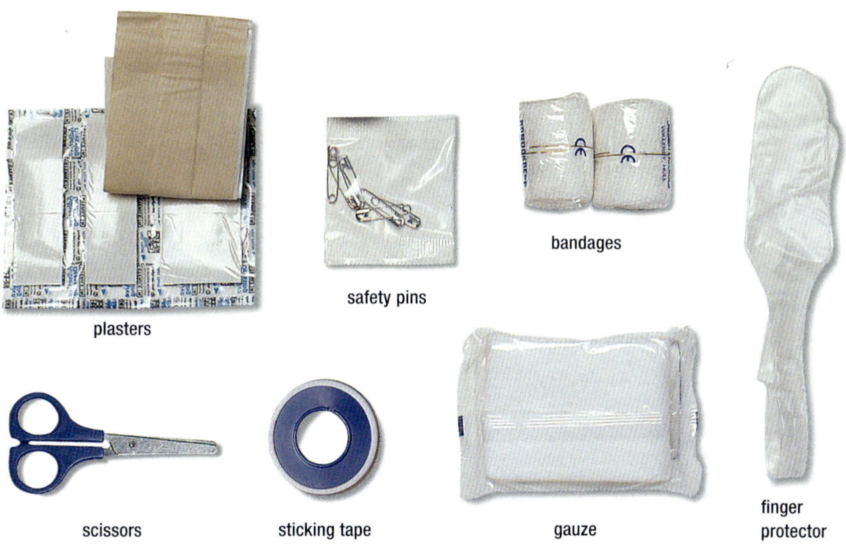

ABOVE: Some of the basic items found in a first aid kit.

ELECTRICAL AND FIRE SAFETY

If used incorrectly, the dangers of electrical equipment can be life threatening, and the dangers of fire are obvious. Always treat the former with respect, and take sensible precautions against the latter.

ELECTRICAL SAFETY

Some tools have removable switches that allow the user to immobilize them and prevent any unauthorized use. Provisions for the use of padlocks are also common on machinery, and it is wise to buy tools with such facilities.

To safeguard against electrocution, which can occur if the flex (power cord) is faulty or is cut accidentally, the ideal precaution is a residual current device (RCD). This is simply plugged into the main supply socket (electrical outlet) before the flex and will give complete protection to the user. Extension leads can be purchased with automatic safety cutouts and insulated sockets, and are ideal for outside and inside work.

The danger of electrocution or damage caused by accidentally drilling into an existing cable or pipe can be largely prevented by using an electronic pipe and cable detector, which will locate and differentiate between metal pipes, wooden studs and live wires through plaster and concrete to a depth of approximately 50mm (2in). These are not too expensive and will be very useful around the home.

LEFT: A simple circuit breaker can save a life by cutting off the power to faulty equipment.

FIRE SAFETY

The danger of fire is ever-present in both the home and workshop, so a fire extinguisher (possibly two or three) is necessary for every do-it-yourself enthusiast. It should be wall-mounted in plain view and serviced regularly.

ABOVE: A fire extinguisher is absolutely essential in the workshop or at home. Make sure the one you have is adequate for the size and type of your workshop, and the type of fire source.

LADDER SAFETY

Steps and ladders can be hazardous, so make sure they are in good condition. Accessories include a roof hook, which slips over the ridge for safety; a ladder stay, which spreads the weight of the ladder across a vertical surface, such as a wall, to prevent slippage; and a standing platform, which is used to provide a more comfortable and safer surface to stand on. The last often has a ribbed rubber surface and can be attached to the rungs of almost all ladders. Even more stable is a movable workstation or a board or staging slung between two pairs of steps or trestles. These can often be used with a safety rail, which prevents the operator from falling even if a slip occurs.

TIPS

- Never overreach when working on steps or a ladder; climb down and reposition it.
- Never allow children or pets into areas where power tools or strong solvents are being used.
- Do not work when you are overtired. This causes lapses in concentration, which can lead to silly and/or dangerous mistakes being made.
- Keep the work environment tidy. Flexes (power cords) should not be walked on or coiled up tightly, because it damages them internally. Moreover, trailing flexes can be a trip hazard, and long extension leads can be prone to overheating.

ABOVE: A ladder platform will provide a firm footing, especially if heavy footwear is worn.

ABOVE: A movable workstation simplifies the process of working at a height.

ABOVE: Platforms supported by trestles offer a safe means of undertaking repair work.

WORKBENCHES AND VICES

A solid and stable surface is essential for producing good work, and serious thought should be given to this by the enthusiast. A good bench need not be too expensive, nor too pretty; the prime requirements are sturdy construction, a flat-top surface and at least one good vice somewhere on the front of the bench. You can make your own or buy one, but beware of cheap benches that may not be up to the job. Suppliers and auctions of used industrial equipment are good sources.

PORTABLE WORKBENCHES

By far the most popular form of portable support is the foldaway workbench. This is really convenient to use, both in the workshop, in the home and outdoors. It has the ingenious feature of a bench top constructed in two halves, which is capable of acting as a vice. It is handy for holding awkward shapes, such as pipes and large dowels.

VICES

Your main workshop vice should be heavy and sturdy. It is normally screwed to the bench, close to one of the legs. If you intend doing a lot of woodworking, buy one with a quick-release action that allows you to open and close the jaws quickly, using the handle for final adjustments. You should certainly be able to fit false wooden jaws to prevent damage to the material you are working with.

ABOVE: Lightweight plastic sawhorses can be useful if you are undertaking small jobs.

ABOVE: A portable foldaway workbench with adjustable bench top.

ABOVE: Wooden sawhorses come in pairs and are often home-made.

Additional ways of protecting the work in the vice take the form of magnetic vice jaws faced with cork, rubber or aluminium, which fit inside the main jaws of the steel bench vice.

Another useful and portable addition to the bench is the swivelling bench-top vice. This can be fitted easily and removed very quickly, usually by means of a screw clamp. It is particularly handy for holding small pieces of work in awkward positions, when carving, for example. However, it is too light in construction to support work that is to be struck with any force.

The mitre clamp can also be considered as a bench vice of sorts and is useful for holding any assemblies that require clamping at 45 degrees, such as picture and mirror frames. Good quality examples are made from metal, since plastic will tend to flex when pressure is applied.

carpenter's vice

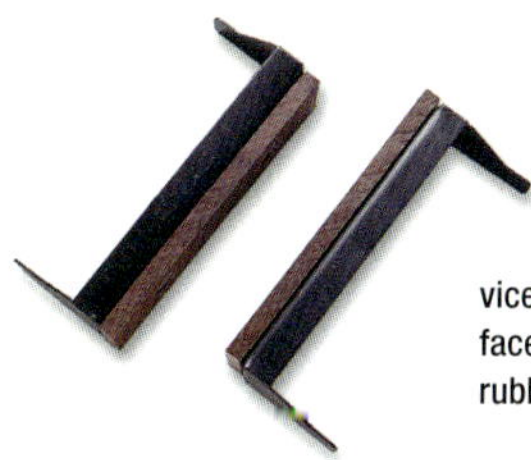
vice jaws faced with rubber

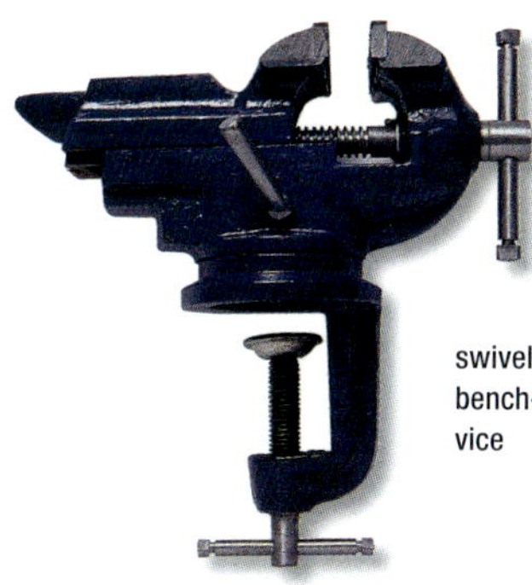
swivelling bench-top vice

mitre clamp

TIPS

- Spend time adjusting your workbench to the exact height that suits you. An incorrect height can prove to be very tiring and is not good for your back. Never shorten the legs of a bench if it is too high; work off a duckboard if necessary.
- Always buy the best-quality vice you can afford; second-hand ones can be particularly good value.

TOOL STORAGE

Tidy and effective storage of your tools pays off in many ways. Properly stored tools will be protected from the atmosphere and will not rust or discolour. The sharp cutting edges of saws and chisels will be protected from damage, as will the potential user's fingers. Moreover, tools will always be easily found near at hand when they are needed.

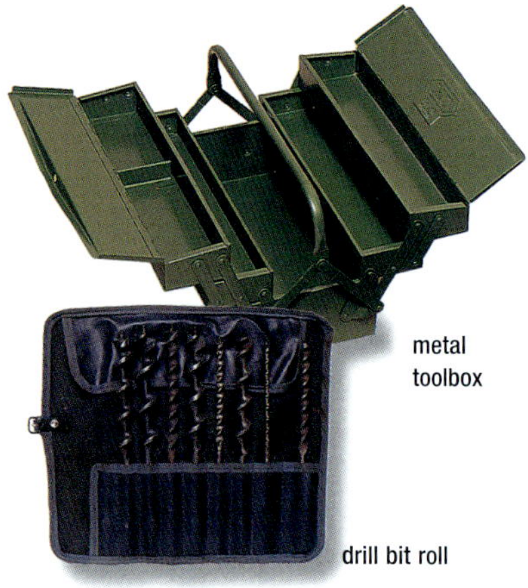

STORAGE

Efficient storage saves bench and floor space for other uses, and tools will be more easily located, saving time and frustration. It is well worth taking the trouble to devise and even make your own storage facilities. There are plenty of benches, cabinets, racks, clips and tool rolls on the market so that you can equip your workshop with exactly what you need. Remember, too, that storage for tools often needs to be portable, so tool pouches and carrying bags also need to be part of the overall picture.

ABOVE: A tool pouch worn around the waist is ideal for carrying tools when working in different parts of the home.

PORTABLE STORAGE

The traditional carpenter's tool bag can still be obtained. Made from heavy canvas, it has two carrying handles and brass eyelets for closing.

Compact, compartmentalized plastic or metal toolboxes with drawers, carrying handles and safety locks are another option for carrying tools from one job to another.

A leather tool pouch can be worn around the waist and has loops and pockets for tools as well as screws and nails. Various sizes and styles are available. They are ideal for use on projects that require you to keep moving about.

Drill bits and chisels should always be carried in a tool roll with their tips covered for protection. Some chisels are provided with individual plastic blade caps, and many saws are sold with a plastic blade guard to protect the teeth when not in use. Always make sure that these are fitted correctly.

STATIC STORAGE

The most important static storage space is that below the workbench top, and often this takes the form of cabinets or drawers. A useful device is a large tilting drawer, which can easily be made and is ideal for storing tools that are in frequent use.

Wall-mounted cabinets with sliding doors are really practical in the workshop. The sliding doors allow them to be sited in confined areas and make it impossible to hit your head on them when they are open, which is especially important above the bench.

Shelving units come in a variety of materials, shapes and sizes, and most can be added to as the need arises.

The tool board has the advantage of not only displaying the tools, but also making it obvious when a tool has not been replaced. To make one, arrange the tools on a flat board and draw around them with a marker pen. Then fit hooks, pegs or clips as necessary.

ABOVE: Specifically made in transparent plastics for easy identification of the contents, storage drawers for screws, nails, clips and a host of other small items are a must.

ABOVE: Use a length of wood to make your own storage block to keep your drill bits tidy.

MAKING A TOOL BOARD

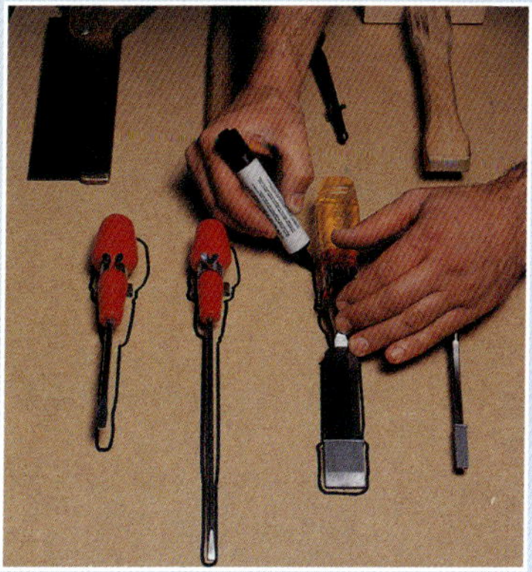

When making a tool board, remember to leave space around each tool so that it can be lifted clear when the board is on the wall. Draw around the tools with a felt-tipped pen to indicate their positions. Hammer in nails or hooks that will hold them in place. Wall hooks will hold larger items, such as saws. Alternatively, you can buy a tool board made from perforated plywood from a local builder's merchant.

MEASURING, SHAPING & CUTTING TOOLS

One of the most crucial skills for do-it-yourself work is the ability to measure accurately. The quality of much of the work you undertake will rely on that skill, so it is worth taking time and care when measuring and marking out. Shaping wood is a task required for many projects, and knowing how to use a plane will pay dividends. Chisels are also used for this purpose, as well as making cut-outs. To be effective, both tools must be kept sharp. A good toolkit will also include a variety of saws and knives; make sure you know which to use and when. Drilling holes is something you will need to do on a regular basis, and there are many types of drill and drill bit to choose from.

MEASURING TOOLS

Accurate measuring is a very basic, but essential, skill for the do-it-yourself enthusiast to master. Time spent on perfecting measuring is never wasted. The golden rule is to measure twice and cut once. Buy good-quality tools – poor measuring and marking devices can lose their accuracy very quickly and spoil your work.

HOW TO MEASURE

There are dozens of types of flat, rigid rule for marking out, most of which are calibrated in both metric and imperial units. They may be wood or steel, although some cheaper varieties are plastic. Where curves are involved, greater accuracy will be achieved with a flexible steel rule or even a retractable steel tape, which can be bent around the work.

The T-square is useful for marking out large sheets of manufactured board such as plywood, MDF (medium-density fiberboard) and blockboard. Remember, however, that it must be used on a perfectly straight edge to produce a 90-degree line across the sheet. Any small discrepancy in the edge will be greatly magnified across the sheet width and even more so along the length.

The combination square incorporates a number of functions in one tool, and is used for both measuring and marking out. It comprises a graduated steel rule that slides within a shaped body. A clamping screw permits the rule to be secured at any point along its length, while the body itself has flat edges that allow guidelines to be marked at 90 and 45 degrees to a straight surface. Many combination squares also feature a spirit bubble, allowing the tool to be used for checking horizontals.

CONVERTING MEASUREMENTS

On small work in particular, never be tempted to convert from metric to imperial or vice versa. Some quite large errors can occur with standard conversions. Always work in the unit specified.

FITTING PRE-MADE STRUCTURES

When fitting previously assembled cabinets or shelving to a wall, the most accurate method is to mark out the wall using a spirit (carpenter's) level. These are available in long and short lengths. Do not rely on existing lines, such as architraves (trims) around doors, picture rails or skirtings (baseboards), as these may not be truly horizontal.

Transferring measurements from one point to another can also be done with a straightedge, and although this is very similar to a heavy steel rule, the bevelled edge gives it the added advantage of being very easy to cut or mark against. Straightedges often have handles, making them easy to hold in place.

retractable steel tape

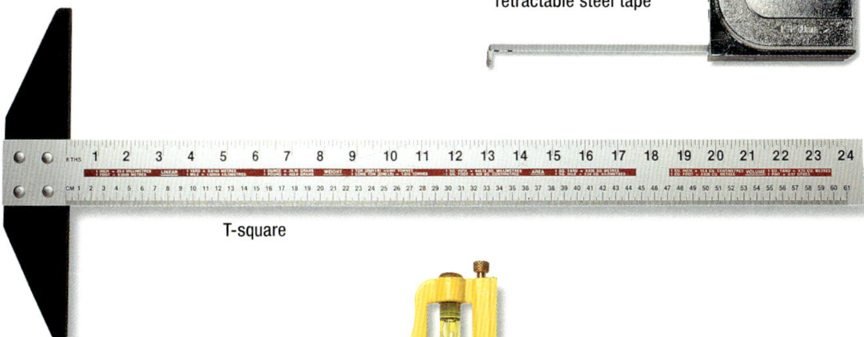

T-square

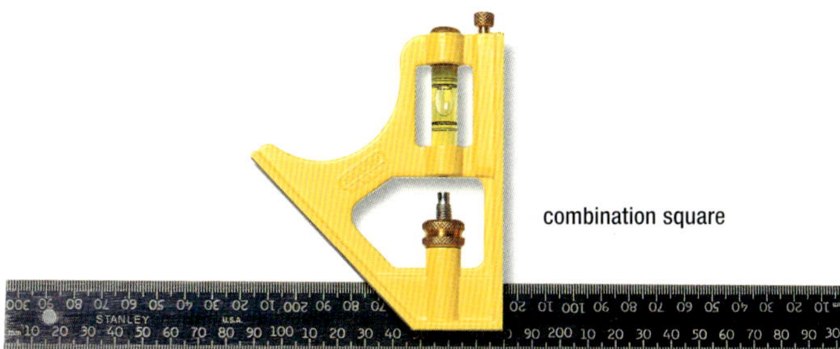

combination square

short spirit (carpenter's) level

long spirit (carpenter's) level

straightedge

MARKING-OUT TOOLS

Another essential do-it-yourself skill is marking out, which can make or mar many projects.

Where you need to mark off a series of equal spacings, simply set a pair of dividers or callipers to the correct distance, using a flat wooden or steel rule, and step off the divisions.

You can mark out your workpiece for cutting and/or shaping with a pencil or a marking knife. The latter is particularly useful for fine work. An ordinary pencil is quite acceptable, but a flat carpenter's pencil will have a chisel-shaped tip when sharpened, making for more accurate marking.

MARKING JOINTS

Marking joints needs a fair degree of accuracy, so the first thing to ascertain is that your prepared wood is flat and square, which is done with a combination square or a try square. Either of these tools should be slid down the length of the wood to be cut, thus ensuring its uniformity and squareness.

For marking out a mortise, use a mortise gauge and set the points to the width of the chisel you intend to use to cut the mortise, not from a rule. This is far more accurate, as well as being much more convenient.

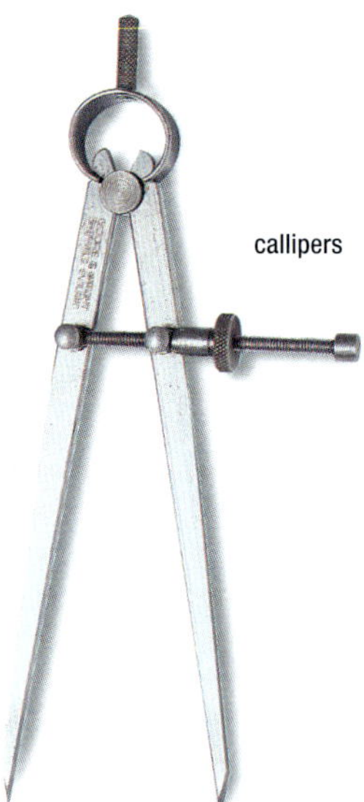
callipers

try square

sliding bevel

mortise gauge

A sliding bevel is a tool used for marking angles on to a square piece of wood. It can be adjusted to any angle, and is especially useful if the angles are to be repeated, such as when setting out treads for a staircase.

A good alternative for marking frequently repeated angles, such as on a staircase, is to make up a jig or template that can be laid on to the stringer (the long diagonal part of the staircase) and mark the treads accordingly. You should be able to buy such templates, in hardboard or Perspex (Plexiglas), from most professional workshops.

THE RIGHT MARKER

Use a carpenter's pencil, ordinary pencil or chinagraph for setting out measurements. Never use a magic marker or a ballpoint pen, since the marks are virtually impossible to remove and will spoil your work. Whichever marking tool you choose, keep it sharp to ensure accuracy.

ABOVE: Use a try square for marking right angles. Keep it clean and make sure the blade is not loose. It can be used with a pencil or a marking knife as required.

ABOVE: Use a mortise gauge to scribe directly on to the wood. The two steel pins of the tool are independently adjustable on accurate brass slides, while the sliding stock runs against the face of the work. There may be a single pin on the opposite side for marking a scribed line, used to gauge thickness.

PLANES

The most commonly used varieties of plane are the jack plane for flattening the faces and edges of boards, and the smoothing plane for fine finishing. Good-quality examples are sufficiently weighty to avoid "chatter", which occurs when the plane skips over the surface of the wood without cutting properly. A block plane is often used for planing end grain because its blade is set at a low angle that severs the wood fibres cleanly.

block plane

smoothing plane

jack plane

PLANING TECHNIQUE

Body weight plays a large part in planing technique. Position your body with your hips and shoulders in line with the plane, and your feet spaced apart.

At the beginning of the stroke, apply pressure to the front handle of the plane, switching to a general downward pressure during the middle of the stroke, and finish off by applying most of the pressure to the back of the plane at the end of the board.

PLANING END GRAIN AND BOARDS

Plane end grain and boards using a block plane. To avoid splitting the ends of the wood, work from each side toward the middle. A useful technique for planing wide boards is to work diagonally, or even at right angles, across the grain. This method will remove material efficiently. To finish, it will be necessary to make fine cuts with the grain to obtain a smooth surface. Run your fingers lightly over the surface to identify any unevenness that needs removing.

TIPS

- Cheap planes often serve to blunt enthusiasm by poor performance. Always buy the best you can afford and keep them sharp.
- Check for sharpness and adjustment each time a plane is used – and make sure the wood to be planed is held firmly.

STARTING TO PLANE

1 The correct body position helps to achieve the desired result. Keep your hips and shoulders parallel to the direction in which you are planing, with your weight balanced on both feet.

2 Apply pressure to the front of the plane as you begin the stroke, equal pressure to front and back in the middle of the stroke, and pressure on the back of the plane at the end of the stroke.

3 When planing a narrow edge, make sure you keep the plane centralized to ensure an even cut. To do this, you can tuck your fingers under the sole plate as a guide.

4 If you have identical edges to plane, clamp them together and work on both at once. Check from time to time that you are planing them square with the aid of a try square.

POWER PLANERS

If you need to remove large amounts of wood, a power planer is very useful. An electric planer should be handled with great care as it is extremely easy to remove too much wood and ruin the work. The depth of cut in one pass ranges from 1.5 to 5mm (1/16 to 3/16in) on more powerful models; 3mm (1/8in) is quite adequate for most general purposes.

Look for a model that offers a dust bag to collect the copious shavings produced. Tungsten-carbide-tipped (TCT) disposable blades are best when working with manufactured boards such as MDF (medium-density fiberboard) and plywood.

power planer

The cutter block, in which the blades are mounted, rotates at very high speed and should be treated with great respect. Always hold the tool with both hands and keep it moving so that it does not cut for too long in one spot.

Although the power planer is very fast, the hand-held version rarely gives the quality of finish that can be achieved with a well-set and sharpened bench plane. Unless you intend doing a lot of work where a power planer will be needed, you may find it less expensive to hire one when you require it. Most tool hirers will have them.

ABOVE: Use two hands to plane end grain with a power planer to ensure complete control.

ABOVE: Plane across wide boards with a power planer to give quick results.

POWER PLANING TECHNIQUES

It is very important to hold a power planer with both hands, as it can be a very aggressive tool. Make sure that the flex (power cord) is well out of the way so that it does not impede the work.

Keep your hands well away from the blades and wait for the cutter block to stop spinning before putting the tool down on the workbench.

Check for sharpness and adjustment each time you use a power planer, and make sure the wood to be planed is held firmly in a vice or clamped down.

As with the hand plane, an electric planer can also be used across the grain of wide boards for quick results, provided that final finishing is with the grain.

1 The depth of cut is controlled by the rotary knob at the front, which doubles as a handle. Push down firmly and evenly on the machine to remove a constant thickness of stock in one pass. The side fence keeps the sole plate square to the edge.

2 Most planers have a V-groove machined in the bottom of the sole plate to permit chamfering. Locate the groove on the square edge of the work to position the cutters at 45 degrees to each adjoining face. The work is in a jig to hold it in position.

3 Some models allow you to form rebates (rabbets) up to 25mm (1in) deep, using the side fence to control the rebate width. The design of the planer body dictates the maximum rebate capacity, so always check that the tool you buy meets your needs.

CHISELS

Each with its own specific use, chisels come in a variety of shapes and sizes. For jobs around the home, only three basic types are required. Most commonly used is the firmer chisel, which is a compromise between a mortise chisel and a bevel-edged chisel. It can be regarded as a general-purpose tool, having a strong blade of rectangular section designed for medium/heavy work. Most home woodworkers will find blade widths of 6mm (¼in), 12mm (½in), 19mm (¾in) and 25mm (1in) sufficient for their needs.

SPECIAL-PURPOSE CHISELS

Bevel-edged chisels have thinner blades than firmer chisels. The tops of the blades are bevelled along their length to allow better access into small recesses and corners, and to permit fine slicing cuts to be made in the wood.

The mortise chisel is a sturdy tool with a lot of steel just below the handle. It is used for chopping deep mortises across the grain, so it has to be able to withstand blows from a heavy mallet. For this reason, a wooden-handled mortise chisel may have a metal band around the top of the handle to prevent it from splitting. The thickness of the steel blade also allows it to be used as a lever for cleaning the waste from the mortise.

Many new chisels have shatter-resistant polypropylene handles that can be struck with a mallet, or even a hammer, without damage since the material is virtually unbreakable.

TIPS

- Always make sure your chisels are sharp. A blunt tool needs more pressure to force it through the work and is more likely to slip, possibly causing an accident.
- Do not leave chisels lying where the blades can touch metal objects. Fit them with blade guards or keep them in a cloth.

firmer chisel

bevel-edged chisel

mortise chisel

plastic-handled chisel

CHISELLING TECHNIQUES

Always aim to remove as much waste wood as possible from the cut before using the chisel. For example, remove the waste with a saw before cleaning up with a chisel or, when cutting a mortise, drill out the waste and use the chisel to clean and square-up the sides.

When using a router to cut slots and rebates (rabbets), square the ends by hand with a chisel.

Remember to cut away from the marked line when chiselling so that any splitting will occur in the waste wood, and always cut away from yourself to avoid injury. Work patiently and never be tempted to make cuts that are too large. The chisel should be pushed or struck with one hand while being guided with the other.

HORIZONTAL PARING

1 Horizontal paring, working from both sides to the middle, prevents "break out" and results in clean work using less pressure.

2 Chamfer an edge, first using the chisel with the bevel down to remove most of the waste. Then make the finishing cuts with the blade held bevel up, taking fine parings.

3 When making the finished cuts, use your thumb to control the cutting edge of the chisel, holding it close to the end of the blade. Make sure the chisel is sharp.

VERTICAL PARING

ABOVE: When paring vertically by hand, guide the chisel blade with one hand while pushing down firmly on the handle with the other.

REMOVING LARGE AMOUNTS

ABOVE: To remove larger amounts of waste wood, hold the chisel vertically and strike the handle firmly with a wooden mallet.

MORTISING

ABOVE: You can form a mortise completely with a chisel, but it is much quicker to remove most of the waste by drilling it out, then use a chisel to clean up the sides and ends of the cutout.

DOVETAILS

ABOVE: Dovetail joints are common in cabinet work. Begin by removing the bulk of the waste with a coping saw before using a narrow, bevel-edged chisel to finish off.

SHARPENING EQUIPMENT

A good sharpening stone is a vital part of the toolkit. Without a sharp edge, a chisel will be not only difficult to work with, but also dangerous. The chisel will follow where the wood directs it, rather than where you want it to go, and can easily slip.

Chisels should be sharpened at the beginning and end of every session. If they are attended to regularly, just a few minutes' work will keep the honed edges in prime condition. Once in a while, a longer honing session might be necessary – if the bevel loses its original angle or if the edge is chipped.

Natural sharpening stones are quite expensive, and synthetic versions are commonly used. Japanese water stones are of natural stone and need water as a lubricant. They can produce a finely ground edge on the best-quality steel. For more general use, however, oilstones are sufficient.

A combination stone is the best buy, two stones of different grades being bonded together back to back.

combination stone

Japanese water stone

SHARPENING PLANE IRONS

To sharpen a plane iron, apply a coat of thin oil to the oilstone, hold the blade at 35 degrees to the stone and maintain this angle while working it backward and forward. Honing jigs, which set the angle exactly, are readily available. Lay the back of the iron flat on the oilstone and rub off the burr formed by the sharpening process. Clean out the inside of the plane before reassembly, and apply a drop of oil to the adjustment mechanism.

1 Hold the iron at a steady angle while rubbing it on the oilstone.

2 Remove the burr from a sharpened blade by rubbing the back flat on the stone.

SAWS

The most common saw used by the do-it-yourselfer is the hand saw. This is used for cross-cutting (across the grain) and ripping (along the grain), and the teeth of the saw are set accordingly, so you will need to ask your tool supplier for the correct one. There are also general-purpose hand saws that are reasonably suited to both tasks. These are quite often hardpoint saws, which cannot be sharpened, but their specially hardened teeth give them a long life.

The tenon saw, sometimes called a backsaw because of the solid strengthening bar along its top edge, is made specifically for cutting the tenons of mortise-and-tenon joints and other fine work. Really fine work is done with a dovetail saw, which is similar to a tenon saw, but has more teeth to the inch to give a finer cut.

The tenon saw is often used with a bench hook for making cross-cuts in small pieces, and one can be made quite easily as a do-it-yourself project. They usually measure about 300 x 150mm (12 x 6in). The mitre box is another handy aid for use with a tenon saw, allowing 90- and 45-degree angles to be cut accurately, but the beginner is best advised to buy one rather than attempt to make one.

A mitre saw makes short work of cutting accurate angles and offers fine adjustment. It is well worth the investment if working with delicate mouldings or making picture frames.

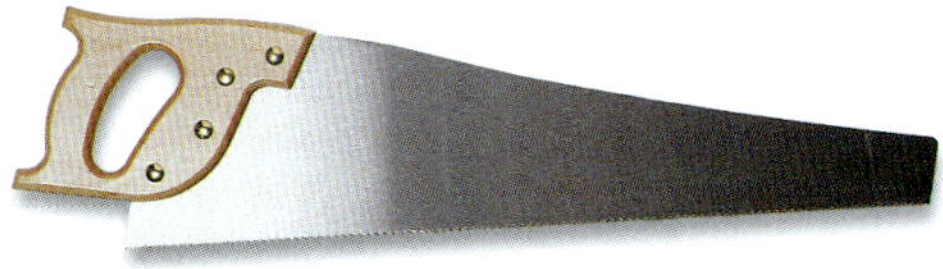

cross-cut hand saw

hardpoint saw

tenon saw

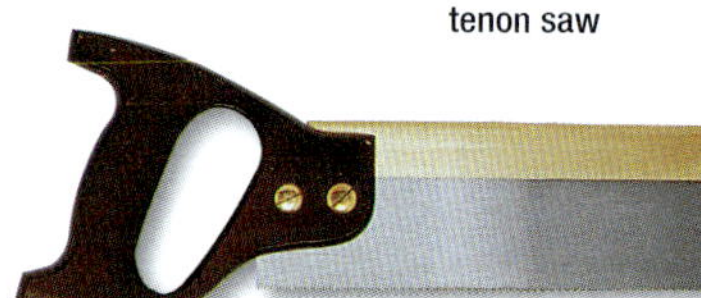

dovetail saw

bench hook

mitre box

mitre saw

SAWING TECHNIQUES

When beginning a cut with a hand saw, draw the saw back toward your body to sever the wood fibres and produce a small kerf – the groove in which the saw blade will run. Always cut on the waste side of the marked line for perfect results.

When using a mitre box to make an angled cut, begin with the back of the saw raised slightly. This will make the cut easier to start.

ABOVE: Draw the saw back a few times to start the cut, using your thumb to support the blade until a kerf has formed.

TIP

Always find a comfortable position in which to saw. It will produce better results and reduce the risks of back strain or other injury.

ABOVE: Use a tenon saw for cutting small components or sawing tenons and the like. A bench hook aids the cross-cutting.

ABOVE: A standard mitre box permits 90- and 45-degree angled cuts to be made with a tenon saw for a variety of applications.

POWER SAWS

Invaluable for saving a lot of time and hard work, a power saw can also do a lot of damage if used incorrectly. Never force a saw through the work. If the blade is not sharp, or the motor is underpowered, not only will the cut be inaccurate, but also you'll be putting your safety at risk. Let the saw do the work, guiding it slowly, but surely, along the line. Use an adjustable fence if possible when making straight parallel cuts.

circular saw

CIRCULAR SAWS

A hand-held circular saw can be used for both cross-cutting and ripping, and many are supplied with a dual-purpose, tungsten-carbide-tipped blade for a long life. It is almost a necessity for the home woodworker and is an excellent investment; there are many quite inexpensive and reliable brands.

CIRCULAR SAW BLADES

Check that the bore of the blade (the diameter of the central hole that fits over the spindle) is compatible with the machine, as different makes vary. As with hand saws, the type of blade should suit the material and the cutting action, whether ripping along the grain, cross-cutting, or making fine cuts in veneered or laminated panels. Carbide teeth are cheaper for most general-purpose work; tungsten-carbide-tipped blades are sharper and much harder wearing. The latter should be used when cutting composite materials and manufactured boards such as plywood and MDF (medium-density fiberboard).

ABOVE: A circular saw will make light work of cutting wood, but be sure not to overload it, and always have the guards in place. Use a good-quality hand saw for smaller jobs.

JIGSAWS

Another very handy tool is the jigsaw (saber saw). It is suitable for both straight and curved cuts, saving a lot of hard work.

jigsaw (saber saw)

Most jigsaws come into their own when cutting out curved shapes from manufactured boards, such as MDF (medium-density fiberboard) and plywood.

If large amounts of curved or shaped work are envisaged, a small bandsaw is a useful addition to the workshop. These can be inexpensive. Fret/scroll saws are very similar to jigsaws, being fitted with a reciprocating movement. They are used for fine pierced and detail work, and are capable of turning out very delicate results.

ABOVE: A jigsaw (saber saw) is very good for making curved cuts. Most have adjustable cutting angles. Be sure your work is securely clamped to keep it firmly in place.

JIGSAW BLADES

Jigsaw (saber saw) blades are made for many purposes, but check that the model of jigsaw you buy will accept standard-fitting blades. Many specialized blades are available for cutting all kinds of material, such as wood, manufactured boards, metal, ceramics, plastics and laminates. A knife blade has no teeth, and is designed for cutting leather and rubber sheeting. Bi-metal blades, although more expensive, will last longer and are less inclined to bend. Most blades are 100mm (4in) long, allowing a depth of cut of 50–65mm (2–2½in), but heavy-duty blades are available up to 150mm (6in) long. These should only be fitted to a machine with a powerful motor designed to accept the extra load.

KNIVES

The do-it-yourself enthusiast will need a variety of knives, some of which have very specific functions. Some do not actually conform to the conventional idea of a knife at all, but all have metal blades and are essentially cutting tools.

MARKING KNIVES

The purpose of a marking knife is to mark a sawing line, by lightly cutting the surface wood fibres, and assist in the beginning of a saw cut. Not only does this provide a permanent guide line, but it also prevents the fibres from splintering as the saw cuts through. These tools are usually about 200mm (8in) long and make a much finer line than a pencil.

They are normally used in conjunction with a steel rule, straightedge or try square and are bevelled on one side only so that they can be used tightly against the steel edge for accuracy. They are available in both left- and right-handed versions.

Marking knives without pointed ends are also frequently used, and these are bevelled on either the left- or right-hand side, depending on the needs of the user.

Twin-bladed knives are available and are adjusted by a set screw and locking knob. Typically, the blades can be set to a spacing of 3–19mm ($\frac{1}{8}$–$\frac{3}{4}$in). This type of knife is used for marking parallel lines, gauging mortises and cutting thin strips from veneers for decorative inlay work.

GENERAL-PURPOSE KNIVES

By far the most common and useful general-purpose knife is the craft knife, which has a store of replacement blades in the handle. This is an indispensable tool which can be used for many purposes.

Another very handy tool is the scalpel. More delicate and invasive than the craft knife, a scalpel is ideal for cutting out templates and particularly useful for cleaning up deeply indented

marking knife with bevel on one side

scalpel

twin-bladed adjustable marking knife

putty knife

craft knife

filling knife

MARKING OUT

ABOVE: Mark a line across the grain with the knife held firmly against the steel edge of a try square. This gives a very fine line of severed wood fibres, which is ideal to work to with either a saw or a chisel.

ABOVE: A typical example of a knife being used with a steel rule. Note how the fingers are spread to keep a firm and even downward pressure on the rule, allowing the knife to be used hard against the rule's edge.

cuts in carvings and routed work. Scalpels are made with a variety of handles and have replaceable blades.

MISCELLANEOUS KNIVES

Putty knives often find their way into the do-it-yourselfer's toolkit. They have specially shaped ends to their blades to make "cutting off" easier. This means withdrawing the knife from the work without damaging the soft putty that is being applied to a window pane or moulding, for example.

The filling knife is a familiar decorator's tool with a flexible spring-tempered blade that is ideal for forcing soft material, such as wood filler, into knot holes, cracks and blemishes in wood, and plaster filler into cracks in walls. These come in a variety of shapes and sizes and are often confused with stripping knives, which have thicker and less flexible blades.

TIPS

- Never use a scalpel or craft knife with excessive pressure. The blade may shatter and sharp pieces fly up into your unprotected eyes.
- Always place the hand not holding the knife behind the blade. This prevents injury if the blade slips.

DRILLS AND BITS

Accurate drilling is an important do-it-yourself technique. It is much easier with a hand-held power drill, and even more so with a bench-mounted pillar drill.

CARPENTER'S BRACE

Drilling by hand with a carpenter's brace still has a place, and a hand drill is useful for smaller jobs, especially in sites far removed from electric power. However, even in these circumstances, the cordless power drill has largely overcome the difficulty of finding a source of electric power.

CORDLESS DRILL/DRIVER

This tool is worth its weight in gold in situations without power, and it is particularly safe near water. It is rechargeable and usually comes with a spare battery. The variable torque and speed settings make it ideal for doubling as a screwdriver. Although generally not as powerful as a mains-powered drill, it is more than adequate for most jobs. Use it for drilling clearance holes for screws, fitting and removing screws, and drilling holes for dowels.

Heavier work, especially that which involves using flat bits or Forstner bits to remove very large areas of wood, is best undertaken with a mains-powered electric drill to save time and avoid the need for constant recharging of the battery.

cordless drill

VARIETIES OF BIT

Great advances have also been made in the pattern of drill bits. For example, there are bits designed for setting dowels. Dowel jointing is often used in projects built with manufactured boards, such as chipboard (particle board) and plywood, and the bits produce flat-bottomed holes.

ABOVE: A carpenter's brace is ideal for boring large holes. Its design provides plenty of leverage to turn flat and auger bits.

dowel bit

flat bit

Forstner bit

plug cutter

countersink bit

There are also flat bits that work with a scraping action, cutting large holes very rapidly, although these are not as accurate as conventional twist bits. The latter are used for making small holes in wood, metal and other rigid materials, but specially hardened types are needed for steel. For the do-it-yourselfer on a limited budget, an adjustable bit is a good investment, but these can only be used in a hand brace.

DRILLING ACCESSORIES

Plug cutters are useful additions to any workshop, especially when quality work is undertaken. The cutter is fitted in a pillar drill and used to remove plugs from a piece of scrap wood. Then the plugs are glued into holes in the workpiece to conceal fixing screws. Most cutters come with a special matching bit that bores a screw clearance hole and plug countersink in one operation.

Another common drilling accessory is the countersink bit. This allows the head of a screw to be set flush with the surface of the wood. Again, this is best used in a pillar drill with a depth stop to ensure accuracy.

Forstner bits are designed to drill large, flat-bottomed holes that do not pass through the wood, such as holes that might be needed to accommodate kitchen cabinet hinges. The bits will drill deep holes accurately, even in the end grain of the wood, which is usually very difficult.

ABOVE: Many drill bits can be sharpened with a specialized grinding attachment designed to be run off a hand-held power drill.

Estwing
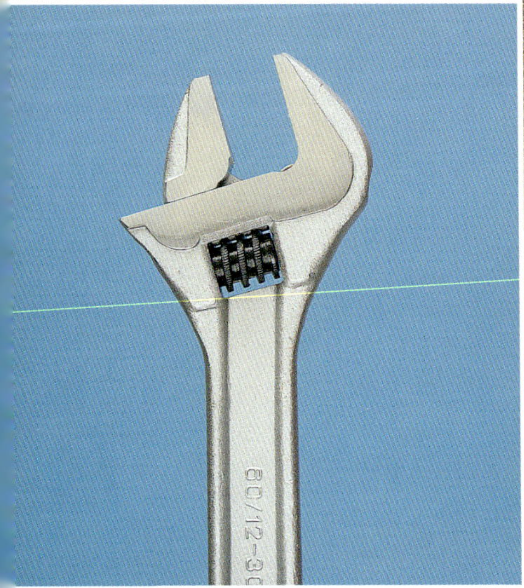

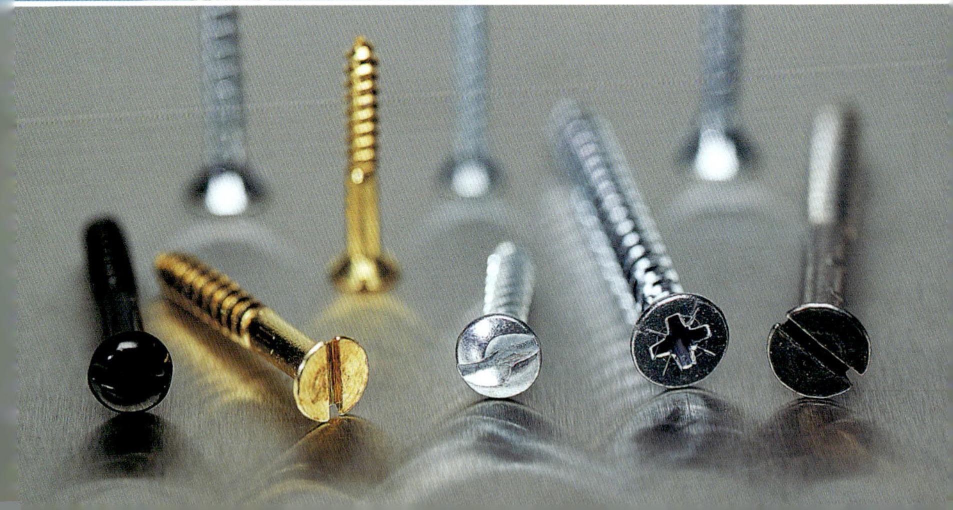

ASSEMBLING & FINISHING TOOLS

Assembling two or more pieces of a workpiece can sometimes be done by forming joints and using glue, clamping the pieces together until the glue is dry. Often some form of mechanical fixing is called for, such as nails and screws, or nuts and bolts. When it comes to finishing a surface, in practically all cases the smoother the surface, the better the finish. A primary method of achieving smoothness is by sanding with abrasive paper, which can be done by hand or by machine.

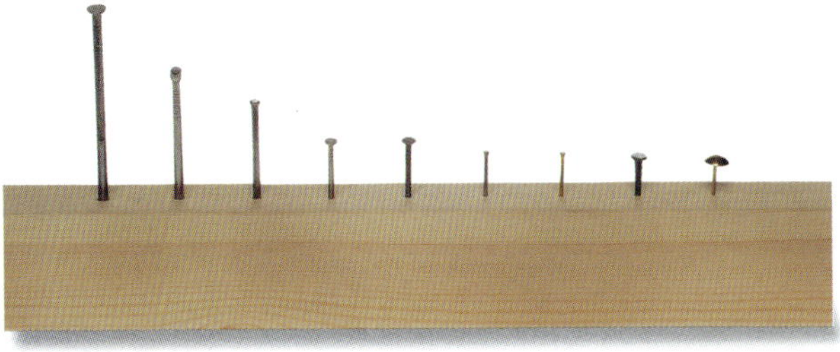

CLAMPS

Many do-it-yourself tasks require two or more sections of a workpiece to be held together temporarily while a more permanent fixing is made, often with glue. A variety of clamps is available for this purpose, many of them with specific uses. Keen woodworkers may make their own clamps (or cramps as they are often called) from scrap wood or other materials.

ABOVE: The G-clamp in a typical application. Note the packing pieces beneath the jaws to prevent bruising of the wood.

COMMONLY USED CLAMPS

The most common clamp in the workshop is the G-clamp. This is a general-purpose tool that is available with a variety of throat sizes. It may be used on its own or in conjunction with others when, for example, working on the surface of a wide board or holding boards together for gluing.

The sash clamp was designed specifically for assembling window frames, or sashes, but it is also often used when edge-jointing boards to form large panels for table tops and similar items.

Sometimes, it is useful to be able to apply a clamp with one hand while holding the workpiece in the other, which is when the single-handed clamp comes into its own. It works on a simple ratchet system, rather like a mastic (caulking) gun.

For picture frames and heavier items with 45-degree mitred joints at the corners, there is the mitre clamp. This can be quite a complex affair with screw handles for tightening or a very simple "clothes-peg" (pin) type arrangement, that can be applied to the work very quickly.

SPECIAL-PURPOSE CLAMPS

There are many of these, but one that the do-it-yourself enthusiast may find useful is the cam clamp, which is wooden with cork faces. This is a quickly operated clamp often used by musical instrument makers. Its advantages are its speed in use, its lightness and its simplicity. The cam clamp is ideal for small holding jobs, although it cannot exert a great deal of pressure.

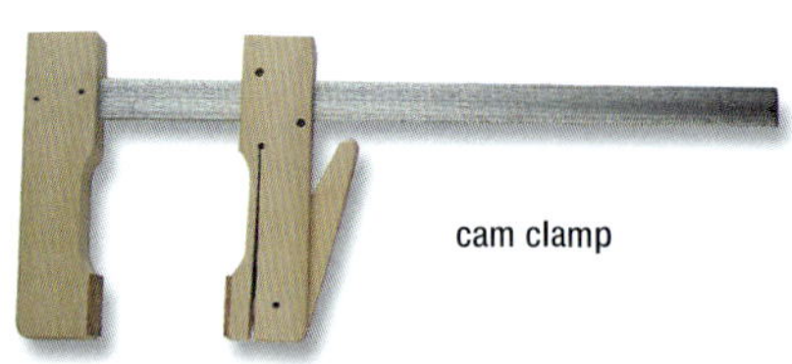

cam clamp

ABOVE: Small wooden picture and mirror frames can be easily assembled with the aid of inexpensive mitre clamps.

ABOVE: This clever little clamp works by means of spring pressure. It can be applied quickly and easily to small assemblies.

ABOVE: Use sash clamps to edge-joint boards to form a panel such as a table top. Reverse the central clamp to even out the pressure.

ABOVE: Home-made clamps used for the same purpose, but this time the pressure is exerted by means of wedges.

CLAMPS IN USE

Apply pressure to a joint or the assembly you are working on as soon as possible after gluing – make a habit of preparing everything you need in advance. Keep a box of small scraps of wood handy and use them to protect the surface of the work. It is often said that you can never have too many clamps, and you will soon start collecting a selection of different types and sizes to suit all kinds of assembly technique. Many can be home-made.

TIPS

- Do not be tempted to release clamps too quickly. Be patient, allowing plenty of drying time for the glue – overnight at least, or as specified by the maker.
- Think through the sequence for the clamping process and make sure you have enough clamps to hand before you apply any glue. With a complex or large structure, you may decide you need another person to help.

NAILS AND HAMMERS

There is no such thing as an "ordinary" nail. All nails have been derived for specific purposes, although some can be put to several uses. Similarly, various types of hammer are available – always use the correct tool for the job. Wooden-handled hammers have a natural spring in the handles, which makes them easier to control than steel-handled types.

NAILS

The wire nail can be used for many simple tasks, such as box-making, fencing and general carpentry. Lost-head and oval nails are useful where there is no need for a flat head, or when it is desirable for the nails to be concealed, such as when fixing cladding or boards.

Oval nails can be driven below the surface of the work with less likelihood of them splitting the wood. They should be inserted with their heads in line with the grain.

The cut nail is stamped from metal sheet and has a tapering, rectangular section, which gives it excellent holding properties. It is largely used for fixing flooring.

Panel pins (brads), as their name suggests, are used for fixing thin panels and cladding. They are nearly always punched out of sight below the surface, as are veneer pins.

When there is a need to secure thin or fragile sheet material, such as roofing felt or plasterboard (gypsum board), large-headed nails are used. These are commonly called clout nails, but may also be found under specific names, such as roofing nails and plasterboard nails. Their large heads spread the pressure and prevent the materials from tearing or crumbling. They are usually galvanized to protect them against rust when used outdoors. Zinc nails are used for roofing because they are rustproof and easy to cut through when renewing slates.

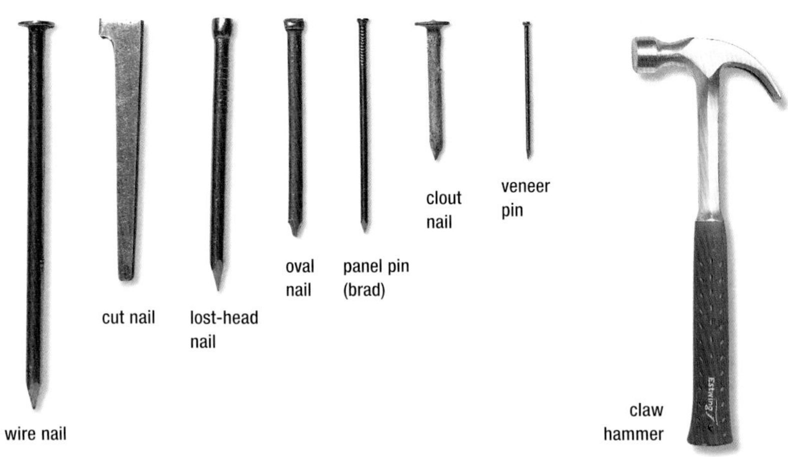

HAMMERS

The essential hammer for the do-it-yourselfer is the claw hammer, the claw being used to extract nails. About 365–450g (13–16oz) is a good weight to aim for, since the hammer should be heavy enough to drive large nails. It is a mistake to use a hammer that is too light, as this tends to bend the nails rather than drive them.

For lighter nails, a cross-pein or Warrington hammer is useful, since the flat head can be used to start the nail or pin without risk of hitting your fingers. For even smaller panel pins, the pin hammer is used.

CARPENTER'S MALLET

It should be remembered that the carpenter's mallet, often made from solid beech, is a form of hammer, but it should never be used for striking anything other than wood or similar soft materials, otherwise serious damage will result.

cross-pein hammer

carpenter's mallet

DOVETAIL NAILING

Cross, or dovetail, nailing is a simple and useful method of holding a butt joint strongly in end grain. When several nails are being driven into one piece of wood, avoid putting them in straight; slanting them will help prevent splitting.

ABOVE: The claw hammer's ability to extract as well as drive nails makes it a useful tool for do-it-yourself projects.

SCREWS AND SCREWDRIVERS

The holding power of screws is much greater than that of nails, and screwed work can easily be taken apart again without damage to any of the components, unless of course it is also glued. Driving screws does take longer than nailing and they are more expensive, but they will give the appearance of quality and craftsmanship to most work.

TYPES OF SCREW

The most common woodscrews may be made of mild steel or brass, often with countersunk heads that may be flat or raised. There are many different plated finishes available, ranging from chrome, used for internal fixings such as mirrors, to zinc, which will resist rust.

flat and raised countersunk screws

Brass screws will not rust at all and are often used in woods such as oak, where steel would cause blue staining due to the tannic acid in the sap.

HEAD PATTERNS AND SCREW SIZES

There are various types of screw head used for both hand and power driving. The most common is the slot-head screw, followed by the Phillips head and the Pozidriv, both of which have a cruciform pattern in the head to take the screwdriver blade.

Screw sizes are complex, combining the length and the diameter (gauge): for example, "inch-and-a-half eight" describes a screw that is 1½in (40mm) long and gauge 8.

TYPES OF SCREWDRIVER

For woodworking, the traditional hand screwdriver has an oval wooden handle and is used to drive slot-head screws only. It is available in a variety of sizes. A range of plastic-handled tools of

slot-head screwdriver

stubby screwdriver

slotted screw head

Phillips screwdriver

Phillips screw head

Pozidriv screwdriver

Pozidriv screw head

various sizes is also available, designed to drive Phillips and Pozidriv screws, as well as slot-heads.

A recent innovation is the screwdriver bit set, containing a handle and a number of interchangeable tips to fit various screw types and sizes.

Power screwdrivers and drill/drivers vastly increase the rate of work. They can offer various torque settings that allow the screw heads to be set just flush with the work surface. Power drivers are also very useful for dismantling screwed joints and furniture because they will run in reverse.

Keeping the head of a slot-head screwdriver correctly ground to prevent it from slipping is very important. Remember also that the blade width must equal the length of the screw slot for the greatest efficiency and to prevent both slipping and damage to the screw head. Always use the correct size of screwdriver with Phillips and Pozidriv screws, otherwise both the screw head and the screwdriver are likely to be damaged.

cordless electric drill/driver

USING SCREWS

Driving a screw is a more skilled task than nailing. It is usually advisable to drill pilot holes first to ease the screws' passage through the wood and to ensure that they go in straight. In hardwoods, pre-drilling is vital, otherwise the screws will shear off when pressure is exerted by the screwdriver. Brass screws are particularly soft, so steel screws of the same size should be inserted to pre-cut the threads.

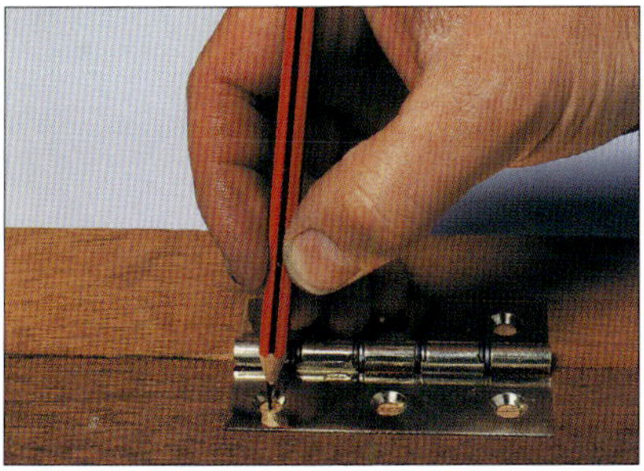

ABOVE: Screw holes should be marked very carefully when fitting hinges.

ABOVE: Where possible, use the screwdriver with both hands to prevent slipping.

PINCERS AND PLIERS

Every do-it-yourself enthusiast's toolkit should include a range of hand tools for gripping small items. Chief among these are pincers, used for removing nails and similar fixings, and general-purpose combination pliers, which offer a variety of gripping and cutting features.

PINCERS

A good pair of pincers will remove nails and tacks with little trouble. The rolling action required to remove a nail with pincers is very similar to that used with a claw hammer. An ideal length is about 175mm (7in) to ensure good leverage, which is essential. The jaws should touch along their entire width and be properly aligned to provide maximum grip.

It is important that pincers do not damage the work, and for this reason, broad jaws – about 25mm (1in) wide – that will spread the load are best.

Some pincers come with a handy tack lifter at the end of one of the handles. Purpose-made tack lifters are very useful for upholstery work, and if you intend doing any furniture making or restoration, it is well worth investing in such a tool.

Another special tack and nail remover is the nail puller, or "cat's-paw", as it is sometimes known. This tool has a standard tack remover at one end and a large, right-angled claw at the other for getting under the heads of stubborn nails. The claw can be tapped under the head of an embedded nail with a small hammer.

pincers

pincers with a tack lifter

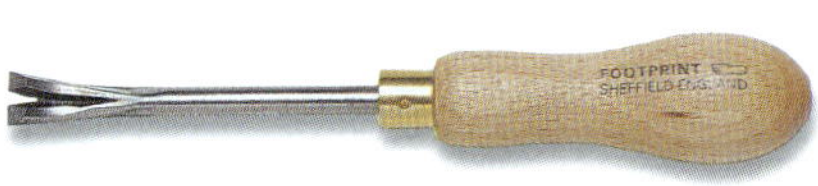

tack lifter

nail puller

combination pliers

heavy-duty pliers

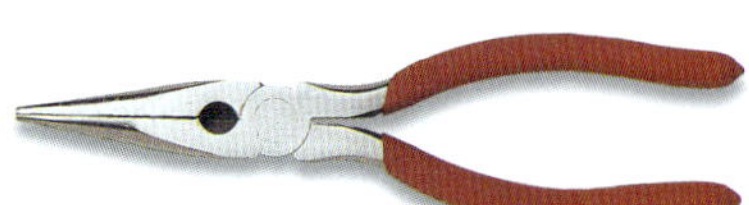
long-nosed (needlenose) pliers

PLIERS

These come in a bewildering range of types and sizes, many of which have very specific uses.

Combination pliers and heavy-duty pliers are used for gripping, twisting and cutting. They come in various sizes, but a good pair would be about 200mm (8in) long and probably have plastic or rubber handle grips for comfort and to provide insulation against electric shock.

Long-nosed (needlenose) pliers are rather more specialized and are used for gripping small objects in confined spaces. Some have cranked jaws at various angles for access to awkward places. They come in many sizes.

ABOVE: When using pincers to remove a nail, protect the wood by slipping a piece of hardboard or plywood below the pincer head.

ABOVE: Remove tacks from wood with a tack lifter. Protect the surface with hardboard or a piece of plywood.

ABOVE: The flat behind the claw of this Japanese nail puller can be tapped with a hammer to drive the claw under the nail head.

ABOVE: When using pliers, hold them firmly, keeping your palm away from the pivot, which can pinch your skin as the jaws close.

SPANNERS AND WRENCHES

Although spanners and wrenches may be thought of as tools for the garage, there are many do-it-yourself tasks that require these gripping and twisting tools, particularly in the kitchen and bathroom, where you are likely to come into contact with pipes and their fittings. All home workshops need at least one comprehensive set of sockets or spanners.

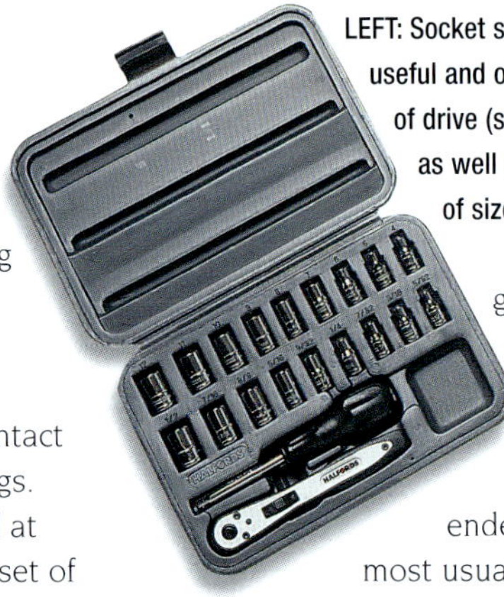

LEFT: Socket sets are extremely useful and offer a choice of types of drive (such as bars and ratchets) as well as sockets in a variety of sizes.

SPANNERS

These are necessary in the home workshop where power tools and machinery are involved. They are needed for changing the blades on circular saws, for adjusting and setting bandsaw guides, and for assembling all manner of machinery stands, tool racks and benches.

A good selection of spanners would include open-ended, ring and combination spanners. These are usually purchased in sets; other tools are bought singly.

It is essential to use a spanner that fits a nut or bolt perfectly, otherwise the fixing will be damaged and you run the risk of skinned knuckles. Spanners are graduated in specific sizes – metric, Whitworth and A/F are the most common. Open-ended spanners are the most usual. Some have jaws that are offset by about 15 degrees to allow them to contact different flats of nuts when working in tight spots.

Ring spanners have enclosed heads that give a more secure grip. They may have six or 12 points, and can be used on square and hexagonal nuts and bolts. The 12-point version needs only a very small movement for it to contact new

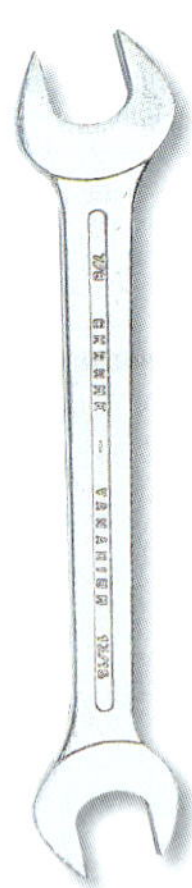

open-ended spanner

ring spanner

combination spanner

adjustable spanner

flats on the nut or bolt head, so it is very useful where there is limited room for movement.

Sockets grip in the same manner as a ring spanner, but are designed to fit a variety of drive handles, of which the ratchet handle is the most useful. This enables the user to continue to turn a nut or bolt without having to remove the socket after each turn. Some large sets offer metric, Whitworth, BSF and A/F sizes. Small sets of additional sockets are available to complement your existing set, allowing you to build up a kit that meets your needs exactly.

WRENCHES

Adjustable spanners and wrenches enable the user to grip various sizes and types of fitting. Some are designed for specific purposes, while others are suitable for more general use.

Basic plumbing tools include adjustable pipe wrenches (known as Stilsons), an adjustable basin wrench and a double-ended basin wrench, both of which will reach up behind a basin to allow removal of the nuts holding taps in place, and water-pump pliers with soft jaws.

Normally, the adjustable spanner is made from forged alloy steel. Self-grip wrenches, or vice grips, can be adjusted to fit pipework or a nut or bolt head, and then can be locked to grip tightly. They are very versatile and useful tools. Water-pump pliers offer five or six settings by virtue of having an adjustable bottom jaw. They are capable of exerting a heavy pressure because of their long handles.

Another variation is the strap wrench, made of a soft pliable material. It is used for gripping container lids.

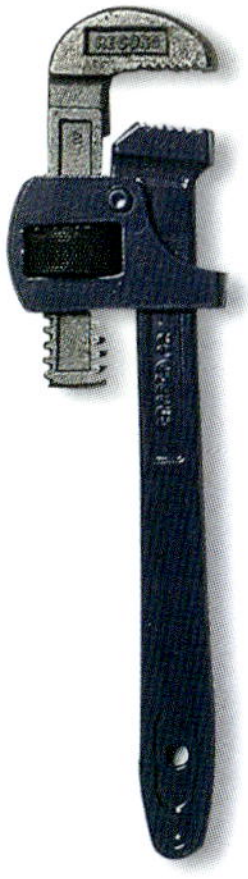

Stilson wrench

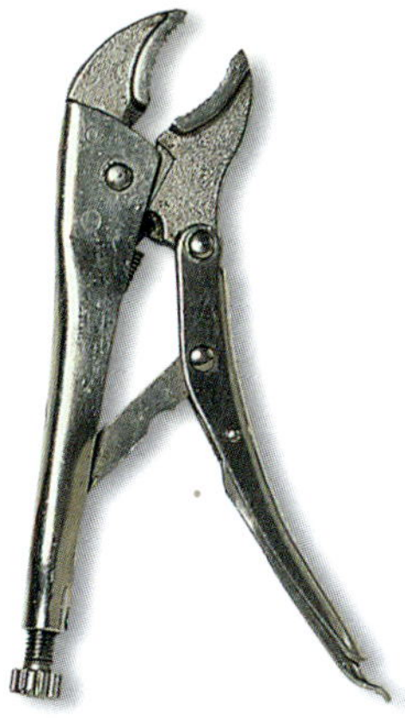

self-grip wrench

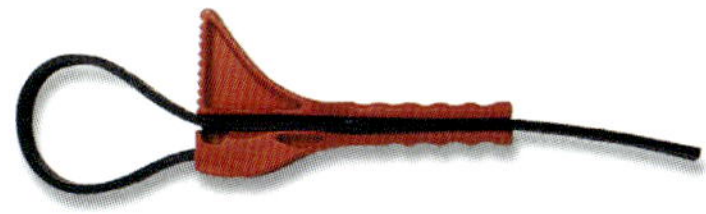

ABOVE: A strap wrench offers a soft pliable grip that can be used for opening containers.

TIP

Never use a wrench on a nut or bolt if a spanner of the correct size is available. Wrenches are essentially for pipe work and will damage the corners of nuts and bolt heads very quickly. Use the correct tool wherever possible.

SANDERS

Although the term "sanding" is generally used for do-it-yourself projects, it is something of a misnomer. A truer description would be "abrading", because what we call "sandpaper" is, in fact, "glasspaper". In addition, we also use garnet paper, and silicon-carbide and aluminium-oxide abrasive papers, all of which shape wood very efficiently.

GRIT SIZE

One thing abrasive papers all have in common is classification by grit size, and the golden rule is to work progressively down through the grit sizes, from coarse to fine, when smoothing a piece of work. For example, 400 grit is finer than 200 grit and should be employed later in the finishing process. Abrasives can be used by hand or with a variety of machines, both hand-held and stationary. Sanders are also suitable for shaping work, using coarse abrasives for rapid material removal.

TYPES OF SANDER

A tool commonly used for heavy-duty shaping and sanding is the belt sander. This normally has a 75mm (3in) wide belt, running continuously over two rollers, and a dust collection facility.

A belt and disc sander is an inexpensive alternative. It is used for shaping and trimming rather than smoothing, as the piece of work is taken to them.

Many do-it-yourselfers are likely to own an orbital sander, which is useful for general light sanding work such as finishing boards. These sanders are designed to accept either half or a third of a standard-size abrasive sheet and quite often have dedicated sheets made for them. Random orbital sanders are similar, but may employ self-adhesive abrasive sheets that are easy to fit. They can be small enough to be used with one hand in tight spots, but still give a good finish.

HAND SANDING

Always wrap abrasive paper around a cork or rubber block when sanding flat surfaces. Clear the dust away as you work to avoid clogging the paper, particularly on resinous and oily wood. To finish off a rounded edge, wrap a square of paper around a section of moulded wood with the correct profile for the job.

belt sander

orbital sander

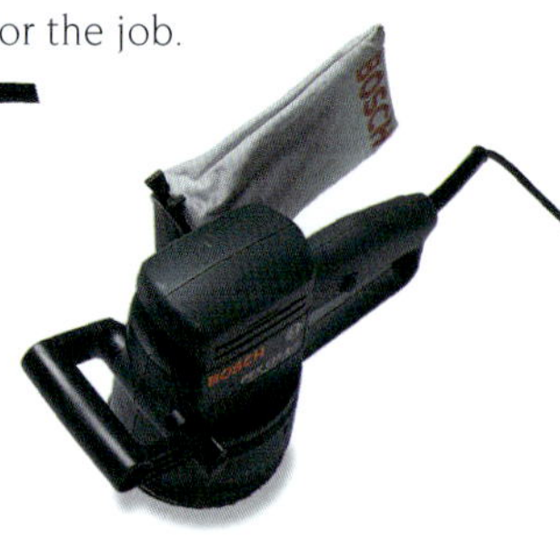

random orbital sander

ABOVE: You should hold a belt sander with both hands to prevent it from running away.

ABOVE: The belt sander can be inverted and secured in a woodworking vice.

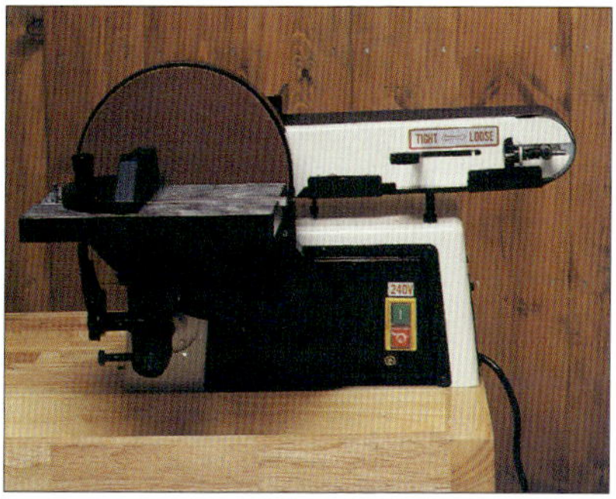

ABOVE: Belt and disc sanders are used for shaping and trimming, and can be aggressive.

ABOVE: The orbital sander is less ferocious than the belt sander and is easy to control.

MAKING A SANDING BLOCK

1 Fold your sheet of abrasive paper to size and tear it along a sharp edge.

2 Wrap the paper around a cork or rubber block before starting to sand.

WOODWORK IN THE HOME

- Woodwork materials
- Wall woodwork
- Doors, locks & windows
- Wood finishing

INTRODUCTION

As a constructional material, wood is invaluable. It is very strong for its weight, and it can be used to create quite complex structures at relatively low cost. Properly looked after, wood will last for years, as an examination of your surroundings will confirm. All homes, no matter how they have been built, will contain a large amount of wood. The basic framework of the house may be made of wood, as well as at least some internal walls and the structure supporting the roof. Floors often have wooden surfaces – the material is warmer underfoot than concrete and stone; walls will be trimmed at floor level and around door openings with wooden mouldings, while the doors themselves will almost certainly be wood; window frames, too, are commonly of wooden construction. Then there is the furniture – shelves, cabinets, chairs, tables and so on. So sooner or later the do-it-yourselfer will be faced with tackling some form of woodworking task.

Fortunately, wood is an easy and forgiving material to work with, requiring few specialized tools unless undertaking cabinet-making or similar complex jobs. Taking the time to develop a few basic, practical

LEFT: Wood possesses a wide range of characteristics in varying degrees – strength, durability, flexibility, brittleness and, of course, beauty. Woodwork is involved in all sorts of jobs around the home, such as putting up shelves, fitting architraves (trims), replacing doors and drawers, and fitting locks.

ABOVE: Skirtings (baseboards) protect wall surfaces at floor level from accidental damage. They receive a lot of wear and tear from feet, vacuum cleaners and furniture legs, and may need replacing.

ABOVE: Renewing old drawer fronts is neither a complex nor a very expensive job. Remove the old drawer front from the carcass with a screwdriver, drill pilot holes in the new front, and screw it into position.

woodworking skills will allow you to tackle a wide variety of do-it-yourself tasks – from simply giving a wooden surface (such as a floor) a new finish, through putting up the simplest of fixtures, to carrying out all manner of repairs around the home.

The following pages contain a selection of simple indoor projects that involve working with wood. By using the information provided, you will gain the confidence you need to complete many do-it-yourself tasks. Just remember that, as with so many things, care and patience are the most important keys to success.

RIGHT: Shelving systems such as these adjustable brackets are capable of holding heavy weights, and have the advantage of being portable when you need to move them. The bracket positions can be adjusted to vary the spacing between the shelves, but remember that a shelf's capacity depends on the strength of the wall fixings employed.

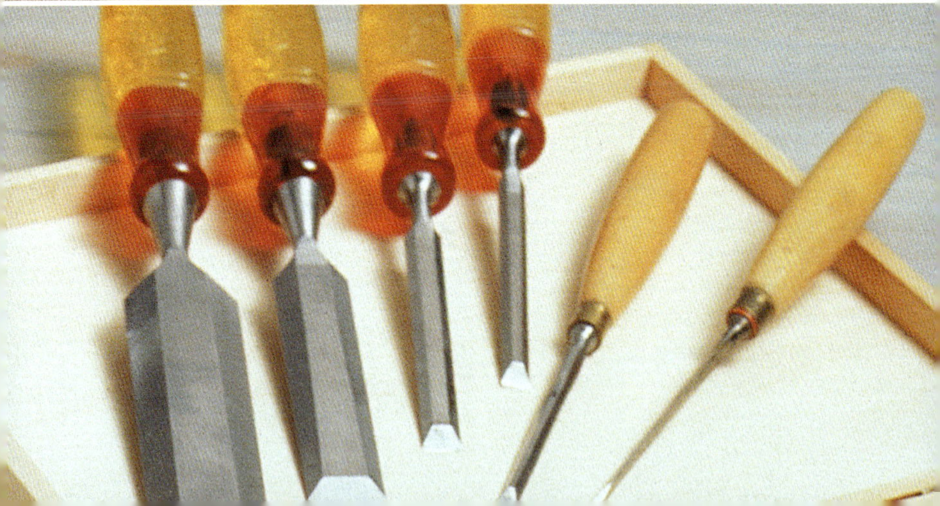

WOODWORK MATERIALS

Wood can be purchased in two basic forms: as sections of natural timber (lumber) sawn and/or planed to shape, or as manufactured boards made from thin veneers, wood particles or blocks. All have their specific uses, and it is important to choose the right type, size and thickness for the job in hand. When joining and hinging pieces of wood, you will also need to choose the correct fittings. Commonly used joint plates include the L-shaped corner plate and the T-shaped fixing plate. There is a wide variety to choose from, as browsing through any catalogue will reveal, and the following pages include most of the types in common use.

WOOD AND MANUFACTURED BOARDS

As they are expensive, hardwoods are often used as veneers over cheaper materials, as lippings around flat surfaces such as shelving and table tops, and for picture framing.

Softwoods, such as pine and, to a lesser extent, Douglas fir, are the most commonly used types of wood for do-it-yourself jobs, such as wall frames, flooring, skirtings (baseboards), picture and dado (chair) rails, and a great variety of cladding, framing and fencing applications. In addition to softwoods, there is a range of inexpensive manufactured boards.

ABOVE: Beech hardwood.

PRACTICAL USES

The two boards most often used are plywood and chipboard (particle board). The former, which has good mechanical strength and can be sawn easily, is suitable for structural work.

Chipboard is more friable and less easy to work accurately, but is cheap. It is adequate for some flooring applications and a host of carcassing jobs, such as kitchen cabinets and bookcases. It is unwise to drive screws or nails into the edge of a chipboard panel, as the material will crumble.

Both plywood and chipboard are available faced with hardwood and coloured melamine veneer for improved appearance.

Blockboard, which consists of solid wooden blocks sandwiched between plywood skins, is a stable and strong structural material often used where some form of weight-bearing capacity is required. As with all manufactured boards, the extremely hard resins used to bond blockboard together rapidly blunt tools unless they are tungsten (carbide) tipped.

Pineboard is like the core of blockboard, but without the outer layers. Small strips of pine are glued together on edge and sanded smooth. It is ideal for shelving and carcassing.

MDF (medium-density fiberboard) is another useful material. Unlike most other boards, it can be worked to fine detail with saws and chisels, and it is often used for delicate mouldings.

Hardboard is ideal for covering floors prior to tiling or carpeting and, as it is light, for making back panels for cabinets and pictures. It can be used for making templates to establish correct shapes, helping to avoid mistakes when using expensive material for a finished piece.

ABOVE: Pine softwood.

ABOVE: Paper-coated MDF skirting (baseboard).

STANDARD SIZES

Nearly all manufactured boards have a standard size of 1220 x 2440mm (4 x 8ft). Some suppliers offer a metric size, which is smaller (1200 x 2400mm), so always check, as this can make a critical difference to your cutting list. Special sizes of plywood and MDF, up to 3m (10ft) in length, are available from some suppliers. Many stores will offer part sheets or cut large sheets into smaller sizes if requested at the time of purchase.

GRAIN DIRECTION

The direction in which the grain runs on the outer layers is always given first when describing plywood. This can be important when planning your cutting list. With birch plywood, for example, 1220 x 2440mm (4 x 8ft) in a supplier's catalogue will indicate that the grain runs across the width of the board, not down its length. Most veneered decorative boards have the grain running across the length, so their catalogue entry would read 2440 x 1220mm (8 x 4ft).

COMMON THICKNESSES OF MANUFACTURED BOARDS

TYPE	3mm ⅛in	6mm ¼in	9mm ⅜in	12mm ½in	16mm ⅝in	19mm ¾in	22mm ⅞in	25mm 1in	32mm 1¼in
Plywood	✓	✓	✓	✓	✓	✓	✓	✓	
Plywood (D. fir)			✓		✓				
Blockboard						✓		✓	
Chipboard				✓	✓	✓	✓	✓	
Hardboard	✓	✓							
MDF		✓	✓	✓		✓		✓	✓

JOINT PLATES AND HINGES

There is a huge range of fittings available for making joints and connecting different materials. These will often prevent the need for making complex joints in wood, allowing the less skilled to produce strong structures or repairs with relative ease.

Hinges will be found all around the home on doors and cabinets, and replacing or refitting them is a common do-it-yourself task.

ABOVE: An L-shaped corner plate.

JOINT PLATES AND BRACKETS

Flat mild-steel plates, drilled and countersunk to take woodscrews, are a common means of making and strengthening butt joints in wooden framing. Some commonly used joint plates are L-shaped corner plates and T-shaped fixing plates.

Brackets such as corner plate fixings, 90-degree angle brackets and joist hangers are also available. They can be used to make right-angled joints, overlapping joints and for hanging joists.

ABOVE: A simple 90-degree angle bracket.

HINGES

Any device that includes a pivot action can be called a hinge, and there are many different variations. Some are designed to be concealed within the framework of a cabinet, or the carcass, while others are intended to act as decorative features in their own right.

It is important to fit the correct number of hinges of a suitable size and robustness when hanging a door so that it is well supported when it swings open. If a hinge or hinge pin is strained in any way, the door will not fit in the frame properly and may even become detached, possibly causing injury.

ABOVE: Hinges are available in a wide range of types, finishes, sizes and materials for a variety of tasks. Some are functional, while others make decorative features in their own right.

ABOVE: A T-shaped fixing plate.

ABOVE: A corner plate fixing.

ABOVE: An overlapping fixing plate.

ABOVE: A joist hanger.

KNOCK-DOWN JOINTS

These fittings are often used with manufactured boards, such as chipboard (particle board) and plywood. They ensure good, square connections, usually by means of pegs, and allow the assembly to be dismantled and reassembled as required. For the best results, at least two joints should be fitted between each pair of panels.

ABOVE: The knock-down joint in its separate parts ready for assembly.

ABOVE: When the parts are connected, they form a strong and accurate joint.

WALL WOODWORK

All walls incorporate wooden fixtures of one form or another. At the very least, there will be skirtings (baseboards) at floor level and wooden trims around door openings. In some cases, there may be dado (chair) rails and, in older properties, picture rails near the ceiling. At some stage, you may find that you need to replace these items, either to effect repairs or give the room a new look. Cladding the walls with wooden boards or panels is another means of giving a room a fresh look, and can provide thermal and acoustic insulation too. Other wall woodwork jobs featured in the following pages include fitting tongued-and-grooved boarding and boxing-in pipes.

USING MOULDINGS

Moulding is the term used to describe any section of wood that has been shaped, either by hand or by machinery, to alter the square profile of the original piece. This may range from simply rounding over the sharp edges of the finished work to adding more decorative detail.

TYPICAL APPLICATIONS

Mouldings have many uses, not only providing protection to vulnerable surfaces, but also adding decoration. The larger mouldings include architraves (trims), dado (chair) rails, picture rails and skirtings (baseboards). Architraves are fitted around flush door and window openings to create decorative and protective borders. Dado and picture rails are horizontal mouldings fixed to wall surfaces, the former to protect the plaster from damage by the backs of chairs, and the latter to allow pictures to be hung. Skirtings are boards fixed at ground level to protect the plaster from damage by feet or furniture.

FIXING MOULDINGS

Generally speaking, it is wise to drill pilot holes in hardwood mouldings before nailing, especially when fixing close to the ends, since small-section hardwoods, especially ramin, which is often used, will split readily.

Softwoods are far more forgiving, and it is unnecessary to drill a softwood architrave before nailing it in place. Simply drive the nails in, punch the heads below the surface, and fill before finishing. Panel pins (brads) or lost-head oval wire nails are the preferred fixings for architraves.

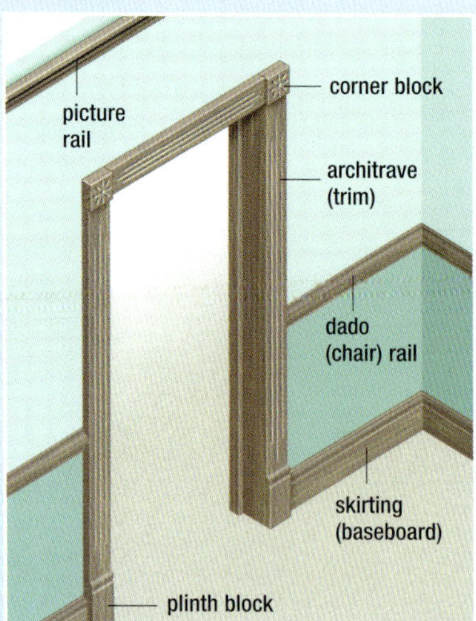

PRACTICALITIES

This is a typical layout showing how architectural mouldings are put to use. They are so called because they would be used to produce a certain effect in the interior of a room rather than for individual items of furniture.

Notice how they combine a decorative effect with good practical points: the plinth blocks and corner blocks around a door frame convey a classic formality, but they also avoid the need to form complex joints where two wooden components meet.

The plinth blocks provide useful protection to more intricate mouldings at floor level where they may be damaged easily.

FITTING A SHELF MOULDING

1 Using a try or combination square, check that the corners of the board are square. If necessary, plane or re-cut the edges to ensure that they are square.

2 Mark the mouldings to length and, using a tenon saw and mitre box, cut their ends at 45 degrees to fit neatly together at the corners of the board.

3 Check the fit of the mouldings, then apply glue to them and the edges of the board. Hold them in place with plenty of masking tape and leave for the glue to dry.

4 When the glue has dried, clamp the board securely to your bench top and carefully clean up any rough edges or slight overlaps with a plane. Finish by sanding lightly.

FITTING AN ARCHITRAVE

Trimming a door is fairly straightforward. Measure the internal width of the door frame and mark out the top piece of architrave (trim) so that its bottom edge is 12mm (½in) longer. Mitre the ends at 45 degrees, using a mitre box, so that the top edge is longer than the bottom.

Pin (tack) the top piece of architrave to the top of the frame so that it projects by an equal amount at each side and is 6mm (¼in) up from the bottom edge of the top frame member. All architrave should be set about 6mm (¼in) back from the inside edge of the door frame.

Measure for each side piece separately, as they can vary quite considerably over the width of a door, especially in older houses. Cut each to length, mitring the top ends to match the horizontal section already fitted. Sand the ends to remove any splinters, then offer them up, checking the fit of the mitred ends. If all is well, pin the mouldings to the frame.

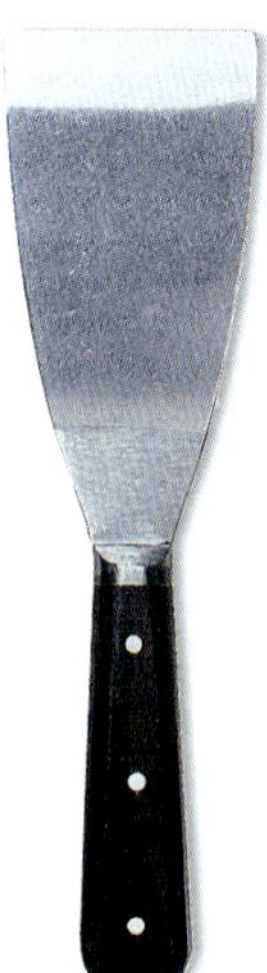

Drive all the pin (tack) heads below the surface of the wood with a nail punch. Then fill the holes and any gaps between the mitred ends of the architrave, using a coloured wood filler if you intend applying a translucent finish. Finally, when the filler is dry, sand it flush with the surrounding surface.

1 Remove the old architrave (trim) with a crowbar (wrecking bar). Place a block of wood beneath the tool's blade to protect the adjacent wall from damage.

4 Pin the new piece of architrave in place, making sure that it is horizontal and about 6mm (¼in) above the bottom face of the top internal frame member.

2 Pull out any remaining nails and scrape away any old wood filler or paint from the face of the opening's frame. Take care, however, not to gouge the wood.

3 Measure the internal width of the door frame and cut the top section of architrave to length, allowing for the 6mm (¼in) projection at each end. Mitre the ends at 45 degrees.

5 Measure, cut and fit the side pieces of architrave in the same manner. Pin (tack) them in position, butting their mitred ends against the ends of the top piece.

6 Punch all the pin (tack) heads below the surface of the wood, apply filler and sand it down. Any gaps between the mitred ends should also be filled and sanded smooth.

REPLACING SKIRTINGS

Skirtings (baseboards) receive a lot of wear and tear from scuffing by feet and furniture, which is why they are there in the first place, of course. From time to time, after replacing floorboards or laying new woodstrip or laminate flooring, for example, the damage may be so great that sections of skirting or even complete lengths of it need to be replaced.

Skirtings may vary from simple rectangular sections of wood to quite ornate moulded profiles.

FITTING NEW SKIRTINGS (BASEBOARDS)

In a rectangular room, it is always best to fit the two long sections of skirting board first, then fit the shorter ones to them. It makes handling, lifting and fixing much easier.

REPLACING STRAIGHT SECTIONS

To replace sections of skirting, first prise the old board partially away from the wall, using a crowbar (wrecking bar), then insert wedges to hold it far enough away to allow you to get at it with a saw. Place a mitre box tight against the board and, with a tenon saw, nibble away at it at 45 degrees until the board is cut in half. Repeat the 45-degree cut at the other end of the section to be replaced and remove the length of old skirting. Then offer up the replacement section, mark each end with a pencil and mitre accordingly. Mitring the ends will make the joints between the new and old boards less obvious and easier to fill if there is any subsequent shrinkage.

A good way to hold the new section in position is to lay a plank so that it butts up against the skirting and kneel on it while driving the nails home. Set all nail heads below the surface before filling and sanding.

DEALING WITH CORNERS

When fitting a moulded shape into a corner, the best way to achieve the joint is to scribe it. This is done by marking the profile of one board on to the back of the other with the aid of a small offcut of the moulding. Then a coping saw is used to cut along the marked line, allowing the board to fit neatly over its neighbour. This technique avoids the mismatch of ends that can occur when some mouldings are mitred at 45 degrees, using a mitre box or mitre saw. However, to form an external corner for a wall return, use a mitre saw or mitre box in the normal way.

TIP

Many skirtings (baseboards) are fixed with flooring, or cut, nails, which are square-edged and grip extremely well. However, they may split a small section of replacement skirting, so use masonry nails instead and drill pilot holes through the skirting.

REPLACING A SECTION OF SKIRTING

1 Prise away the old skirting (baseboard) with a crowbar (wrecking bar) and wedges.

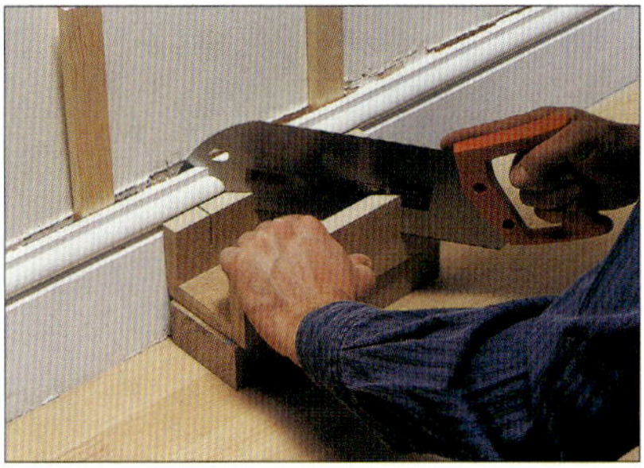

2 Cut away the damaged section with a mitre box and a saw.

3 Hold a new length of board in place and mark it for cutting.

4 Hammer nails into the new section of board while holding a plank against the wood.

INTERNAL AND EXTERNAL MITRES OF A SKIRTING

ABOVE: An internal corner with mitred joint.

ABOVE: A mitred external corner.

REPLACING RAILS

Picture rails and dado rails, sometimes called chair rails because they protect the walls from damage by chair backs, may need to be renewed or repaired. This task is essentially the same as replacing skirtings (baseboards).

REMOVING AND REPLACING RAILS

Use a crowbar (wrecking bar) to prise the old picture or dado (chair) rail away from the wall, inserting a block of wood under its head to protect the plaster and to give extra leverage.

Remove any nails that remain in the wall with a pair of pincers, again using a block of wood to protect the wall. Make good the nail holes with filler, leaving it slightly proud at this stage. When the filler is completely dry, sand it down with abrasive paper wrapped around a cork block, or block of wood, to give a perfectly flat, smooth surface. Fit the new length of rail, scribing or mitring the ends as necessary to ensure a neat finish at the corners.

FIXING METHODS

Cut-nails, such as those used to fix skirtings, have long been used to fix picture rails, dado (chair) rails and the like, but you may find that they are not available in your local store. Any ordinary wire lost-head nail is a good alternative when fixing through plasterwork into stud (dry) walling, as long as you know where the studs are. With a brick or blockwork wall, use masonry nails, drilling clearance holes in the wood to prevent splits.

REPLACING A DADO RAIL

1 Prise the old rail from the wall using a crowbar (wrecking bar) and levering against a block of wood. This will provide additional leverage and prevent damage to the wall.

CUTTING A SCRIBED JOINT

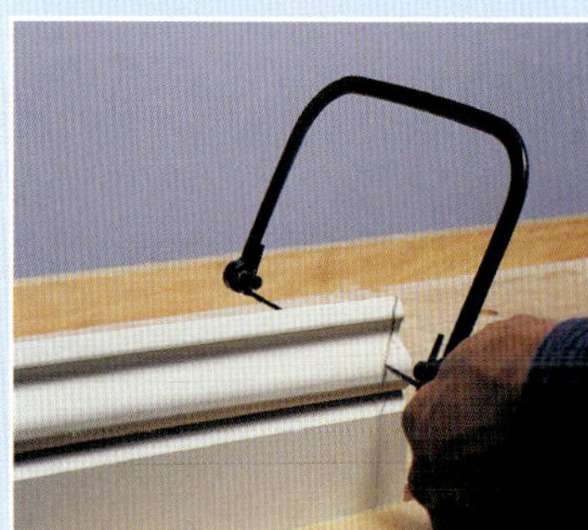

Use a scrap of the moulding as a guide. Hold a pencil against the scrap of wood and run it over the back of the board to transfer the outline. Cut out the waste with a coping saw.

2 Remove any nails that remain in the wall with pincers. Again, lever against a block of wood to prevent the plasterwork from becoming damaged, reducing the amount of making good required.

3 Brush off all dust and loose paint and plaster. Fill any cracks or holes in the plasterwork with filler, working it in well with a filling or putty knife and leaving it slightly proud.

4 Leave the filler to dry. Then sand it with abrasive paper wrapped around a cork or wooden sanding block to obtain a smooth, flat finish. You may need to fill any low spots again.

5 Nail the new rail to the wall, making sure that it is horizontal with a spirit (carpenter's) level. Punch the nail heads below the surface of the wood, fill and sand smooth.

FIXING CLADDING

Wooden cladding may be fixed to walls and ceilings for a variety of reasons. These include: cosmetic, to hide the existing finish; acoustic, to deaden sound; and thermal, to insulate against heat loss. Sometimes cladding has a structural purpose, for example, when it forms part of a stud (dry) wall.

The framework of battens needs to be designed around obstacles (windows and doorways), electrical switches and sockets, and positioned so that whole sheets of cladding join on a stud.

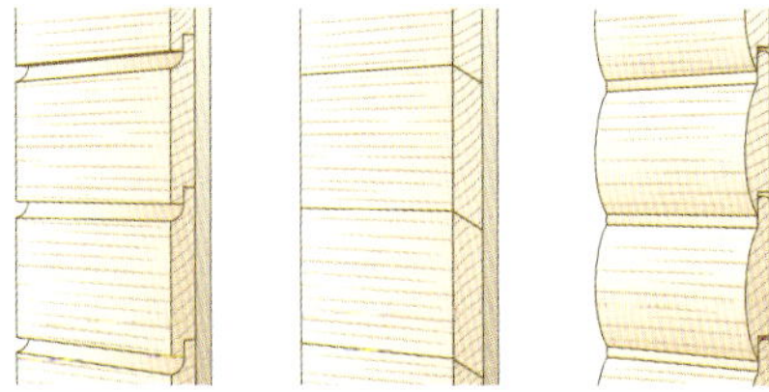

ABOVE: Cladding comes in a range of profiles and can be fixed to a framework of battens using nails, screws or adhesive.

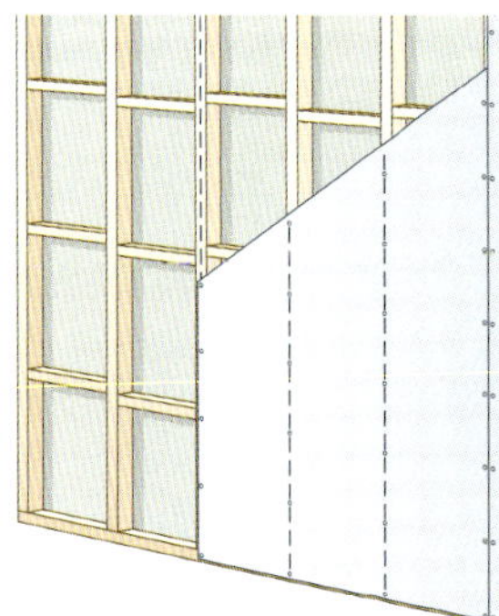

ABOVE: Make sure joints coincide with the centres of studs.

BATTENING A WALL

Drill pilot holes in the battens for the masonry nails, as this will prevent the wood from splitting. Hammer a masonry nail home at one end, level the batten with a spirit (carpenter's) level and drive home a nail at the other end. Finish by driving in more nails along the batten. If the wall is crumbly, you can attach the battens with screws and wall plugs. Secure battening is essential.

FITTING SHEET PANELLING

Cladding can be fixed to the framework of battens using either nails or screws. If screws are used, especially brass ones, a feature can be made of them, so they should be equally spaced to form a pattern. Alternatively, a panel adhesive can be used. If it fails to adhere immediately, tap nails part way through into the battens. The nails can be removed when the panels are secure.

To cut cladding, use either a hand saw or power saw. If using a hand saw, have the decorative face uppermost and cut on the downstroke to limit the chances of damaging it. With a power saw, turn the decorative face of the wood downward. Before using the saw, score the cutting line carefully using a straightedge as a guide. If you need a perfectly straight edge on a cut sheet, where it is to be butted against another board, clamp a straightedge to the board as a guide for the saw.

After cutting, use a fine abrasive paper wrapped around a wood or cork block to smooth down the rough edges.

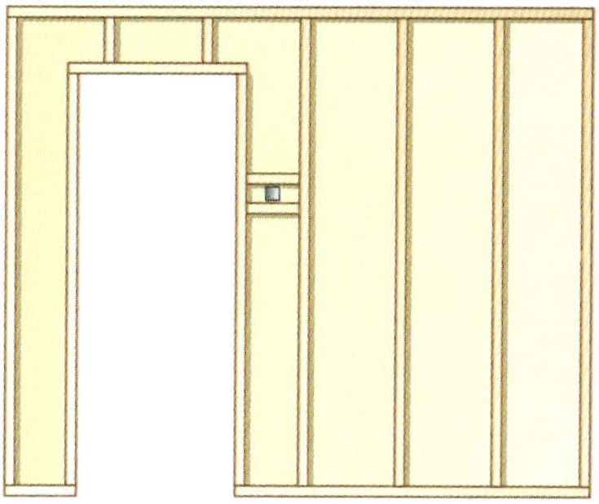

ABOVE: The framework of battens has to be tailored to suit the size and position of obstacles such as doors, windows and electrical fittings. Shown are layouts for vertical cladding (left) with a likely cable point and horizontal cladding (right).

LEFT: Work from each end of the surface to be covered, using cut panels in the middle to retain symmetry.

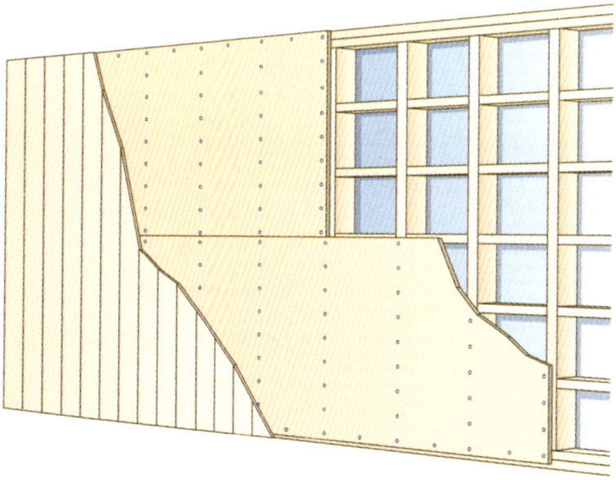

LEFT: Vertical boards fitted to stud (dry) walling with optional intermediate backing sheets. Note how the sheets meet in the centres of the studs.

TONGUED-AND-GROOVED BOARDING

Fitting tongued-and-grooved boarding is more time-consuming than using sheet materials, but the supporting framework can be made simpler because the boards are relatively narrow and rigid. As with all cladding, it is essential to ensure that the battens are fixed securely, and are reasonably spaced for adequate support.

FITTING THE BOARDING

First, square off the ends of the board to ensure that it is at 90 degrees, or 45 degrees if you want to set the boards at an angle. Mark off the length of board required with a craft knife or pencil and cut it to size with a tenon saw.

Place the board in position on the battens, making sure that the tongue is left exposed for the next board to slot over, and in the case of TGV (tongued, grooved and V-jointed) that the correct face side with the chamfer is showing. Secret nail the board by driving panel pins (brads) through the tongue. Repeat this procedure with the remaining boards, tapping each firmly home with a mallet and an offcut of wood to prevent damage to the tongue before nailing.

Leave the second to last board slipped over the previous tongue, but before nailing, use an offcut and pencil to scribe the cutting line on the final board if it needs trimming to fit. Cut and plane the board to width. You might need to fit the last two boards by springing them into place, in which case, both will have to be nailed through the face, since the tongues will not be accessible. Punch the nail heads down and fill.

At internal and external corners, the joints between boards can be concealed by pinning (tacking) on a decorative moulding, which can also be used along the ceiling. Fit normal skirtings (baseboards) at floor level.

DEALING WITH CORNERS

ABOVE: Neaten internal corners by pinning or gluing a length of scotia (cove) moulding into the angle. Use this at ceiling level too.

ABOVE: Butt-join the two boards that form an external corner, and conceal the joint with a length of birdsmouth (corner bead) moulding.

1 Tap fixing nails into each support batten at 300mm (12in) intervals. Check the batten is level and drive in the nails.

2 If the walls are out of true, insert slim packing pieces between the battens and the wall to ensure that the faces of the strips are vertical.

3 Scribe the wall outline on to the face of the first board by holding its grooved edge to the wall and running a block and pencil down it.

4 Fix the boards by interlocking their tongued-and-grooved edges and driving nails through the exposed tongue of each board into the battens.

5 When fixing subsequent boards, close up the joints by tapping the board edges with a hammer and a scrap of wood.

6 Saw or plane the final board down to the required width and spring the last two boards into place. Secure the last board.

BOXING-IN PIPES

Some people regard visible pipes in the home as an eyesore, but with a little time and minimal woodworking skills they can be hidden from view.

ACCESSIBILITY

Bear in mind that stopcocks, drain taps, pumps, hand-operated valves and the like will need to be readily accessible and require some form of removable box system. For this reason, the boxing around them should be assembled with screws rather than nails. If a panel needs to be regularly or quickly removed, turn buttons or magnetic catches are a good idea.

BOXING BASICS

Steel anchor plates and screws can be used to secure the sides of boxing to walls. Battens, either 50 x 25mm (2 x 1in) or 25 x 25mm (1 x 1in), can be used to fix boards at skirting (baseboard) level.

Measure the distance the pipes project from the wall. Cut the side panels from 25mm (1in) plywood or MDF (medium-density fiberboard) slightly over this measurement and to their correct length. Fix small anchor plates flush with the back edge of each panel and spaced at about 600mm (2ft) intervals.

Hold the panels against the wall and mark the screw holes. Drill them and fix the panels with plugs and screws.

Cut the front panel to size from 6mm (¼in) plywood. Drill screw holes in the panel and fix it in place.

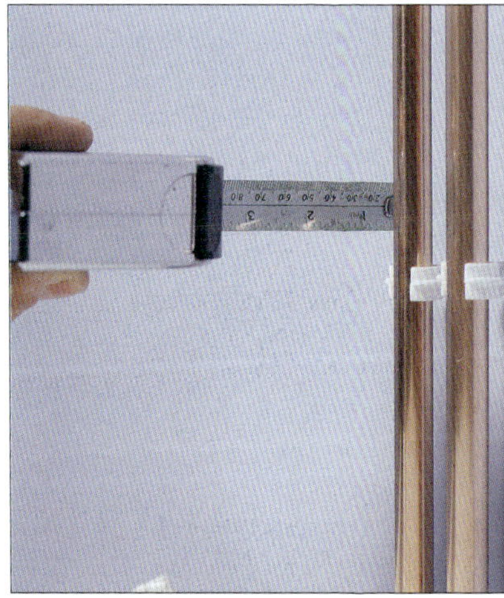

1 Measure the distance that the pipes protrude from the wall, making an allowance for any clips, brackets or fittings such as valves. Make the side panels slightly wider than this measurement.

4 Cut the front panel of the box from 6mm (¼in) plywood, using a jigsaw or circular saw. Offer it up and check the fit. If the panel does not need to be removed again, it can be nailed in place.

2 If the panels are narrow, you may be able to drive the screws through their edges – mark the positions with a pencil. If not, fix anchor plates flush with the back edges of the panels.

3 Attach the side panels, screwing them firmly into position. If screwing to a plywood panel, you may need to make pilot holes; in masonry, you need to drill and plug the holes.

5 If the panel needs to be removable, drill screw holes and secure it with 19mm (¾in) screws. Cup washers under the screw heads will protect the panel if it is likely to be removed often.

6 Trim the edges of the front panel flush with the side panels with a block plane. Then drive any nail heads below the surface and fill. Sand the entire box prior to applying a finish.

Yale

DOORS, LOCKS & WINDOWS

Among the wooden items in the home that receive a considerable amount of wear and tear are the doors. In time, you may need to replace them, either because they are damaged or to spruce up a room. Their hinges, too, can become worn and loose, or even broken. Even the doors of cabinets can suffer the same ailments, while their drawer fronts may have to be changed to match any new doors fitted. An important consideration for every householder is security – making sure that the doors and windows of your home are fitted with sturdy locks and catches that will deter a thief from breaking in. Fortunately, a wide range is available and they are not difficult to fit. A weekend's work is all that is necessary to ensure that your home is well protected.

HANGING DOORS

Installing a new door is not a difficult task, but the job does need patience, precision and organization if it is to go smoothly. A methodical step-by-step approach will pay off. The following sequence relates to hanging a new door, which may or may not need trimming on one or more sides.

TYPES OF DOOR

Many modern internal doors are hollow structures with "egg-box" centres and solid edges. They offer little flexibility for trimming to fit frames that are out of square, which is often a problem in old buildings. For this reason, as well as for aesthetic appeal, use only solid doors in older houses.

PUTTING IN A NEW DOOR

Measure the frame top to bottom and side to side, then choose a door that will fit as closely as possible. Even so, it will probably need to be cut to fit.

Joggles, or horns, may project from the ends of the door to protect it in transit. Mark these off level with the ends of the door, using a try square. Place the door on a flat surface and cut the joggles flush with the ends of the door, using a hand saw. Offer up the door to the frame, placing wedges underneath (chisels are handy) to raise it off the floor by about 12mm (½in) to allow for a carpet or other floor covering.

Mark the door in pencil while it is wedged in place to allow for a 3mm (⅛in) clearance at the top and sides. Place the door back on the flat surface and saw off the bulk of the waste, leaving the marked lines still visible. Plane down the edges of the door to the marked lines, working with the grain, then plane the top, working in from each side to avoid splintering the wood. Replace the door in the frame, wedging it once more to hold it. If you are satisfied with the fit, you can hang it.

Hold each hinge in position, about 150mm (6in) from the top and 225mm (9in) from the bottom of the door, with the knuckle projecting just beyond the face of the door; mark it with a knife. For a heavy door, a third hinge will be needed, positioned centrally between the other two.

Working around the outline, cut down vertically into the wood to the depth of the hinge flap with a chisel. Make a series of cuts across the width of the recess, to the same depth, and remove the waste. Place the hinge in the recess, drill small pilot holes for the screws, then screw the hinge to the door. Repeat with the other hinge.

Offer the hinge side of the door to the frame, placing wedges under it to raise it to the correct height. Press the free flap of each hinge against the frame and mark around it in pencil. Cut the recesses. Drill pilot holes and hang the door, fitting only one screw in each hinge flap. When you are satisfied with the operation of the door, insert all the screws, making sure that the heads lie flat in the countersinks of the hinges, otherwise the door will not close properly.

1 Measure the height and width of the door frame to assess the size of the door you require. If you cannot find the exact size needed, choose one that is slightly larger.

2 If there are protective joggles projecting from the top and bottom of the door, square them off accurately with the ends of the door, using a pencil and try or combination square.

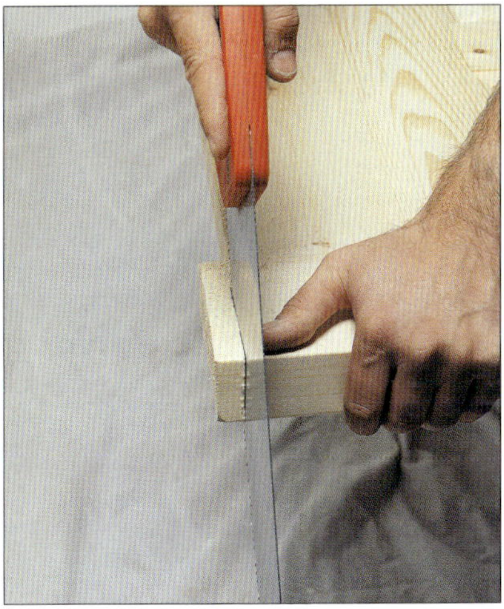

3 Remove the joggles with a hand saw, making a clean, square cut. Saw on the waste side of the line and finish off with a plane or sanding block, working in toward the centre of the door.

4 Offer the door into the frame. Use wedges to square it up if necessary. Make sure you allow a gap of about 12mm (½in) at the bottom to accommodate the thickness of any floor covering. ►

5 Mark the clearance between the door and frame across the top and along the sides, using a pencil and a 3mm (⅛in) washer as a guide. Join the pencil marks with a straightedge.

6 Support the door on sturdy trestles or a similar firm surface. Then saw off the bulk of the waste, using a hand saw and keeping to the waste side of the marked lines.

9 Set a marking gauge to the thickness of the hinge flap and use the gauge to mark this dimension on the face of the door, allowing the flap recess to be cut to the correct depth.

10 Chop out the waste with a sharp chisel, cutting vertically along the scribed lines first, then across the waste before scooping it out. Work carefully down to the depth of the flap.

7 Plane the edges of the door down to the marked lines. When planing the top edge, work in from both sides to prevent splintering at the ends. Offer the door into the frame to check its fit.

8 Hold each hinge on the edge of the door so that its knuckle projects just beyond the face of the door. Mark around the flap with a sharp knife or pencil.

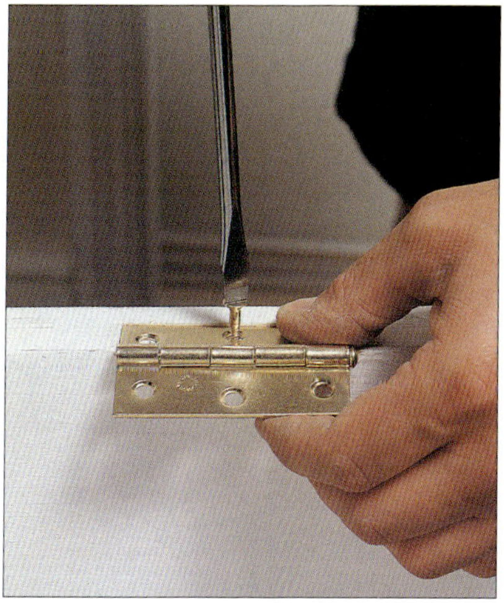

11 Check that the flap fits snugly in the recess, flush with the door edge, making any necessary adjustments. Then make pilot holes for the screws and fix the hinge securely.

12 Mark the positions of the hinges on the door frame with a pencil. Cut the recesses and offer up the door. Fix each hinge with one screw only until you are happy with the fit.

REPLACING CABINET FRONTS

Even if they are not damaged or worn, changing the doors and drawer fronts of storage cabinets is an easy way of giving a room a new look.

NEW DRAWER FRONTS

The drawers of modern furniture are often made with false fronts that allow a basic carcass to be used in a number of different styles. To replace a front, open the drawer or, better still, remove it completely. From inside the drawer, slacken the screws holding the false front to the carcass and remove it. Place the old front over the new one, aligning it exactly, drill down through the screw holes and into the new front to make pilot holes for the fixing screws. Take care not to drill right through the new face and spoil the finish. Use a depth stop to prevent this. Finally, screw the new front to the carcass from the inside.

NEW DOORS

Replacing a chipboard (particle board) door may be necessary if the hinges have failed, which can occur with kitchen furniture after a number of years because of its heavy workload. If you replace old chipboard doors with new ones, they must be exactly the same size and be hung in the same way as the originals, since they cannot be trimmed to fit. Doors such as these are readily available, along with the chipboard hinges necessary to fit them. It is important to ensure that the hinge positions are perfectly accurate and that their recesses are of the correct depth, so careful measuring and a reliable drill stand or pillar drill is essential. You will also need a special bit to cut the blind hole for the hinge in the door. Transfer the hinge positions from the old door.

REPLACING A DRAWER FRONT

1 Remove the old drawer front by unscrewing it from behind.

REPLACING A DOOR

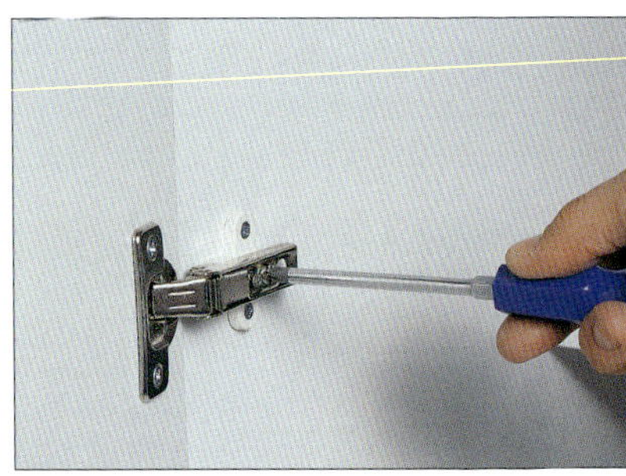

1 Remove the old hinge simply by unscrewing it from the side.

2 Drill pilot holes in the new front, using the existing holes in the old one as a guide.

3 Screw the new drawer front into position from behind. Offer up the drawer and check the fit.

2 Measure accurately from the edge of the old door to the centre of the hinge hole.

3 Transfer the position to the new door to ensure that the new hinge is placed accurately.

4 Drill a new hole, preferably using a drill stand for accuracy.

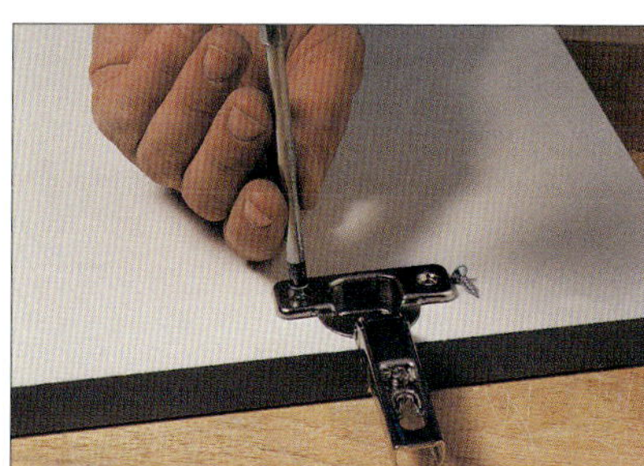

5 Attach the new hinge to the new door. Then fit the door.

FITTING MORTISE DOOR LOCKS

Doors, especially those at the rear of the house, often provide an easy entrance and exit point for intruders. Good locks, properly fitted to a strong door and door frame, are the basic requirements for ensuring that house doors are secure, while additional security devices may help you feel safer at home. A mortise lock is fitted into a slot cut in the edge of a door, where it cannot easily be tampered with.

1 Mark out the dimensions of a mortise lock on the door edge.

INSTALLING MORTISE LOCKS

Align the mortise lock with the centre rail of the door and use the lock body as a template for marking the top and bottom of the mortise.

Draw a line down the middle of the door edge and, using a drill bit the width of the lock body, drill a series of overlapping holes along the centre-line to the depth of the lock. Chisel out the mortise so that the lock body fits snugly.

Insert the lock, mark the outline of the faceplate with a pencil and chisel out a recess so that it fits flush with the door edge.

Mark and drill the holes for the key and spindle; enlarge the keyhole with a padsaw. Assemble and check the lock works.

With the latch and bolt open, mark their positions on the frame. Measure from the outside of the door to the centre of the bolt, mark that distance on the jamb and cut mortises in this position. Chisel a recess for the striking plate (keeper) and check that the door closes properly before fixing.

4 Insert the lock, then mark and chisel out the recess for the faceplate.

TIP

"Measure twice and cut once." Accuracy is vital when marking out for door locks, so take your time with this part of the job and you will experience fewer problems later.

2 Using a mortise gauge, mark a vertical line in the centre of the door between the pencil lines.

3 Drill a line of holes along the centre-line to the depth of the lock body.

5 Using the lock as a guide, mark the positions of the spindle and keyholes.

6 Drill the holes, then use a padsaw to form the keyhole. Fit the covers.

7 Cut mortises for the latch and the deadbolt on the door jamb.

8 Cut out a recess for the striking plate (keeper) so that it fits flush in the door jamb.

FITTING RIM DOOR LOCKS

A rim door lock is an alternative to a mortise lock. It locks automatically as the door is closed, and the bolt cannot be forced back without a key.

INSTALLING RIM LOCKS

Mark the position of the lock on the door, using any template provided, and bore a hole with a flat bit for the key cylinder. Push the cylinder into the hole, connect the lock backplate and secure it with screws. The cylinder connecting bar will protrude through the backplate. If necessary, cut it to length using a hacksaw.

If necessary, mark and chisel out the lock recess in the door edge, then fit the lock and screw it to the door, making sure that the cylinder connecting bar has engaged in the lock.

With the door closed, mark the position of the striking plate (keeper), then chisel out the recess so that the plate fits flush with the frame. Fix the striking plate with the screws provided and check that the door closes properly.

1 Mark the position of the cylinder on the door and drill its hole.

4 If necessary, mark the length of the connecting bar to be cut off.

FITTING A RACK BOLT

A rack bolt allows you to lock a door from the inside, and is unobtrusive and secure.

Mark the position of the rack bolt in the centre of the door edge and on the inner face of the door, using a try or combination square to ensure that the two marks are level. Drill a hole of suitable size horizontally into the door edge to the depth of the body of the bolt. Push the bolt into the hole, mark the outline of the faceplate, then withdraw the bolt and chisel out a recess for the plate. Hold the bolt level with the guideline on the inside of the door, and mark and drill a hole for the key.

Fit the bolt, check that it works properly and screw the keyhole plate to the door. Close the door and wind out the bolt so that it leaves a mark. Drill a hole at this point and fit a recessed cover plate.

2 Insert the barrel of the lock cylinder into the drilled hole.

3 Fit the backplate to the door and secure it tightly with screws.

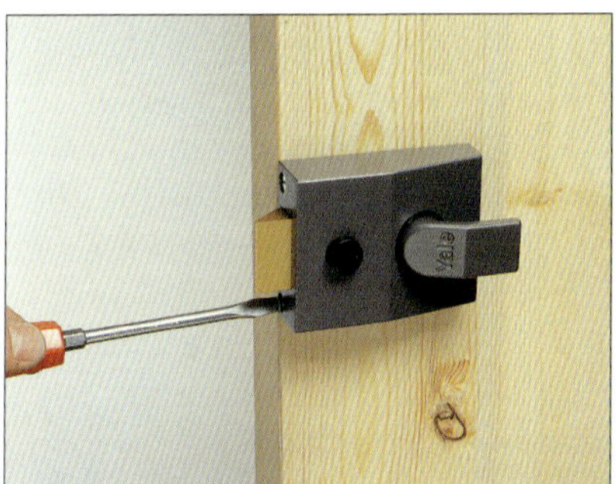

5 Fit the lock case to the connecting plate and screw together.

6 Mark the position of the striking plate (keeper). Chisel out its recess in the frame.

1 Use tape to mark the drilling depth and keep the bit horizontal. Push in the bolt.

2 Mark the outline of the faceplate, then withdraw the bolt to chisel out the recess.

WINDOW SECURITY

Over half of all home burglaries occur through a window, and even the smallest is vulnerable, so good locks are very important. The first line of defence is to fit good-quality handles and stays, followed by key-operated locks to all ground-floor windows, and those first-floor windows that are easily accessible. It is also essential to provide a secure means of ventilation around your home.

BASIC HARDWARE

The most common items of hardware fitted on hinged windows are a rotating cockspur handle, which is used simply to fasten the window, and a casement stay, which props it open in several different positions. On sliding sash windows, the basic hardware is a catch that locks the two sashes together when they are closed.

CHOOSING AND FITTING WINDOW LOCKS

Many window locks are surface-mounted, using screws, and are quick and easy to fit, although for some types a drilled hole for a bolt or recess chiselled for a striking plate (keeper) may be required. Mortised locks and dual screws that fit into holes drilled in the window frame take longer to install, but they are very secure.

When buying locks for windows, bear in mind the thickness of the frames. In some cases, these may be too thin to accommodate a recessed lock without seriously weakening the frame. If in any doubt, buy surface-mounted fittings.

All window locks are supplied with fixing screws, but these should often be discarded in favour of longer, more secure fixings. Some locks come with special security screws that can only be tightened, but not unscrewed. In this case, the lock should be fitted with ordinary screws first and the proper screws only added when you are happy that the lock functions correctly. In other cases, the screws are concealed by plastic plugs. For extra security, it is also a good idea to fit two locks on casement windows more than 1m (3ft) high, while all locking devices for sash windows are best used in pairs.

For secure ventilation, if the window has a stay pierced with holes, you can replace the plain peg with a casement stay lock. Attach the screw-on lock to the threaded peg with the key supplied. This will allow you to secure the window in any position.

If fitting lockable window catches and stays, do not leave keys in the locks where they might be seen by an intruder; they may also fall out as the window is opened and closed. Instead, hang them on a hook close to the window where they are readily accessible, but can't be seen from outside.

TIP

Ensure you have the right screws: a lock intended for wooden window frames requires woodscrews; metal window frames will require self-tapping screws.

FITTING A WINDOW HANDLE AND STAY

1 Choose the position of the cockspur handle on the casement and make pilot holes through it with a bradawl (awl). Then screw the handle firmly to the casement.

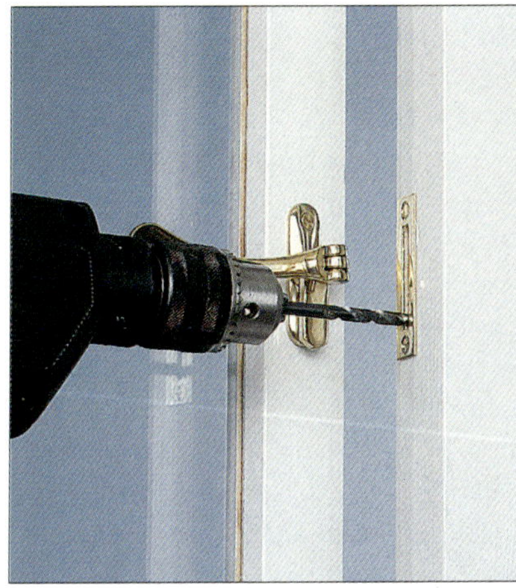

2 Fit the striking plate (keeper) to the frame so that it will engage with the cockspur. Drill out the frame to a depth of 20mm (¾in) through the slot in the plate.

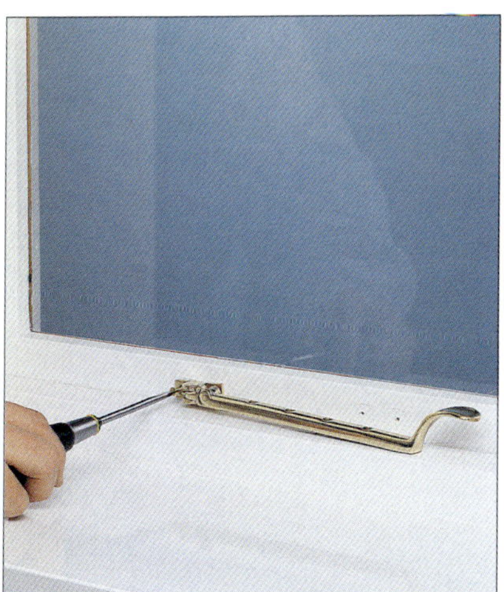

3 Fit the casement stay by screwing its baseplate to the bottom rail of the casement, about one-third along from the hinged edge.

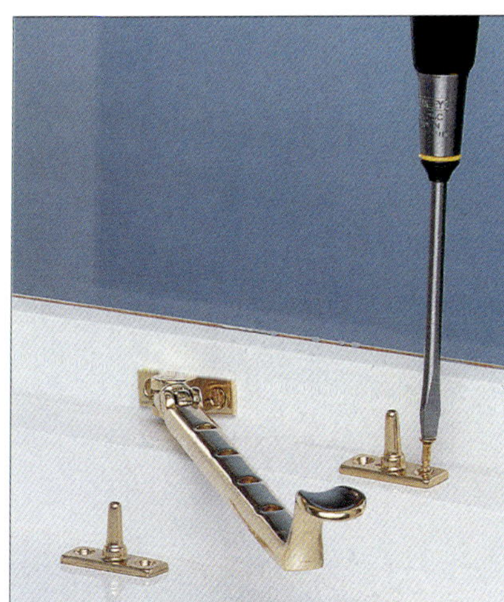

4 Open the window to find the correct position for the pegs on the frame. Attach the pegs, then fit the stay rest to the casement rail.

CASEMENT WINDOW LOCKS

Locks for wooden casement windows may be surface-mounted or set in the frame. If surface-mounted, the lockplate is attached to the fixed frame, and the body of the lock to the opening frame. With the window closed, mark the positions of the lock and plate on both frames, then screw them in place. For those with a locking bolt, you will have to cut a rebate (rabbet) or drill a hole to receive the bolt. Some surface-mounted locks are also suitable for fitting to metal casement windows. Check the instructions.

Locks that are designed to be set in the frame normally require holes to be drilled in both fixed and opening frames. Also, a hole must be drilled through the face of the frame to allow insertion of the key.

1 With the lock assembled, mark its position on the fixed and opening frames. Separate the two parts of the lock and screw the body to the opening frame.

2 Fit the cover plate and insert the screws. You may want to use longer screws than those provided to ensure a strong fixing.

3 Some makes come with small covers or plugs to hide the screws. Tap these into place when you are happy with the fit of the lock.

SASH WINDOW LOCKS

Some types of casement window lock will also work with sash windows. An effective security device for sash windows is the sash stop, which actually allows the window to be opened slightly for ventilation. To fit the device, it is necessary to drill a hole in the upper sash to accommodate its bolt. Then a protective plate is added to the top of the lower sash. In operation, turning the key releases the spring-loaded bolt, which prevents the sashes from sliding past each other.

Another option is key-operated dual screws (shown below), which bolt both sashes together. Use a flat bit the width of the lock barrel to drill through the inner meeting rail (mullion) into the outer rail to the required depth, then tap the barrels into place with a hammer and piece of wood. Fit the longer barrel into the inner rail, the shorter into the outer rail, and screw the bolt into the barrel with the key.

FIRE SAFETY

Wherever possible, fit window locks that all use the same standard key so that any key can be used to open a window in the event of an emergency. Keep keys in accessible positions.

1 Mark the drill bit with tape to the required depth and drill through the inner meeting rail (mullion) of a sash window, into the outer rail.

2 Separate the two sections of the lock and tap the barrels of the dual screw into place in the meeting rails.

WOOD FINISHING

Practically all wooden structures need finishing with some form of protective film that prevents them from becoming dirty, discoloured, or damaged by moisture or slight knocks. Some finishes, such as wax, allow the decorative pattern of the grain to show through, while others, such as paint, conceal it. Although there are many techniques for finishing wood, a number of basic steps are common to all of them. Carry out preparation work well away from the finishing area, and be prepared to move the work back and forth several times as you apply and rub down successive coats. Remember that any finish on wood will enhance defects as well as good points, so preparation is important.

PREPARING WOOD FOR FINISHING

Many different types of wood will need filling. This can be as simple as rubbing in a grain filler, which will give a more even and less absorbent surface. It may involve using a wood filler, which can be bought to match the colour of the wood being used, to fill cracks, blemishes and knot holes. Soft interior stopping is fine for tiny cracks, and a two-part exterior-grade wood filler for making good large holes.

The tools required for finishing are simple, and most of the work can be done entirely by hand. A few scrapers, some abrasive paper in various grades, wire (steel) wool, soft cloth, a cork sanding block and some filler or stopping are the basic requirements.

Apply any filler that is necessary to knot holes and blemishes in the wood, allow to dry and remove the excess gently with a chisel. With this done, the wood can be rubbed down with abrasive paper wrapped around a cork block, working along the grain.

Wipe over the surface with a clean, damp rag to raise the grain very slightly, allow it to dry, then cut it back lightly with 400-grit abrasive paper, again working along the grain.

ESSENTIAL REQUIREMENTS

Not often mentioned is the fact that wood must be dry, regardless of the treatment applied. Another requirement is that when several applications of a finish are called for, they must be rubbed down, or "flatted", between coats.

1 Apply filler to match the colour of the wood. Scrape away any excess with a sharp chisel.

2 Sand down with abrasive paper wrapped around a cork block, working along the grain, not across it.

3 To remove dust, wipe down with a soft, damp cloth, using long strokes parallel to the grain.

STAINING AND VARNISHING WOOD

If you want to stain your wood, test the stain on a spare piece of the same wood to check the final colour and depth.

Remember that end grain will absorb a lot more of the stain and will be much darker. Stain can be applied with a soft cloth or brush. Keep a wet edge all the time to avoid a patchy finish. Apply the stain in short circular motions.

Varnishes, such as polyurethane or acrylic, which are quick drying, should be applied along the grain with a soft brush. Be sure to get into all recesses, but do not leave pools or runs. Allow to dry and flat down with 320-grit abrasive paper or a fine grade of wire (steel) wool.

Varnish is best applied in a cool environment; otherwise problems with a "ripple" finish can occur.

APPLYING STAIN

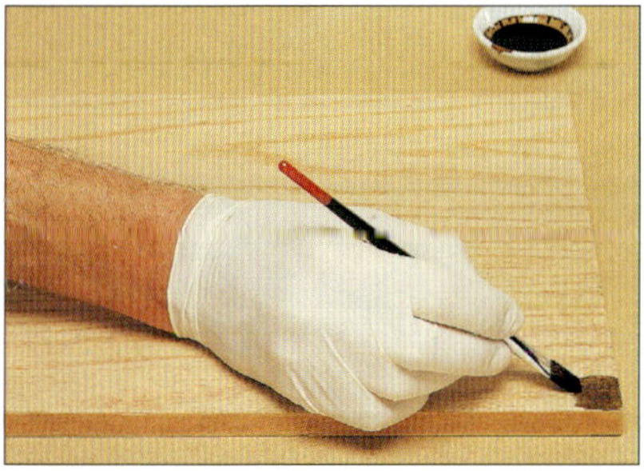

1 Use a small brush to test the colour on a spare piece of wood. Dilute the stain when treating end grain, otherwise it will be too dark.

2 If satisfied with the colour, apply the stain with a soft cloth in quick, circular motions. Don't allow the stain to "puddle".

APPLYING VARNISH

1 For large panels, use a wide brush to apply varnish with long strokes.

2 Rub down the surface using 320-grit silicon-carbide paper, varnish and repeat.

WAXING WOOD

With the wood sanded down, apply a coat of sanding sealer, lightly sanding it when dry. This provides a good base for the wax, preventing it from soaking too deeply into the wood and improving the durability of the final finish.

Apply a coat of wax to the wood with a soft cloth or a ball of very fine wire (steel) wool, using a circular motion, followed by strokes along the grain, to work it well into the wood.

Allow the wax to dry for an hour or so, then polish off with a soft cloth. Add a second, thinner, coat of wax, working in the direction of the grain only. Polish this off lightly and leave for a few hours before giving it a final vigorous polishing.

1 Apply a thin coat of clear shellac or a proprietary sanding sealer to the wood to provide a stable base for the wax. Leave this to dry, then sand lightly.

2 Apply the wax with a ball of fine wire (steel) wool, using a strong circular motion to work it into the wood. Then finish off with strokes in the direction of the grain. Allow the wax to dry.

3 Buff the wax vigorously with a polishing pad made from a soft duster. Add a second, thinner coat of wax and polish it off lightly before leaving it for a few hours. Finally, buff well.

PAINTING WOOD

Start by priming any bare areas, then apply an undercoat and finally one or two coats of gloss (oil) paint. With a standard gloss paint, begin by applying the paint vertically, and then use sideways strokes to blend it well. Work in the direction of the grain, blending in the wet edges for a uniform finish. If you are using a one-coat paint, apply the finish quite thickly in close, parallel strips and do not over-brush.

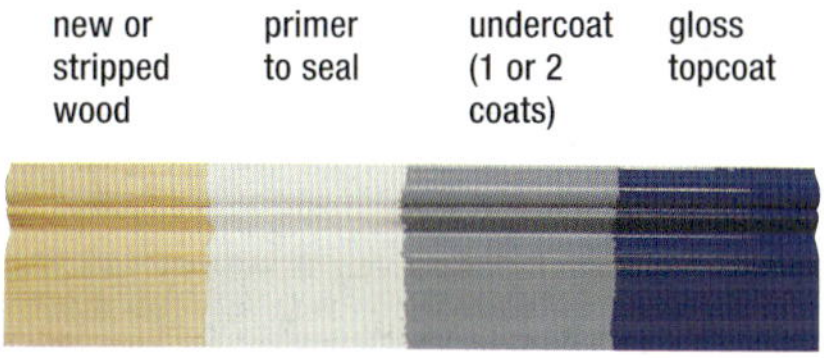

ABOVE: The sequence for painting wood.

1 Apply a suitable primer to all areas of bare wood and allow to dry completely before over-painting. The primer will prevent the paint from soaking into the wood and leaving a patchy finish.

2 Apply one or two undercoats and lightly rub down with fine-grade abrasive paper between coats. To avoid problems, always use the same make of undercoat as topcoat.

3 Finally, apply the topcoat. When painting a panelled door, do the mouldings and panelled areas first, then move on to the cross rails, and finish with the vertical stiles.

SHELVES & STORAGE

- Shelves
- Cabinets & wardrobes
- Storage projects

INTRODUCTION

Finding suitable storage space around the home for all the personal and household belongings every family accumulates can be quite a challenge. One difficulty is making a sensible compromise between tidiness and accessibility; it is no good having a place for everything if that means spending hours each day laboriously taking things out and putting them back again.

The solution is to tailor-make storage to suit its purpose. Some things need a temporary resting place where they remain readily accessible. Others need long-term storage, perhaps being retrieved and used only occasionally. And there is a third storage category, that of display – simply to show things off.

In a typical home, possessions are stored in one of three main ways: on shelves, in cupboards (closets) or in drawers. These may be combined in a variety of storage or display units, and the amount of each type of space that is required will vary from one house to another. For example, the avid bookworm will have miles of bookshelves, while the clothes horse will need more wardrobe space.

The storage that is needed can be provided in one of two ways. One is to buy or make pieces of freestanding furniture that match the required storage function. The other is to use raw materials such as wood and manufactured boards plus the

BELOW: Planned storage is essential in a kitchen to make the most of available space.

ABOVE: A system of shelves provides a useful means of storage in a living room.

ABOVE: For an office/study area, consider using wire baskets for storage.

appropriate hardware to create built-in storage space – arrays of shelving, cupboards in alcoves and so on. The former is the best solution for those who value furniture more than function, since the pieces can be moved from one home to another. However, built-in storage is generally more effective in providing the most space for the least money, since the walls of a room can often be used as part of the structure. In this chapter, you will find a wide variety of storage options that you can use to good effect.

Apart from obvious places such as kitchen cabinets and bedroom wardrobes, there are many places in the main rooms of the home where items can be stored. This can be done without spoiling the look of the room. Properly planned storage space can be not only practical and capacious, but positively elegant.

LIVING ROOM

Here, storage needs are likely to be firmly leisure-oriented. There has to be room for books, tapes, CDs, videotapes and DVDs, not to mention display space for ornaments and other treasures. The choice is between freestanding and built-in furniture, and it is worth spending time looking at different possibilities because here looks are as important as performance.

Built-in furniture can make optimum use of alcoves and other recesses. A more radical option is a complete wall of storage units, which could incorporate space for home entertainment equipment, as well as features such as a drinks cabinet. This also offers the opportunity to include a home office section – some desk space, room for a computer, plus somewhere to file away all the essential paperwork that every household generates.

KITCHEN

Storage is a serious business here, and what is needed and how it is provided depends on what kind of kitchen it is and how it is used. The fully fitted kitchen is still popular because it packs the most storage into the least space, although there is now a discernible movement back to farmhouse-style kitchens fitted with freestanding rather than built-in furniture. This is suitable only for people who are either very tidy and well organized or, on the other hand, happy to live in chaos. The style of such kitchens restricts the amount of storage space they can offer at the expense of the look of the room, so for those who have a lot of kitchen utensils and like to keep large stocks

ABOVE: The traditional dresser is ideal for creating the country kitchen look.

ABOVE: A fitted kitchen unit provides made-to-measure storage space under a work counter.

of food, a fitted kitchen is a better idea. However, there is one big advantage with freestanding furniture: it can be taken along when moving house.

In deciding what is wanted, analyse storage needs thoroughly. Think about food, utensils and small appliances for a start; all need a place close to cooking and food preparation areas. Move on to items like china, cutlery and glassware; do they need to be in the kitchen at all, or would the dining room be a better place to keep them? Then consider non-culinary items – things like cleaning materials, table linen and so on – and make sure there is enough space for them.

Remember that ceiling-height cupboards (closets) are always a better bet than ones that finish just above head height, even if some small steps or a box are needed to reach them. It is best to use the top shelves for storing seldom-used items.

Always aim to make the best possible use of cupboard space. Fit extra shelves where necessary, use wire baskets for ventilated storage, hang small racks on the backs of cupboard doors and use swing-out carousels to gain access to corner cupboards.

If there is a separate laundry room, it is often easier to split cooking and non-cooking storage needs by moving all home laundry and cleaning equipment out of the kitchen altogether. Such a room can also act as a useful back porch if it has access to a garden.

ABOVE: A collection of glasses can be seen to best advantage in a glass-fronted display case.

DINING ROOM

Here, storage needs relate mainly to providing places for china, glassware and cutlery – especially any that is kept for special occasions. Think too about storage for tablemats, cloths and other table accessories. There may also be a need for somewhere to store small appliances such as toasters, coffee makers and hotplates. Once again, the choice is between built-in storage units and freestanding furniture; this is largely a matter of taste.

HALLWAY

Simple hooks and an umbrella stand are the bare minimum, but consider providing an enclosed cupboard (closet) that is built-in rather than freestanding. It is simple to borrow some porch or hall floor space to create an enclosure. If it is fitted with a door to match others leading to the rest of the house, it will blend in perfectly. Make sure it is ventilated so that damp clothes can dry.

ABOVE: A hallway needs storage for items you will use outdoors, such as umbrellas and shoes.

BEDROOM

Now take a look at your storage requirements in the bedroom. Here, the main need is for space to store clothes, and this is one area where built-in (and ideally, walk-in) storage is the perfect solution. If there are two bedrooms, space can often be poached by forming a deep partition wall, accessible from one or both rooms. This can actually save money in the long run, as there is no furniture to buy. If you have bedrooms upstairs and the overall upstairs floor space is large enough, you could also consider creating a separate dressing room.

ABOVE: Wardrobes need an arrangement of hanging rails, shelves and drawers.

Bedrooms built under the roof slope offer an opportunity to make use of the space behind the walls by creating fully lined eaves cupboards (closets). These are particularly useful for long-term storage of items such as luggage, which may be needed only occasionally, as well as providing a home for toys and games in children's rooms.

Do not just restrict bedroom storage to clothes and bedlinen, though. There is no reason why it should not also allow for books, ornaments, or even a small television or computer.

LEFT: In a bedroom, small shelves can provide useful room for a variety of bits and pieces.

RIGHT: In a home workshop, use perforated wall boards to store hand tools.

BATHROOM

Next, look at the bathroom. Here requirements are likely to be relatively low-key – somewhere to keep toiletries and cleaning materials, for example. It is not a good idea to store towels and the like in a potentially damp and steamy atmosphere. The choice is likely to be between a floor-standing vanity unit and some wall cabinets, although if space permits some thought might be given to the growing number of fully fitted bathroom furniture ranges.

ROOF SPACE

It is worth boarding over at least the area around the access hatch so that luggage, boxes and the like can be put there. If the roof construction permits, however, there is a chance to create almost unlimited storage capacity. Fit a proper ladder for safe and easy access.

WORKSHOP

An area where some storage space is certainly needed is a home workshop, whether this is a spare room, an area at the back of the garage or a separate building. The basic need is for shelf space, to take everything from cans of paint to garden products, and also some form of tool storage to keep everything in order.

LEFT: A corner cabinet makes a versatile bathroom storage unit because it uses literally every corner of space. In this bathroom, bottles and soaps have been neatly stored in an aluminium accessory holder.

RIGHT: Storage can be stylish and attractive as well as functional, as these painted bathroom hooks show.

SHELVES

The most basic form of storage is shelving, but even so, there are options to consider. Adjustable shelving systems are very versatile, making use of slotted wall uprights that accept special shelf brackets. They allow you to add or remove shelves or adjust their spacing at will. Individual brackets are ideal for single shelves, but can be utilitarian in appearance. If you intend fitting shelves into an alcove, they can be fixed to battens screwed to the wall. In a freestanding unit, shelves can be held by special studs, bookcase strips or dowel-reinforced butt joints. In a garage or home workshop, shelves can be supported on sturdy "ladder" frames to create flexible storage systems.

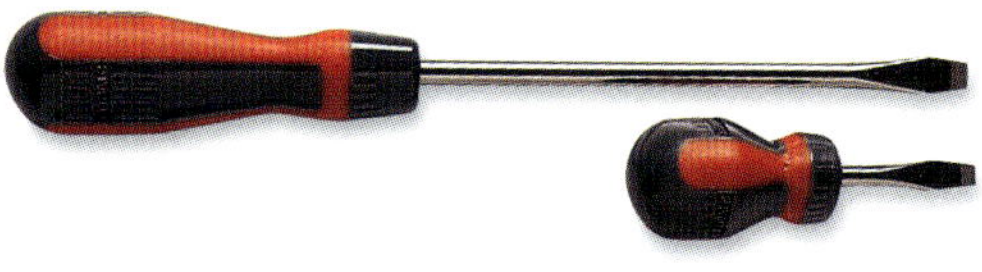

ADJUSTABLE SHELVING

Shelving systems abound in do-it-yourself stores for those who prefer simply to fit rather than to make the shelving. There is a range of brackets on the market to cater for every need, and these clip into slotted uprights screwed to the wall. The bracket positions can be adjusted to vary the spacing between the shelves to accommodate your needs.

Shelving systems are a versatile way of dealing with changing requirements, and they have the distinct advantage of being portable when you need to move them. They are capable of holding heavy weights, but remember that ultimately a shelf's capacity depends on the strength of the wall fixing employed.

First measure the distance between the shelving uprights, bearing in mind the thickness and material to be used for the shelf. Books can be very heavy, so do not set the uprights too far apart, otherwise the shelf will sag in the middle. About a quarter of the length of the shelf can overhang each end. If necessary, cut the uprights to length. Drill and plug the wall so that you can attach one upright by its topmost hole. Do not tighten the screw fully at this stage. Simply allow the upright to hang freely.

Hold your spirit (carpenter's) level against the side of the upright, and when you are satisfied that it is vertical, mark its position lightly on the wall with a pencil. Mark in the remaining screw positions, then drill and plug the rest of the screw holes.

You may find that when you tighten the screws, the upright needs a little packing here and there to keep it vertical in the other plane. If these discrepancies are not too large, this adjustment can be done by varying the relative tightness of the screws, which will pull the upright into line. You can mark off the position for the second upright and any others, using a spirit level on top of a shelf with a couple of brackets slipped into position. Fitting the second upright entails the same procedure as before.

PLANNING SHELVES

Aim to keep everyday items within easy reach and position deep shelves near the bottom so that it is easy to see and reach the back. Allow 25–50mm (1–2in) of clearance on top of the height of objects, so that they are easy to take down.

Think about weight too. If the shelves will store heavy objects, the shelving material must be chosen with care. With 12mm (½in) chipboard (particle board) and ready-made veneered or melamine-faced shelves, space brackets at 450mm (18in) for heavy loads or 600mm (2ft) for light loads. With 19mm (¾in) chipboard or 12mm (½in) plywood, increase the spacing to 600mm (2ft) and 750mm (2ft 6in) respectively. For 19mm (¾in) plywood, blockboard, MDF (medium-density fiberboard) or natural wood, the bracket spacing can be 750mm (2ft 6in) for heavy loads, 900mm (3ft) for light ones.

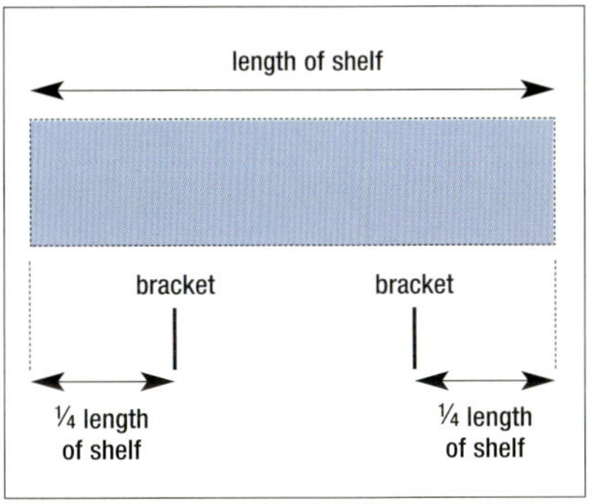

1 Measure the distance between the uprights. Allow a quarter length of shelf at each end.

2 Fix the first screw loosely in the top hole and let the upright hang.

3 Check the bracket is absolutely vertical with a spirit (carpenter's) level.

4 A little packing card may be necessary if the wall is uneven.

5 Mark the position for the second upright using the first as a guide.

6 The shelf brackets can be inserted at different heights and can be easily moved.

USING SHELF BRACKETS

With a little thought, shelving can be made to be decorative as well as functional, and a variety of materials, including wood, metal and glass, can be used to good effect.

All require firm wall fixings. Always use a spirit (carpenter's) level when fitting shelves.

1 Mark the position of the shelf by drawing a line across the wall, using a long, straight batten as a guide. Make sure it is perfectly horizontal with a spirit (carpenter's) level.

SIMPLE SHELVING

Ready-made shelving systems can be employed, both wall-mounted and freestanding. The basic methods of fitting shelving are the same, no matter what material is used. Essential requirements are establishing a truly level surface with a spirit level, obtaining firm fixings in the wall, and being able to fit the shelving accurately into an alcove.

The simplest form of shelf is a wooden board supported by a pair of metal or wooden brackets. The latter are available in a range of sizes and in styles that vary from purely functional to quite decorative. Consider carefully before buying; the brackets will be in plain view, so make sure they fit in with their surroundings. You can make them less obvious, however, by painting them to match the wall colour.

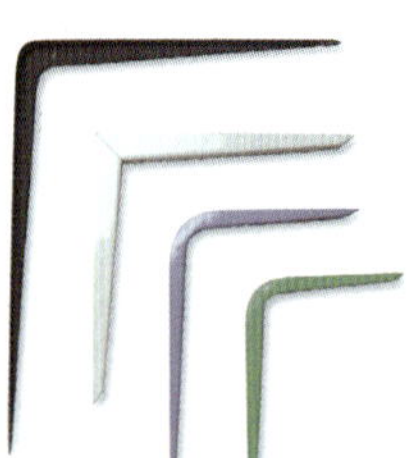

Make sure that you match the size of bracket to the width of board you intend using – if too narrow, the shelf will not be supported fully and may actually collapse when loaded. Choose brackets that will span between two-thirds and three-quarters of the width of the board.

Use your spirit level to ascertain the height and horizontal run of the shelf, then mark the positions for the brackets. Mark the positions of the screws through the holes in the brackets, drill with a masonry bit and insert wall plugs. Hold each bracket in place and start all the screws into the wall plugs before tightening them fully.

If fitting more than one shelf on an uninterrupted run of wall, mark them out at the same time, using a try or combination square. Cut them to size, then screw them to the shelf brackets.

2 Mark the positions of the fixing screws on the wall through the bracket holes. For accuracy, lay a short piece of wood on top of each bracket, aligning it with the pencil line.

3 Drill the holes for the screws, using a masonry bit if necessary, and insert wall plugs. Hold each bracket in place and start all of its screws before tightening them fully.

4 Lay the shelf on top of the brackets, making sure the overhang is equal at each end. Use a bradawl (awl) to make pilot holes and screw through the brackets into the shelf.

5 You can also attach the shelf to the brackets before mounting the brackets to the wall. If you do this, make sure that the back edge of the shelf aligns with the bracket mounting faces.

FITTING SHELVES IN ALCOVES

Alcoves beside chimney breasts (fireplace projections) or other obstructions make perfect sites for shelves, since the back and side walls can be used as supports. Although it is easy to use fixed shelf brackets or an adjustable shelving system to support shelves here, it is cheaper to fix slim wood or metal support strips directly to the alcove walls and rest the shelves on top of these.

If using wooden supports, cut their front ends at an angle so that they are less noticeable when the shelves are fitted. Paint them the same colour as the walls (or to tone with the wall covering) to make them even less obtrusive. If using L-shaped metal strips for the supports, choose a size that matches the shelf thickness so they are almost invisible once the shelves have been fitted.

The actual job is quite simple. Mark the shelf level on the alcove walls, cut the supports to the required lengths and screw them to the walls. Then cut your shelf to size and slip it into place, resting on the supports. It can be nailed, screwed or glued in place for extra stability. The only difficult part is in making the shelf a good fit, since the alcove walls may not be truly square. Accurate measuring of the alcove width at front and back, plus some careful scribing of the rear edge of the shelf, will ensure good results.

When fitting more than one shelf, measure for each separately, since the alcove may not be uniform in size.

1 Decide on the shelf positions, then use a spirit (carpenter's) level to mark the position of the first shelf support on one alcove wall.

4 Screw the second support in place as before, marking the positions of the fixing holes on the wall. Check again that it is level.

7 Repeat step 5 to measure the width at the point where the front edge of the shelf will be, then transfer the measurement to the shelf.

2 Drill clearance holes in the supports, and use one to mark its fixing hole positions on the wall. Drill the holes and fix this support.

3 Rest a shelf on the first support, hold it level and mark the shelf position on the opposite wall. Then prepare the second shelf support.

5 Make a set of gauge rods from scrap wood, held together with a rubber band. Extend the rods to span the rear wall of the alcove.

6 Lift the rods out carefully without disturbing their positions and lay them on the rear edge of the shelf. Mark the width of the alcove on it.

8 Cut the shelf to width and lay it in place. If the fit is poor against the back wall, use a block and pencil to scribe the wall outline on it.

9 Saw carefully along the scribed line with a power jigsaw (saber saw). Sand the cut edge smooth and fit the shelf back in position.

USING SHELF SUPPORT STRIPS

This is an ingenious method of providing support for single shelves. It consists of a specially shaped channel that is screwed to the wall at the required position; then the shelf is simply knocked into place with a soft-faced mallet.

The channel grips the shelf securely and can support surprisingly heavy loads. For lighter loads such as ornaments you can use small shelf support blocks. The shelf is clamped in place by tightening a locking screw underneath the block.

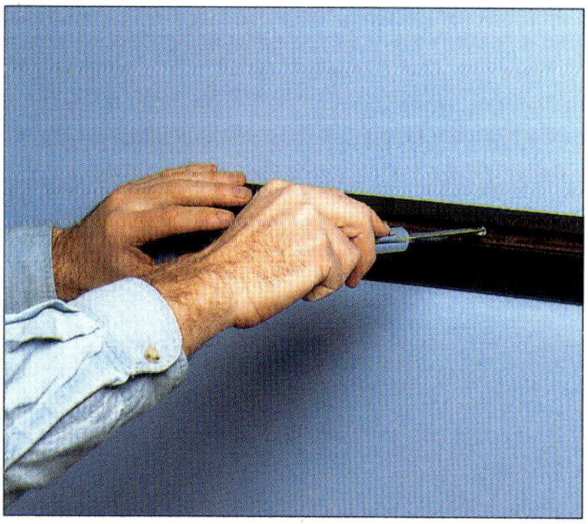

1 Hold the support strip against the wall at the desired level and mark the position of the central screw hole. Drill and plug the hole, then attach the strip.

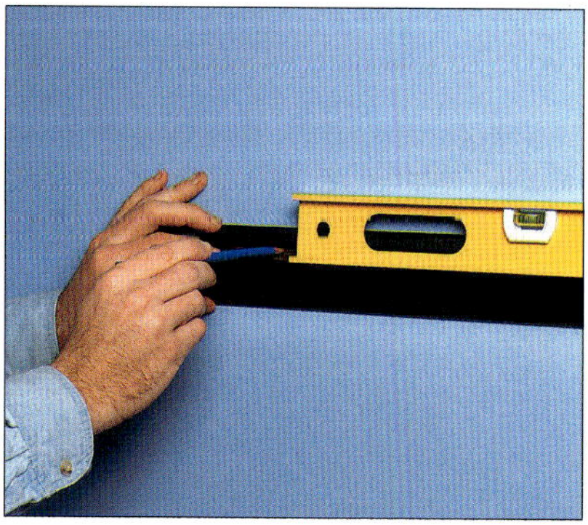

2 Place a spirit (carpenter's) level on top of the strip. Swivel the strip until it is precisely level, then mark the positions of the remaining screw holes on the wall.

3 Swivel the strip out of the way and drill the other holes. Insert wall plugs. Then secure the strip with the remaining screws and slot the shelf into place.

4 Shelf support blocks are also available for mounting small display shelves. The shelf is clamped in the block by tightening a locking screw from underneath.

USING STUDS AND BOOKCASE STRIPS

Adjustable shelves may also be wanted inside a storage unit. There are two options. The first involves drilling a series of carefully aligned holes in each side of the unit, then inserting small plastic or metal shelf support studs. The second uses what is known as bookcase strip – a metal moulding with slots into which small pegs or tongues are fitted to support the shelves. Two strips are needed at each side of the unit. In both cases, accurate marking out is essential to ensure that the supports line up.

USING SHELF SUPPORT STUDS

1 Use a simple predrilled jig to make the holes for the shelf supports in the sides of the unit. A depth stop will prevent you from drilling too deep and breaking through.

2 Drill two sets of holes in each side of the unit, with the top of the jig held against the top of the unit to guarantee alignment. Insert the supports and fit the shelves.

USING BOOKCASE STRIPS

1 Mark the positions of the top ends of the strips to ensure that they are level, then mark the screw positions to a true vertical. Make pilot holes and screw on the strips.

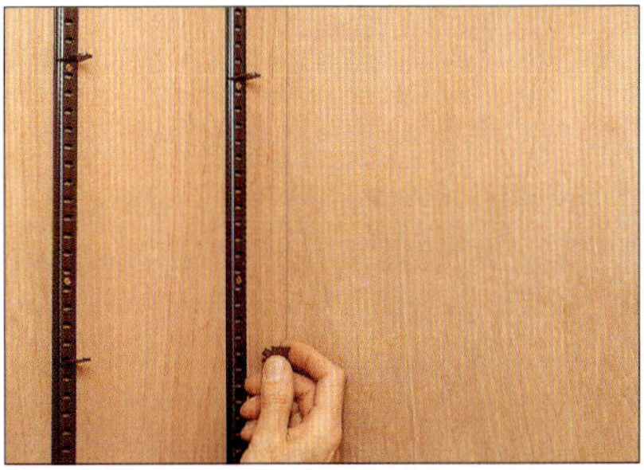

2 Insert pairs of pegs into the bookcase strip at each shelf position, checking that their lugs are properly engaged in the slots. Then lift the shelf into place on the pegs.

FREESTANDING SHELVING

Freestanding shelf units can easily be moved if the room layout is changed or when painting or papering. However, they have drawbacks too. Some manufactured shelving and display units are rather flimsy, and may twist out of square or sag if they are heavily loaded. In general, better results come from building units from stronger materials such as natural wood and plywood.

The other problem is getting units to stand upright against the wall; skirtings (baseboards) prevent standard units from being pushed back flush with the wall surface, and carpet gripper strips make them lean forwards slightly. The answer is to design the side supports on the cantilever principle with just one point of contact with the floor. This point should be as far as possible from the wall, so that the unit presses more firmly against the wall as the load on the shelves is increased. Fix the unit to the wall with brackets for safety, particularly if there are children around.

Since a shelf unit is basically a box with internal dividers, it can be constructed in several different ways, using simple butt joints or more complicated housings. Perhaps the best compromise between strength and ease of construction is to use glued butt joints reinforced with hardwood dowels, which give the joints the extra rigidity they need in a unit of this sort.

Start by deciding on the dimensions of the unit, then select materials to suit the loading the shelves will support.

1 Clamp groups of identical parts together. Mark them to length and cut them in one go to ensure that they are all the same.

4 Glue the dowels and tap them into the holes in the shelf ends. Check that they all project by the same amount, and cut down any that may be too long.

2 Mark the positions of the shelf dowel holes on the unit sides. Drill them all to the required depth, using a drill stand if possible.

3 Use a dowelling jig to drill the dowel holes in the shelf ends. This ensures that the holes are correctly positioned and are drilled straight.

5 Assemble the unit by gluing one end of each of the three shelves and joining them to one of the side panels. Then glue the other ends and add the second side panel.

6 Cut a hardboard or plywood backing panel. Use a try square to check that the angles are correct, then pin the board into position on the back of the unit.

MAKING UTILITY SHELVING

Storage space in workshops, garages, basements and attics is best provided by building simple but sturdy shelves from inexpensive materials. Use wood that is sawn, not planed (dressed), for the framework, and cut the shelves from scrap plywood. Damaged boards and offcuts (scraps) are often available cheaply from timber merchants (lumberyards).

The shelving units shown here are made from 50mm (2in) square wood, with shelves of 19mm (¾in) plywood. The only other materials needed are some scraps of 9mm (⅜in) thick plywood for the small triangular braces that help to stiffen the structure.

The uprights should be spaced about 760mm (2ft 6in) apart so that the shelves will not sag; they can reach right to ceiling level if desired. Match the depth of the unit to whatever is to be stored and to the amount of space available. Remember that it can be difficult reaching things at the back of deep shelves.

1 Start by deciding on the height the uprights should be, and on how many "ladders" are needed. Cut them all to length with a power saw.

2 Make up the ladders by gluing and nailing the rungs between pairs of uprights. Reinforce the joints by gluing and screwing on plywood triangles.

3 Stand the assembled ladders against the wall, check that they are truly vertical, and screw them to the wall into wooden studs or masonry anchors.

4 Cut as many plywood shelves as are needed so they span between the centre lines of the rungs; notch the corners so they will fit neatly.

MAKING A STORAGE RACK

This tool storage rack is basically a wall-mounted backing board of 19mm (¾in) thick plywood. Tools are hung on various supports, as shown in the illustration. These are located in, and slide along, horizontal channels formed by pinning 38 x 12mm (1½ x ½in) plywood to the backing panel and then pinning 75 x 19mm (3 x ¾in) softwood strips to the plywood. Make the trays for small tools from 12mm (½in) plywood, and use hardwood dowel pegs or old wire coat hangers to form support hooks for larger tools. Slide the backplate of each support into its channel at the sides of the rack, and push them to where they are needed.

BELOW: This versatile storage rack is easy to make and can be tailored exactly to accommodate a variety of hand tools. Its design allows the arrangement of fixtures to be adjusted at any time to meet changing needs.

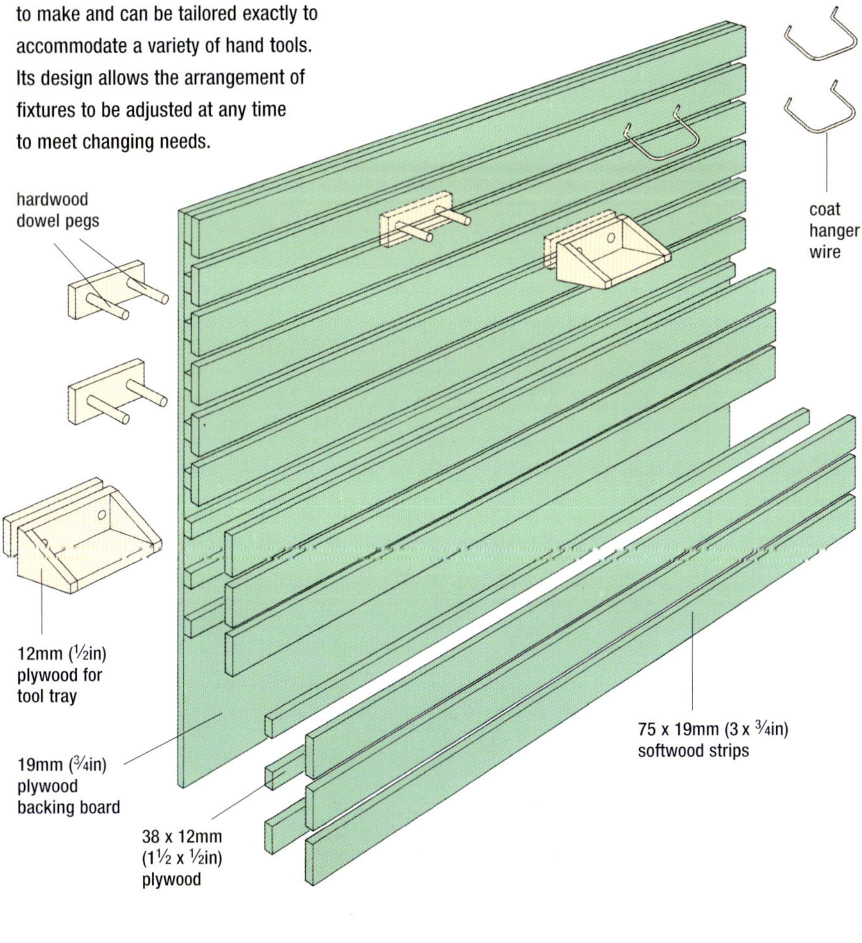

MAKING A GARAGE STORAGE WALL

The garage is a favourite place to store all manner of things, including tools and materials for do-it-yourself, gardening and car maintenance tasks. Unless these are kept under control, they will spill over until there is no room for the car. The solution is to build a shallow full-height storage unit along either the side or the end wall of the garage, tailor-made to suit whatever will be stored there.

The design concept of the storage wall is quite simple. The structure is based on ladder frames fixed to the wall to support shelves, drawers and

BELOW: This simple storage wall unit is the ideal home for all the various tools, equipment and do-it-yourself materials that are likely to find a home in your garage, keeping the floor area clear for your car. You can easily adapt its design to fit your own garage and particular needs.

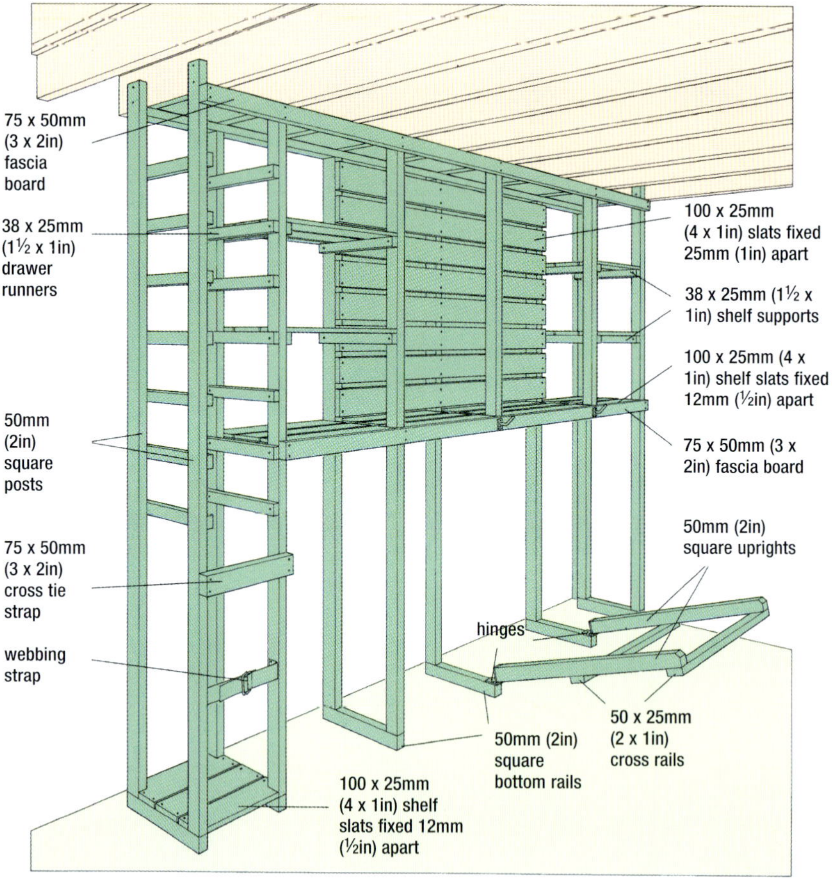

whatever else is required. The frame is made mainly from 50mm (2in) square sawn softwood, with 75 x 25mm (3 x 1in) wood for the shelves and the slatted hanging rack. The hinged section drops down to allow sheets of plywood and the like to be placed on edge behind it, and is held shut with a simple hasp and staple at each side. The wall-mounted rack allows heavy items to be hung out of the way, yet be readily to hand, on metal S-hooks.

1 Start by securing the uprights to the garage wall to form the various bays. Check that each is vertical before fixing it in place.

2 Set sole plates on something damp-proof (here sheet vinyl flooring has been used), and screw them down into expanding wall plugs in holes drilled in the garage floor.

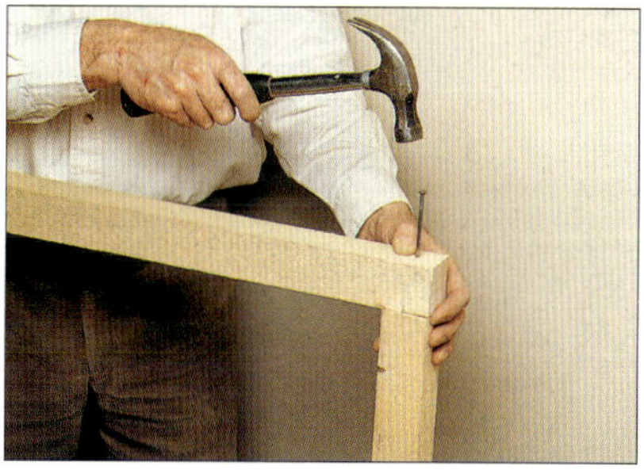

3 Simply nail the components together as required to form the frames that make up each bay. Add horizontals to support wooden shelves or plastic bowl drawers.

4 To make the drop-down flap for the sheet materials storage bay, hinge the two front uprights to their baseplates and add a cross rail.

5 To make the wall rack, nail on the slats, using an offcut (scrap) as a spacer. Make the shelves in the same way.

CABINETS & WARDROBES

Cabinet-making is a skilled craft, but the ready availability of man-made boards faced with veneer or melamine and ready-made doors in a variety of styles has made it possible for any competent do-it-yourselfer to create attractive, functional cabinets for any room of the home. Panels can be joined by simple glued butt joints reinforced with nails, screws or wooden dowels, while doors can be hung with flush or concealed hinges. Even drawers can be added, using kits of plastic parts. Wardrobe space is invariably in short supply in the bedroom, but it is relatively simple to add doors, shelves and hanging rails to an alcove, or even across the entire end wall of a room.

MAKING CABINETS

Freestanding storage units consist simply of a basic box, fitted out internally as required. For example, this can include one or more shelves, vertical dividers, hanging rails, drawers and doors. All this applies to units as diverse in scale as a small hi-fi cabinet and a large double wardrobe. A pair of boxes can be placed under a counter top to create a desk or dressing table.

Units will probably be made from manufactured boards. It is difficult to get natural wood wider than about 225mm (9in), which rather restricts its scope; it is also more expensive. The most popular material for making box furniture is chipboard (particle board), especially the veneered and melamine-faced varieties. It is sold in planks and boards of various sizes with the long edges (and sometimes the ends) already veneered or faced. Its main disadvantage is that it will sag under its own weight across spans of more than about 900mm (3ft).

Stronger alternatives are plywood, MDF (medium-density fiberboard) and blockboard. Blockboard is the strongest and can be used unsupported over spans twice as great as for chipboard. Sheets of blockboard sold as door blanks usually have the long edges faced.

Plywood offers the best of both worlds – it is almost as strong as blockboard, and has edges that can be neatly finished. It is also available in thicknesses from 4mm (just over ⅛in) to 19mm (¾in), so there should be a perfect match for any application.

MDF is a popular choice for box furniture as well as shelves, since it cuts beautifully without the need for finishing sawn edges. It is a medium-strength material and its very smooth surface finish can be painted, varnished or stained. Available in 2440 x 1220mm (8 x 4ft) sheets and in thicknesses

MAKING BUTT JOINTS

1 To make a box, take measurements and start by cutting the components to size. Use a circular saw or a jigsaw (saber saw).

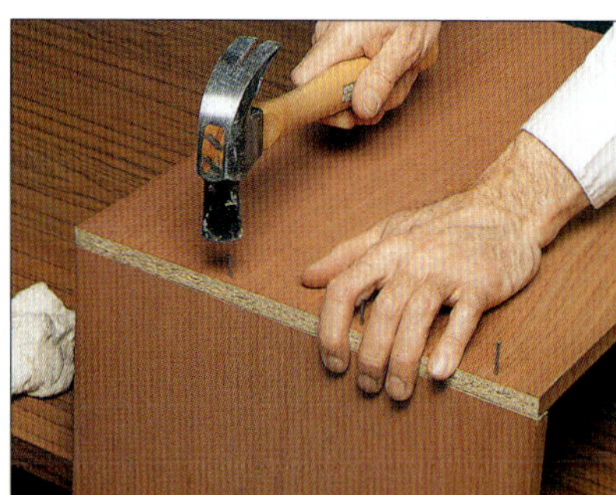

4 Reinforce a glued joint with nails driven in so that they pass into the centre of the panel underneath. Use a damp cloth to remove any excess adhesive.

ranging from 6 to 25mm (¼ to 1in), MDF falls into the medium price range.

Those who are inexperienced in using power tools to make rebates (rabbets) and housing joints will be making boxes using glued butt joints, nailed or screwed for extra strength. These are adequate for small items, but will need reinforcing on larger pieces. The ideal way of doing this is with hardwood dowels. It is advisable to use dowels for chipboard, in which nails and even screws will not hold well. Alternatives, for light loads only, are special chipboard screws, or ordinary screws set in glued-in fibre wall plugs.

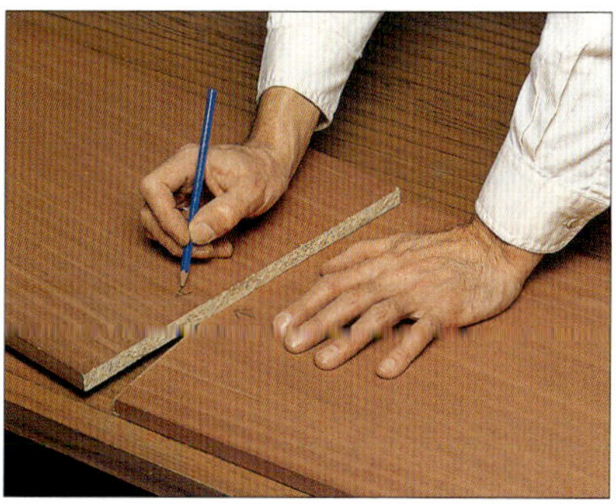

2 Label each piece in pencil and mark both halves of each joint with matching letters to avoid mix-ups during assembly.

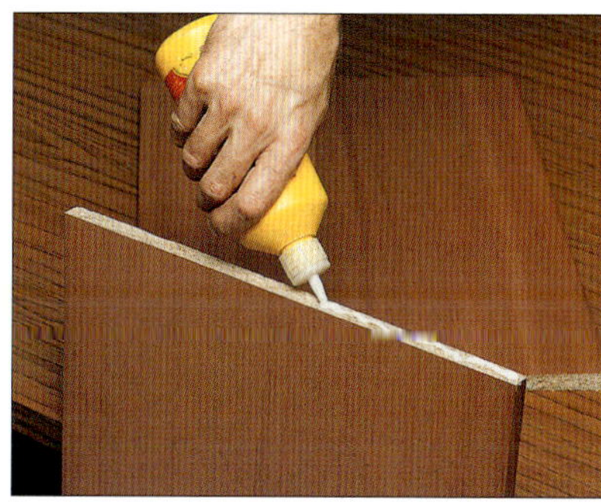

3 To make a glued butt joint, spread adhesive along the edge of one component. Assemble the joint and clamp it to keep it square.

5 Screwed joints are stronger than nailed ones. Place the edge component against the face component and mark its position on the latter. Mark the screw positions carefully.

6 Drill clearance holes through the face component, then pilot holes in the edge component. Countersink the clearance holes and drive in chipboard (particle board) screws.

USING DOWELS

Hardwood dowels are an effective means of reinforcing butt joints between panels, and you can buy them in various sizes. Since they are glued into blind holes, it is essential to allow glue to escape as they are pushed home. This can be achieved by sanding a "flat" along the length of the dowel or by using ready-grooved dowels.

Careful marking out and drilling is essential to ensure correct alignment of the dowel holes in adjacent panels. Various devices are available to make this possible. The simplest is the dowel pin. This is fitted into the dowel hole in one panel, which is pushed against the adjoining panel; a sharp point on the pin effectively marks the centre of the dowel hole in that panel, ensuring perfect alignment. Another method is a dowelling jig, which fits over the edges of the panels to align the holes.

1 Draw a pencil line along the centre of the joint position, then align the two components carefully and mark corresponding dowel hole positions on both pieces.

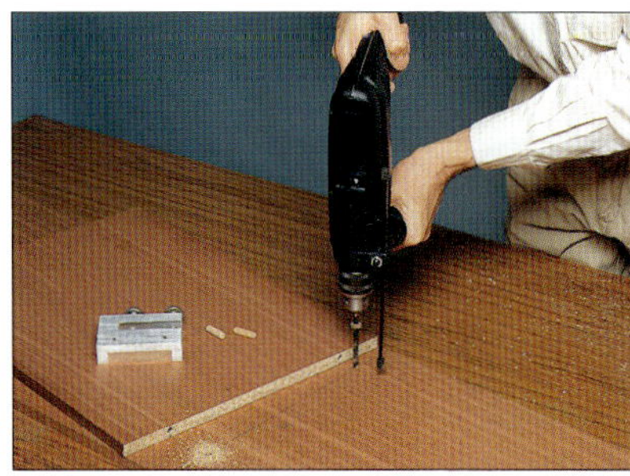

2 Drill the dowel holes in the face component, using a depth stop to avoid drilling too deep and breaking through the panel. Use a dowelling jig to drill holes in board edges.

3 Insert glued dowels in the holes in the edge component, then glue this to the face component. Add more glue along the joint line to provide extra strength.

4 A back panel will give any box extra strength, and also helps to resist skewing. Cut the panel fractionally undersize, then nail it in place, making sure the assembly is square first.

FITTING FLUSH HINGES

Adding doors and drawers to a basic storage box will turn it into a cabinet or a chest. Doors can be hung on any one of the many types of hinge available, but two of the most versatile are the flush hinge and the concealed hinge. The former has one leaf fitting into a cut-out in the other, and so can be surface-mounted to the door edge and the frame, without the need to cut recesses.

These hinges have countersunk mounting screw holes in their leaves, so it is essential to buy screws that have heads that fit the countersinks exactly. If the heads are too big, they will prevent the screws from sitting flush with the faces of the hinge leaves and will stop the doors from closing.

1 Mark the hinge position on the door edge, then make pilot holes and screw the smaller flap to the door. Check that the hinge knuckle faces the right way.

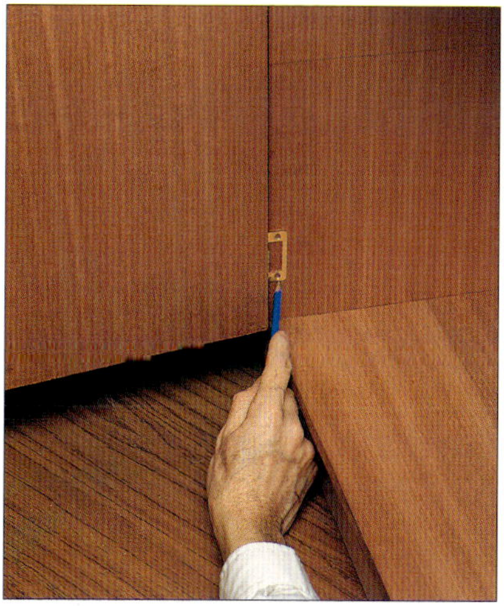

2 Hold the door in position against the cabinet carcass, and mark the hinge position on it. Mark the screw holes too, then drill pilot holes for the screws.

3 Reposition the door and attach the larger hinge leaf to the carcass. Check the door alignment carefully, then attach the other hinge in the same way.

FITTING CONCEALED HINGES

The concealed hinge is a little more complex to fit – the hinge body sits in a round hole bored in the rear face of the door, while the hinge arm is attached to a baseplate fitted to the side of the cabinet carcass – but it can be adjusted after fitting to ensure perfect alignment on multi-door installations.

Make in-out adjustments to the door by loosening the mounting screw and repositioning the door. Make side-to-side adjustments with the smaller screw.

1 Mark the centre line of the hinge baseplate on the side of the cabinet, then lay the door flat against the carcass and extend the line on to it.

2 Use a power drill fitted with an end mill, held in a drill stand, to bore the recess for the hinge body to the required depth in the rear face of the cabinet door.

3 Press the hinge body into the recess, check that the arm is at right angles to the door edge and make pilot holes for the fixing screws. Drive these in.

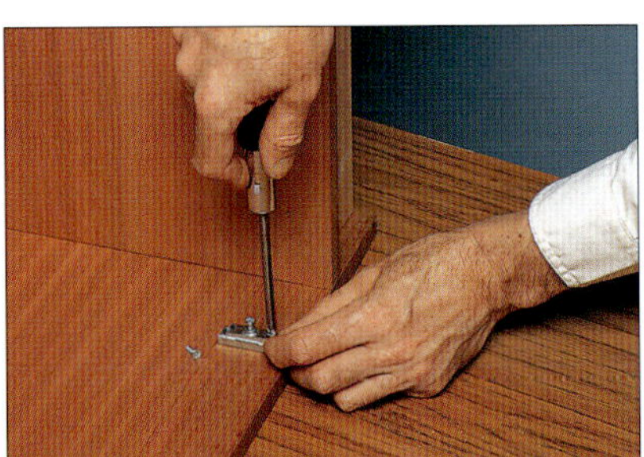

4 Next, attach the baseplate to the side of the cabinet, centred on the guideline drawn earlier. Check that it is fitted correctly.

5 Hold the door against the cabinet, slot the hinge arm over the screw on the baseplate and tighten the screw to lock the hinge arm in place.

MAKING UP DRAWER KITS

When it comes to adding drawers to your cabinets, the simplest solution is to use plastic drawer kits. These consist of moulded sections that interlock to form the sides and back of the drawer, special corner blocks to allow a drawer front of any chosen material to be attached, and a base (usually a piece of enamelled hardboard). The drawer sides are grooved to fit over plastic runners that are screwed to the cabinet sides. The sides, back and base can be cut down to size if necessary.

1 Cut the sides and back to size if necessary, then stick the side and back sections together, using the clips and adhesive provided in the kit.

2 Cut the base down in size too if the drawer size was altered. Then slide the panel into place in the grooves in the side and back sections.

3 Screw the two corner joint blocks to the inner face of the drawer front, stick on the drawer base support channel, and glue the front to the ends of the side sections.

4 Hold the drawer within the cabinet to mark the positions of its side grooves on the side walls. Then attach the plastic drawer runners with the screws provided.

FITTING BUILT-IN WARDROBES

The walls of a room can be used to create larger storage spaces. These can range from filling in an alcove, through a unit in the corner of a room, to one running right across the room to the opposite wall. If the room has a central chimney breast (fireplace projection) with an alcove at each side, both alcoves can be used for storage and the chimney breast can be concealed with dummy doors.

In each case, the most important part is a frame to support the doors; these can be hinged conventionally or suspended from ceiling-mounted track. Remember that hinged doors allow unlimited access, but need floor space in front of them so they can be opened easily. Sliding doors do not need this floor space, but they do have the minor disadvantage that access to the interior is sometimes restricted – when one door is open, it blocks access to the next section.

Such a flexible structure affords an opportunity to meet storage needs precisely. Start by selecting the depth needed for clothes to hang freely on hanging rails, then work out what width should be given to hanging space and what to shelving, drawers or basket space for storing other items of clothing. Shoe racks can be added at floor level.

Doors can be made into a feature of the room, or painted or covered to blend unobtrusively with the room's colour scheme. Large flat-surfaced doors become almost invisible if decorated with a wallcovering.

1 Screw a track support strip to the ceiling joists, levelling it with packing, then add the top track. Leave a gap at the wall for the side upright.

4 Use a spirit (carpenter's) level to check that the upright is vertical, mark its position on the wall and drill the clearance and fixing holes.

7 Hang each door by engaging the hanger wheels on the track as shown and lowering the door to the vertical position. Finally, fit the floor guides provided.

2 Hold the lengths of wood that will form the side frame uprights against the wall, and mark on them the profile of the skirting (baseboard).

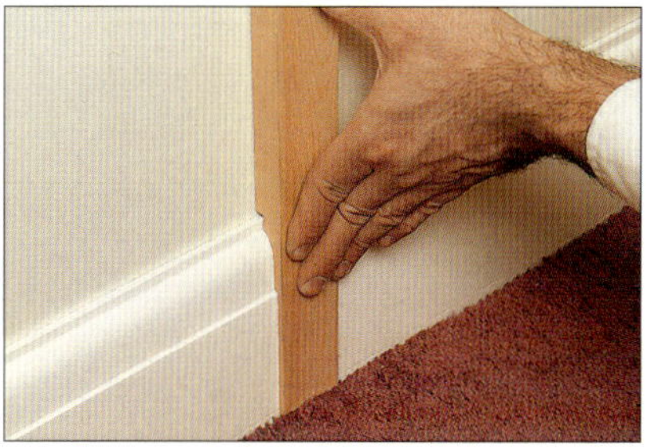

3 Use a coping saw or power jigsaw (saber saw) to cut away the waste wood from the foot of the upright, then test fit against the wall.

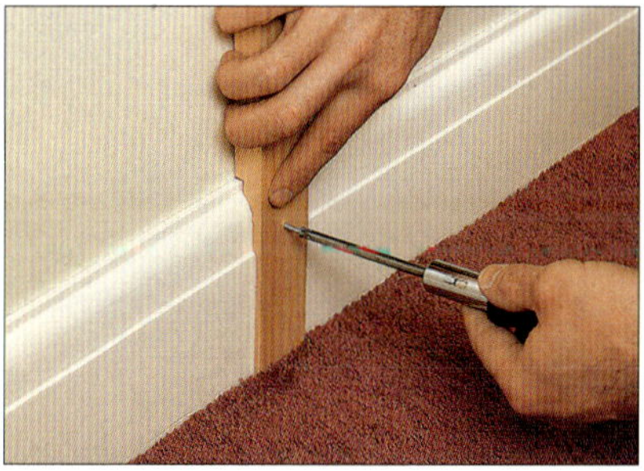

5 Realign the upright with the positioning marks made earlier and screw it to the wall. Repeat the process at the other side of the opening.

6 Cut the doors to size if necessary, allowing for clearances or overlaps as required in the door gear instructions, then fit the door hangers.

8 Conceal the track and door hangers by pinning (tacking) a decorative moulding to the track support batten. Some tracks come complete with a metal pelmet strip.

9 Finish off the installation by pinning slim wooden mouldings to the front edges of the side uprights. These hide any slight gaps when the doors are closed.

FITTING CLOTHES ORGANIZERS

In both freestanding and built-in wardrobes, best use of the interior space can be made by creating tailor-made hanging and shelving sections. Clothes organizers of this kind can be professionally made to measure, but in fact they can be constructed from the simplest of materials, at a great saving in cost. A wardrobe up to 2400mm (8ft) wide can be "organized" with just four standard lengths of veneered or plastic-coated chipboard (particle board), a length of clothes pole and some 75 x 25mm (3 x 1in) wood to act as shelf supports.

Start by marking and cutting out the components. All are 300mm (12in) wide. There are two uprights 1930mm (6 ft 4in) long, two shelves long enough to span the wardrobe or alcove, and six small shelves 300mm (12in) square. Sand all the cut edges.

Next, cut two sets of shelf supports to fit the back and side walls of the wardrobe or alcove. Nail or screw the first supports in place so that their top edges are 2140mm (7ft) above the floor. Add the second set 1930mm (6ft 4in) above the floor. Then make up the central shelf unit, using the two uprights and the six small shelves, spacing these to suit the storage requirements. Notch the top rear corners of the unit so that they will fit around the lower shelf support, and stand it in place. Add the lower shelf first, then the upper one, and complete the unit by adding upper (and, if desired, lower) hanging rails at each side of the central unit.

1 Fix the upper set of shelf supports to the sides and back of the wardrobe or alcove, with their top edges 2140mm (7ft) above floor level.

4 Mark the height of the uprights and the length of the shelves required on the components. Square cutting lines across them, using a try square.

7 Stand the unit against the back of the wardrobe or alcove. Mark the position of the lower shelf support on the uprights. Cut notches to fit around the support.

2 Add the lower set of shelf supports with their top edges 1930mm (6ft 4in) above floor level. Check that they are all horizontal.

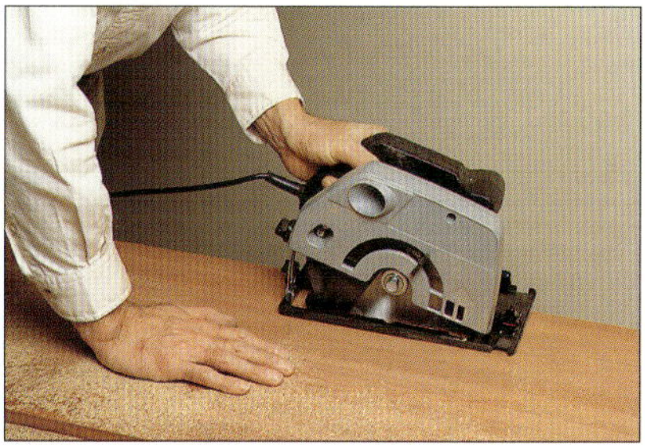

3 Next, cut the components to width, using a circular saw with a fence or a guide strip clamped across it to keep the cuts straight.

5 Cut the shelves and uprights to the lengths required with the circular saw. Then cut the six small squares for the central shelf unit.

6 Make the central shelf unit by gluing and nailing or screwing the shelves between the uprights. Space the shelves as required.

8 Reposition the central shelf unit, then lay the lower shelf on its supports. Drill pilot holes, then nail or screw down through it into the supports and the shelf unit.

9 Fit hangers to support the clothes rail beneath the lower shelf. Add a second lower rail if wished. Complete the unit by fixing the top shelf to its supports.

STORAGE PROJECTS

Although storage units are functional, they can often be attractive too. On the following pages you will find three simple storage projects that are just that. A magazine rack is a must for any home, providing a place for newspapers and magazines that have yet to be read. The rack shown has a large capacity, but can be folded up and stored when not needed. A small double-shelf wall unit will have many uses around the home, for books, ornaments and the like. It is made from board and trimmed with decorative moulding. Finally, there is an unusual sloping CD rack, which can be made from wood left over from other projects.

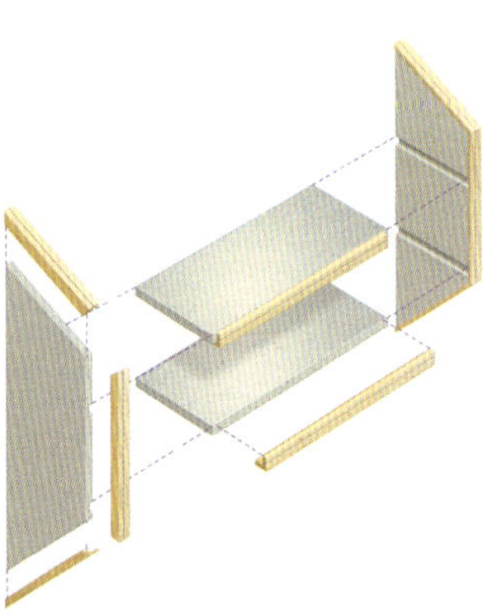

MAGAZINE RACK

This folding rack takes little time to construct and uses a few basic techniques. There are no joints to make, and no expensive tools are required; all you need are the basics of accurate marking out, cutting and fitting together. The interlocking design allows the rack to be opened up or folded flat and stowed away, with no need for clips or catches.

The rack consists of two separate assemblies that form the sides. One slides inside the other and is attached with the two bolts that form the pivot mechanism. It can be made to any convenient size, but if you follow the diagrams, you will not have to calculate the dimensions and angles required for the legs. Draw it out full size on plywood or MDF (medium-density fiberboard) to create a template for marking out.

Materials

- 2.7m (9ft) of 50 x 25mm (2 x 1in) planed (dressed) softwood for the legs
- 4.2m (14ft) of 75 x 12mm (3 x ½in) planed (dressed) softwood for the slats
- 6mm (¼in) MDF (medium-density fiberboard) for the template
- 16 25mm (1in) brass woodscrews
- 2 50mm (2in) brass woodscrews
- Panel pin (brad)
- 2 65mm (2½in) coachbolts (carriage bolts), nuts and washers
- Thin cord

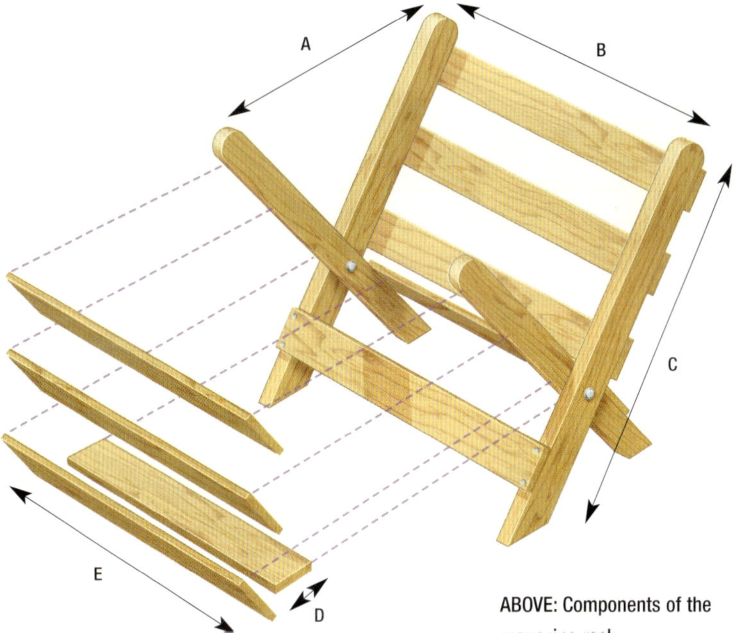

ABOVE: Components of the magazine rack.

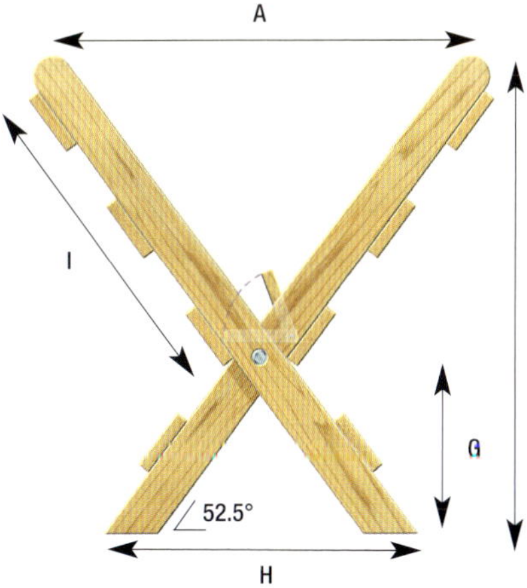

ABOVE: End profile.

KEY

A 510mm (20in)
B 490mm (19¼in)
C 660mm (26in)
D 75mm (3in)
E 435mm (17⅛in)
F 520mm (20½in)
G 190mm (7½in)
H 345mm (13½in)
I 400mm (16in)

1 Cut the legs and the slats to their overall length. The slats for the inner frame are 55mm (2⅛in) shorter than those used for the outer frame, allowing them to slide easily within the latter. Cut a rounded profile at the top of each leg if wished, using the first as a pattern for the others so that they will be uniform. ▶

2 Lay each pair of legs in turn over the template drawn on a sheet of MDF (medium-density fiberboard) and mark the positions of the slats and pivot point. Support the upper leg with an offcut (scrap) of wood to keep it level. Drill a pilot hole through the pivot point of each leg at this stage.

3 Assemble the inner frame. Insert one screw at each end of the top slat, then use a try square to adjust the assembly before you proceed. It is essential that the frames are absolutely square. Make sure the ends of the slats do not protrude over the sides of the frame.

6 Use two small offcuts of 12mm (½in) thick wood at each side to support the outer legs at the correct level. Screw the top and third slats in place on the outer legs, checking that they are square as before. All four legs of the rack should be parallel with each other to allow the assembly to open and close freely without any binding. If necessary, make adjustments.

7 Turn the assembly over to fit the bottom slat. At this stage, the two frames should enclose each other, but they can still be slid apart if required. Now is a good time to clean up any rough edges with medium-grade abrasive paper, wrapped around a cork sanding block, before proceeding. You could also apply a coat of clear sealer or varnish at this stage.

4 Add the third slat, then turn the frame over to attach the bottom slat. The final assembly will be easier if you omit the second slat at this stage; it can be added when the rack is bolted together. Three slats are sufficient at this stage to keep the assembly square.

5 Use the inner frame as a building jig for the outer frame. Position the components carefully, making sure that the pivot holes are in line. Insert a small panel pin (brad) to keep the legs aligned as you work. Note how the angled ends of the legs face in opposite directions.

8 Drill through the legs for the coachbolts (carriage bolts), using the pilot holes to guide the drill bit. Fit a coachbolt to each side, inserting a large washer between the moving parts to reduce the amount of friction. Fit the nuts on the inside, but do not over-tighten them or you will distort the framework. Note how the bottom slat on the outer frame will act as a stop to hold the rack open.

9 Insert the bottom piece, which acts as a floor for the rack. Cut it to fit between the legs of the inner frame and attach with two long brass screws. It should pivot easily, allowing the rack to be folded flat for storage. Add the remaining two slats. Fix a couple of lengths of thin cord between the bottom slats as a final touch to secure the legs in their open position.

BOOKSHELF

Manufactured boards with veneered faces, sometimes called decorative boards, can make quick work of any project. However, the exposed edges of veneered plywood and MDF (medium-density fiberboard) are vulnerable to damage and not at all attractive. To overcome this drawback, you can buy solid wood trim to match most common types of veneer, or you can make your own if you have the right tools. This bookshelf was made from boards veneered with American white oak, edged with darker oak trim.

The dimensions of this small shelf unit are provided as a guide only. You can alter them to suit your own books or any other items you may wish to display. A suitable height for most paperbacks is 205–255mm (8–10in). Bear in mind that 12mm (½in) boards will sag under heavy loads if you make the shelves too wide. Restrict unsupported widths to 600m (24in).

Materials

- 760 x 610mm (30 x 24in) of 12mm (½in) veneered plywood or MDF (medium-density fiberboard)
- 2.7m (9ft) of 19mm (¾in) angled moulding for edge trim
- PVA (white) wood glue
- Panel pins (brads)

BELOW: Bookshelf components.

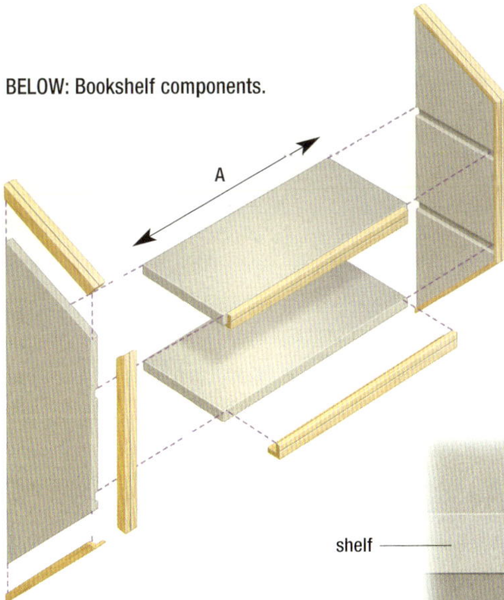

KEY

A 405mm (16in)

B 610mm (24in)

C 90mm (3½in)

D 12mm (½in)

E 205mm (8in)

F 190mm (7½in)

G 190mm (7½in)

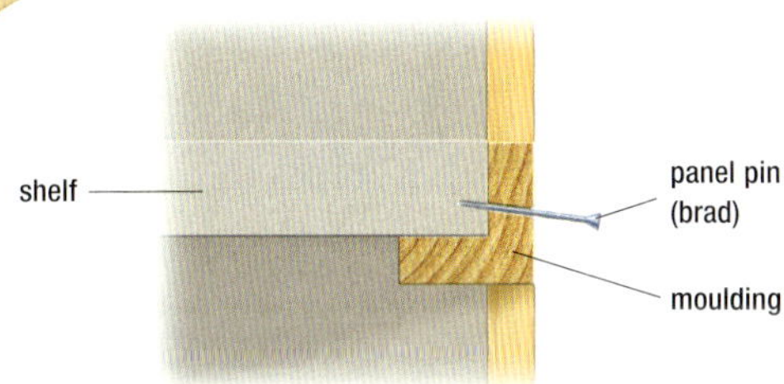

ABOVE: Section.

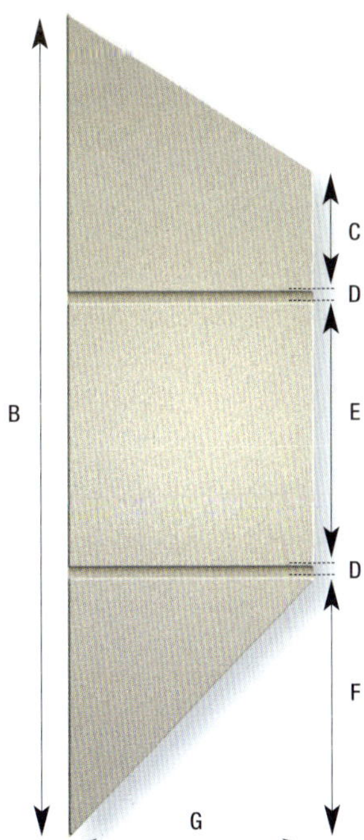

ABOVE: Side view.

1 Set out the profile on one end of the unit, cut it out and use it as a pattern for the other end to ensure that they are a perfect match. Scribe the angled cuts across the grain with a sharp knife to avoid tearing the grain of the thin veneer. Cut just outside the line with a jigsaw (saber saw), if you have one, or sharp panel (crosscut) saw. ▶

2 Clamp the angled ends in a vice so that they are horizontal, then plane them down to the scribed lines with a block plane. Work with the grain angled away from you to avoid damaging the veneer. The block plane, with a finely set, sharp blade, is the ideal tool for working this material.

3 Form the housings for the shelves with a router, running it along a straightedge pinned (tacked) to the inner face. To ensure accuracy, clamp the two ends together and cut the grooves in one operation. Pin a strip of scrap wood to the board edge to prevent breakout at the end of the groove.

6 Sash clamps are ideal for holding the assembly steady while pinning the shelves in place. Small panel pins (brads) are sufficient for a small unit such as this. Check that all corners are square – measuring the diagonals is the easiest way of doing this; they should be equal – and leave overnight for the glue to set. Note the small scraps of wood inserted beneath the clamp heads to protect the veneer.

7 Cut two lengths of decorative angled moulding to trim the front edges of the shelves. The moulding shown has a small shadow line, or "quirk", running along its length. This is designed to help conceal the heads of the panel pins after they have been punched down with a nail punch. When buying mouldings for this purpose, always check that their design provides a means of concealing the fixings.

4 The boards can vary in thickness depending on the type of veneer. It is not always possible to match the size of board exactly to the diameter of the router cutter. If necessary, plane small rebates (rabbets) on the underside of each shelf until it fits the grooves perfectly.

5 Apply glue to the housings and slot the unit together. It is good practice to use the glue sparingly. Any excess will have to be removed completely to prevent discoloration of the veneer at the finishing stage. Wipe off with a slightly damp cloth, and avoid rubbing glue into the grain.

8 The same moulding is used to trim the end panels. Mitre the ends at the corners with a tenon saw or adjustable mitre saw. To determine the angle for the mitred corners, place a short section of moulding in position and use it to mark pencil lines on the end panel, parallel to the front edges. Draw a line from the corner to the point of intersection to bisect the angle exactly. Use this as a guide for setting an adjustable bevel gauge.

9 Apply PVA (white) wood glue to the front edges of the end panels and pin (tack) the mouldings in place. Notice how the minimum of glue has been used. This is to prevent any excess from being squeezed on to the veneer surface when the pins are punched in with the nail punch. When the glue has dried, apply coloured stopping to each pinhole before sanding smooth all over, ready for finishing.

CD RACK

The idea for this compact disc storage system came about because a piece of cherry wood, with distinctive figure in the grain, and a short offcut (scrap) of waney-edged yew with an interesting shape was left over in the workshop. You can use any type of wood, of course, possibly something left over from another job. With a little imagination, you can turn short lengths of wood into all manner of items.

The design is simplicity itself – it uses the cantilever principle to support the weight of the CDs. A width of 255mm (10in) will allow two columns to be stacked side by side. The rack can be any height you like, provided the base is wide enough to make it stable.

Materials

- 760mm (30in) of 125 x 25mm (5 x 1in) hardwood for the rack
- 760mm (30in) of 25 x 12mm (1 x ½in) hardwood for the sides
- 280mm (11in) of 150 x 19mm (6 x ¾in) hardwood for the base
- PVA (white) wood glue
- Brass panel pins (brads)

As a guide, ensure that the top of the rack, inclined at 10 degrees, is vertically above the back edge of the base. The diagram shows how to set out the ingenious dovetailed housing joint that holds the unit together.

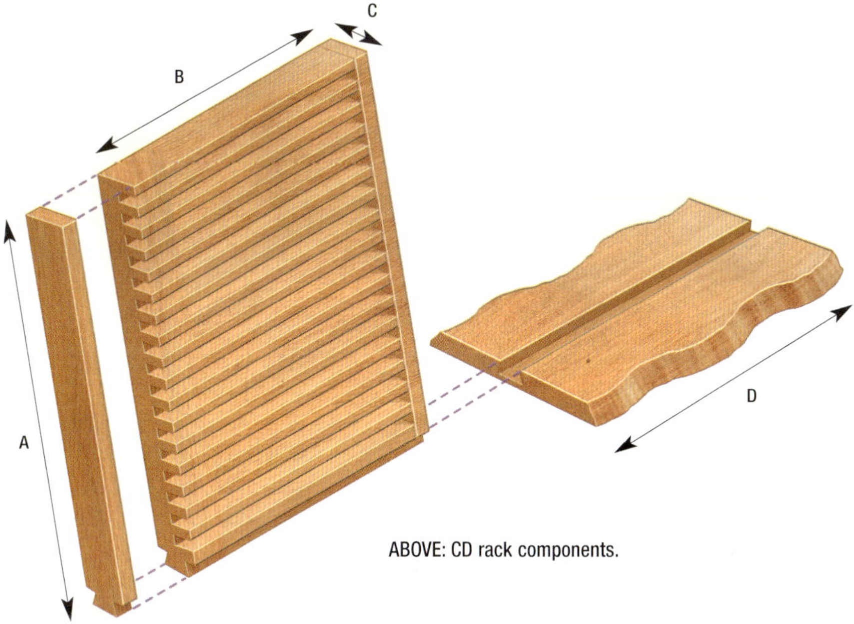

ABOVE: CD rack components.

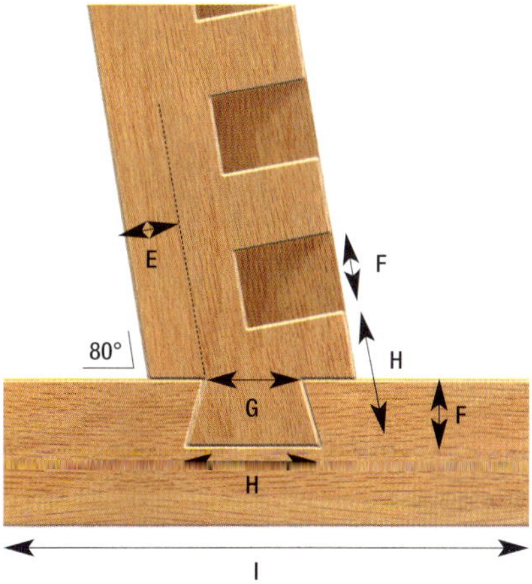

ABOVE: Section.

KEY

A 370mm (14½in)	E 6mm (¼in)
B 255mm (10in)	F 9mm (⅜in)
C 25mm (1in)	G 12mm (½in)
D 280mm (11in)	H 19mm (¾in)
	I 150mm (6in)

1 Cut the 125 x 25mm (5 x 1in) hardwood into two pieces 370mm (14½in) long for the main portion of the rack. Plane the edges square, glue and clamp them together. Simple butt joints are sufficient in this case. To make sure that the board remains absolutely flat, clamp a stout batten over the top of the assembly before finally tightening the sash clamps. ▶

2 Use a 9mm (⅜in) router bit to rout a slot 19mm (¾in) up from the bottom edge. Make a routing jig for the other slots by fixing a 9mm (⅜in) strip of hardwood to the router base, 9mm (⅜in) from the cutter's edge.

3 It is a simple matter to run the hardwood strip along each slot to position the next groove correctly. Continue in this way to the end of the board. Make sure the work is clamped firmly to the bench when doing this, or use a bench stop.

6 Use the same template to mark out the bottom edge of the main upright. Scribe the shoulders along its length with a marking gauge, and clamp a straightedge along the shoulder line to guide the tenon saw. Keep the saw blade perfectly level to ensure the shoulders are straight and parallel.

7 To form the tail on the upright, plane the required angle on a scrap piece of wood to make an accurate guide for a small shoulder plane. Use a paring chisel to remove the waste from the corners. The angles are different on each face because of the sloping profile and should match those on the two side pieces.

4 Use a dovetail cutter to rout the housing groove in the base. To deal with a waney edge, pin a straight-edged piece of plywood to the underside and run the router fence along it. Screw it down to the work surface so that it cannot move.

5 Cut the tails on the two side pieces with a fine dovetail saw. Use a bevel gauge to set the shoulders at an angle of 10 degrees. Then make a small template to mark the shape of the tails to suit the profile of the dovetail groove.

8 Plane the bottom edge of the tail to the required angle to complete the joint, paring it down until the tail achieves a good sliding fit in the housing. Before fitting the side pieces, you should clean up each groove with a small sanding block. Make this from a thin strip of wood and wrap it with abrasive paper.

9 Pin (tack) and glue the side pieces to the upright, using small brass panel pins (brads). Align the dovetails accurately and position the pins so that they avoid the slots. Apply glue to the dovetailed housing in the base and slide the rack into place. Wipe off excess glue with a damp cloth. When the glue is dry, apply the desired finish.

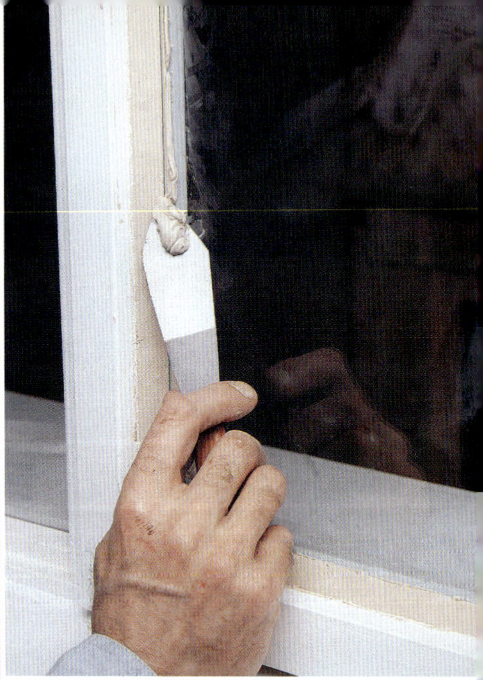

HOME REPAIRS

- Repairing walls & ceilings
- Repairing windows & doors
- Repairing floors & stairs

INTRODUCTION

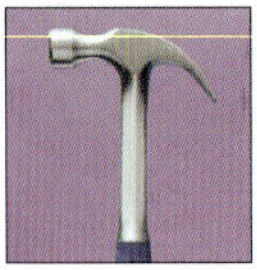

Where your home is concerned, prevention is often better, and certainly less expensive, than cure. A regular programme of inspection and maintenance will prevent small problems from becoming large and costly ones. From time to time, however, repairs will be necessary, and their successful completion depends on having all the relevant tools and equipment to hand, and understanding how to use them.

The following pages will guide you through a wide range of common repairs that may be needed to walls, ceilings, doors, windows, floors and stairs, showing you a variety of simple techniques for achieving professional results. By following its advice, and applying a little forethought, care and patience, you will not only save money, but will also have the satisfaction of knowing that you have done the jobs yourself. Moreover, the basic skills you learn will provide a core of knowledge that should give you the confidence to tackle more ambitious do-it-yourself projects.

PREPARATION

When beginning a repair job, be sure that everything is to hand; it is no use beginning to repair a wall, then finding that you are too short to reach the top and that you need to go looking for a trestle or a pair of steps. All your

LEFT: A beautiful home will stay that way only if it is well looked after. Sooner or later, however, repairs will be necessary; the various tasks shown on the following pages will help you to keep your home looking pristine.

RIGHT: The secret of success for any do-it-yourself job is preparation and planning. Before you start your repair job, lay out all the materials and equipment that you will be using, and try to keep your workplace tidy.

tools and equipment should be well prepared and in position. It is also important to keep your workplace tidy, and do not allow children or pets into areas where power tools or strong solvents are being used.

PROTECTIVE CLOTHING

When doing repair jobs around the home, wear old clothes or overalls, and knee pads if you are laying, stripping or varnishing floors. If removing glass from windows, always wear a pair of industrial gloves, and a dust mask is essential when sawing and sanding wood.

FIRST AID

It is inevitable that minor cuts and abrasions will occur at some point, so a basic first aid kit is an essential for the home or workshop. Keep your kit in a prominent position ready for use. If any of the contents are used, replace them immediately.

first aid kit

REPAIRING WALLS & CEILINGS

Most walls and ceilings have some form of plaster surface, whether it be plaster on a backing of wooden laths or plasterboard (gypsum board) on a wooden framework. This rigid material may suffer from cracking and damage due to building settlement or accidental impact. Fortunately, this is relatively easy to repair, either with a filler material or a plasterboard patch. Walls also feature wooden skirtings (baseboards) and decorative architraves (trims) around door openings. These, too, can become damaged and may need repairing or replacing. The following pages show you how to do a range of wall and ceiling repair jobs, as well as how to use coving (crown molding) to hide ceiling-to-wall joints.

PREPARATION AND MINOR REPAIRS

Walls and ceilings need to be prepared carefully so that the surfaces are in as good a condition as possible. The better the surface, the better the new finish.

If the room was papered originally, the first job is to remove all the old wallcovering. With vinyl, it should be possible to peel off the outer layer to leave the backing behind. If this is in good condition, you can paper over it again, but if you wish to paint the walls, it should be removed too.

Painted surfaces can be painted over, but make sure that any loose or flaking paint is removed first. Then you can begin to repair any cracks or other damage in the surfaces.

A general-purpose filler can be used for the majority of cracks in ceilings and walls. This comes ready-mixed in tubs or as a powder for mixing with water. Simply apply the filler with a filling or putty knife, pressing it into the cracks and smoothing it flush with the surface. Some cracks need enlarging slightly to give the filler something to grip; fine cracks can be filled with special hairline-crack filler.

Normal fillers are quite adequate if you are papering the ceiling or wall, but for paint, a fine surface filler is better. Most fillers take a short while to dry, after which they can be sanded flush with the surrounding surface.

1 Strip wallcoverings by soaking them with water or by using a steam stripper, then remove with scrapers. Peel off the top layer of vinyl types to leave the backing behind.

4 When dry, sand the filled area smooth with fine abrasive paper. On flat surfaces, wrap the abrasive paper around a sanding block. You may need to add more filler to fill any remaining defects.

2 Remove flaking paint with a scraper. Take care not to dig the blade into soft surfaces. Feather the edges of the sound paint by sanding lightly. This will disguise them under the new finish.

3 Fill any cracks and gaps in plasterwork with all-purpose filler. Press the filler firmly into the gap and finish off by leaving it slightly proud of the surrounding surface.

5 Give the walls a thorough wash with a solution of sugar soap (all-purpose cleaner). This will remove all dust and grease. Allow the liquid to dry completely before decorating the wall.

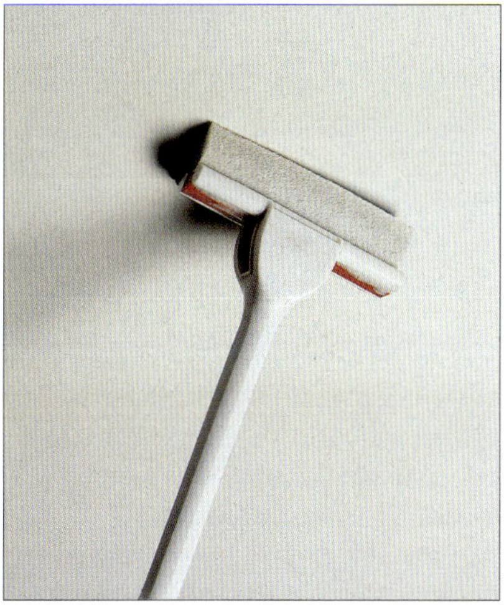

6 Using a squeegee mop to clean ceilings will allow you to work at ground level. Make sure you spread dust sheets (drop cloths) on the floor to protect it from drips.

FILLING HOLES IN PLASTER

Small holes, especially those left by screws, can be filled in the same way as cracks. Cut off any protruding wall plugs or, better still, remove them altogether so that you can obtain a smooth finish.

Larger holes are more of a problem. The kind of hole left by removing a waste pipe from a wall can be made good with do-it-yourself repair plaster, which can usually be applied in layers up to 50mm (2in) thick. Smaller recesses up to 20mm (¾in) deep can be treated with a special deep-gap filler, while really deep cavities can be filled with an expanding foam filler. Once set, this can be cut and sanded smooth, then painted or papered over. If an area of plaster has fallen off the wall, use a repair plaster, levelling it with the surrounding sound plaster with a straight length of wood.

For larger areas, nail wooden battens to the wall. These should be equal in depth to the surrounding original plaster. By running a long wooden straightedge up the battens, using a sawing action, you will be able to level off the fresh plaster to the correct depth. When the plaster has set partially, the battens can be prised from the wall and the resulting gaps in the plaster filled.

You may need to divide a really large area of wall into workable "bays" using this technique.

ABOVE: Use a paintbrush to remove dust from holes and deep cracks prior to filling, then rinse and work the damp bristles into the hole. This will prevent moisture from being sucked from the filler, which would cause it to dry too quickly, weakening it and leading to poor adhesion.

ABOVE: Use a repair plaster for a deep hole, applied with a plasterer's trowel. Work the plaster well into the hole and smooth it off flush with the surrounding surface. Allow to dry slightly, then polish smooth with a wet trowel.

REPAIRING LATH-AND-PLASTER

Holes in lath-and-plaster ceilings and walls can be repaired in the same way as holes in normal plastered surfaces, provided the laths are intact.

First brush the laths with diluted PVA (white) glue to reduce absorbency, then repair with general-purpose filler, deep-gap filler or repair plaster.

If the laths have broken, cut back the plaster until you expose the vertical studs. Cut a piece of plasterboard (gypsum board) to size and nail it in place before filling the hole.

If the damage covers a large area, it may be necessary to nail battens between the studs or joists to support the long edges of the patch. Nail them in place so that the nails project halfway into the opening.

This sort of repair can also be made using expanded aluminium mesh to support the repair plaster.

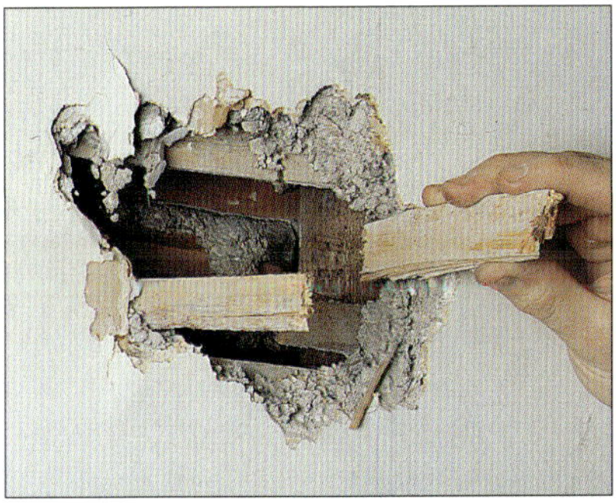

1 If the wood laths are split or broken, pull them away from the surface. Remove any loose sections of plaster.

2 Continue cutting back the old plaster and the laths behind it to expose the studs or ceiling joists at each side of the hole. Square off the edges.

3 Cut a plasterboard (gypsum board) patch to fit the hole, and nail it in place. Add two support strips if the panel is large.

4 Complete the repair by plastering over the patch after filling and taping the cut edges all around. Polish the repair with a steel float.

REPAIRING PLASTERBOARD

Surface damage and small holes in plasterboard (gypsum board) can be repaired in the same way as cracks and holes in solid plaster, but if a large hole has been punched in the material – by a door handle, for example – a different solution is required. In this case, a patch must be placed behind the hole to provide support for a layer of filler.

First, use a padsaw to open out the hole, squaring the sides. Then cut a section of fresh plasterboard to a length slightly less than the diagonal dimension of the hole. This will allow you to pass it through the hole at an angle. Drill a tiny hole in the middle of the plasterboard patch and pass a piece of knotted string through it before adding filler or coving (crown molding) adhesive to the edges on the grey side of the plasterboard. This will secure it firmly to the back of the existing plasterboard panel.

Pass the patch through the hole and pull it back against the edges. Hold the string taut while adding filler to the hole, then leave this to set. Cut off the projecting string and make good with a final smooth coat of general-purpose filler or finish plaster, ensuring the surface is level.

If the area of damage in a plasterboard wall or ceiling is substantial, it is much more sensible to work back to the nearest studs or joists, using a padsaw to cut the cladding flush with the wood. Then nail 50mm (2in) square noggings between the studs or joists so that they project halfway into the opening. Nail 50 x 25mm (2 x 1in) battens to the studs or joists, flush with the faces of the noggings.

Cut a patch of plasterboard to fill the opening and nail this to the noggings and battens, using galvanized plasterboard nails.

Apply a layer of filler around the edges of the patch, bedding jointing tape into it as you go. Feather the edges with a damp sponge and apply another layer when it has dried to leave a perfect surface.

1 Use a padsaw to square up a hole in damaged plasterboard (gypsum board). Keep the size of the hole to the minimum necessary to accommodate the damaged plasterboard.

2 Attach a piece of string to the patch, knotting it at the back so that it cannot be pulled through the hole. It may help to insert a galvanized nail through the knot for extra security.

3 Butter the back of the patch with a layer of filler or coving (crown molding) adhesive, making sure the edges are covered and keeping the free end of the string out of the way.

4 Pass the plasterboard patch through the hole while holding the free end of the string. Use the string to pull the patch firmly against the back of the existing plasterboard surface.

5 Add more filler or repair plaster to the hole while holding the patch tightly in place with the string. Leave the filler just below the surface of the wall and add a final thin layer when it has set.

REPLACING SKIRTINGS

Skirtings (baseboards) protect wall surfaces at floor level from accidental damage. They can be plain or ornate, and can be painted, stained or varnished. They may need replacing if they are damaged or simply look unfashionable.

Skirtings are often fixed directly to masonry walls with large cut nails in older homes, or with masonry nails in more recent ones. Alternatively, they may be nailed to rough timber fixing blocks or grounds (furrings), which are themselves nailed to the masonry. Boards fixed to blocks are much easier to remove than those nailed directly to the wall, since both cut and masonry nails can have a ferocious grip. In the latter situation, it is often easier to punch the nails through the boards and into the walls than to try to prise them out. Boards on wood-framed walls are simply nailed to the frame and are easy to remove.

Provided the correct profile is available, small lengths of skirting can be replaced by levering the damaged section from the wall with a crowbar (wrecking bar), holding it clear of the wall with wooden wedges and sawing down through the moulding at each side of the damage with a tenon saw. For best results, the cuts should be made at 45 degrees with the aid of a mitre box, and the ends of the new piece cut in the same manner so that they overlap. Nails should be driven through the overlaps into wooden supporting blocks behind.

1 To replace a small area of damaged skirting (baseboard), prise it away from the wall slightly, wedge it and use a tenon saw and mitre box to cut out a section.

4 Nail the replacement board to the support blocks. If using plain wood, pin (tack) on decorative mouldings to build up a close match to the existing board.

2 Nail small support blocks behind the cut ends of the board, using masonry nails in brick and block walls, and then nail the cut ends to the support blocks.

3 Cut a piece of replacement board to fit, with its ends mitred to match the cut ends of the original board. Use plain wood if the skirting profile cannot be matched.

5 When replacing whole lengths, use mitre joints at external corners. Fix the first length, then mark the inside of the mitre on the back of the next board.

6 Cut the mitre joints with a power saw. At internal corners, fit the first length right into the corner. Then scribe its profile on to the second board; cut this with a coping saw, and fit it.

REPLACING ARCHITRAVES

Architraves (trims) are used around door and window openings to frame the opening and disguise the joint between the frame and the wall surface. Like skirtings (baseboards), they may need replacing if they are damaged or unfashionable.

Architraves are pinned (tacked) in place to the edges of the door or window frame. It is an easy job to prise the trims away with a bolster (stonecutter's chisel) without causing undue damage to the frame or the surrounding wall surface.

Once the old architrave has been removed, the edges of the wooden lining of the opening should be tidied up by scraping off ridges of old paint and filler.

Take careful measurements when cutting the new architrave, bearing in mind that mitred joints are normally used where the uprights meet the horizontal section above the opening.

If the new moulding is particularly ornate, it could be difficult to obtain neat joints, and you may prefer to add decorative corner blocks instead. These could also be fitted at the bottoms of the uprights if they are narrower than the originals and will not meet the skirtings.

Fit the new sections of architrave 6mm (¼in) back from the edges of the lining of the opening.

1 Prise off the old mouldings. They should come away easily. If necessary, lever against a wooden block to avoid damaging the wall.

4 Fix the uprights to the frame by driving in nails at 300mm (12in) intervals. Recess the heads with a nail punch and fill the holes later.

2 Hold an upright against the frame so that the inside of the mitre joint can be marked on it. Repeat for the other upright.

3 Cut the end of the moulding, using a mitre block or box. Alternatively, mark the line across the moulding with a protractor or combination square.

5 Hold the top piece above the two uprights to mark the position for the mitre cut at each end. Make the cuts as before and test the piece for fit.

6 Nail the top piece to the frame, checking that the mitre joints are aligned accurately. Then drive a nail through each corner to secure the joint.

HIDING CEILING-TO-WALL JOINTS

Coving (crown molding), a quadrant-shaped moulding made from polystyrene, plaster or wood can be fitted between the walls and ceiling of a room. It has two functions: to be decorative and to conceal unsightly joints between the walls and ceiling. An ornate coving may be referred to as a cornice; old plaster cornices may be clogged with several layers of paint and need cleaning to reveal the detail.

Coving normally comes in long lengths and you will find it easier to fit if you have someone on hand to help place it in position. Where lengths meet at corners, the ends should be mitred for neat joints. The manufacturer may provide a cutting template; if not, use a large mitre box.

1 Mark guidelines on the ceiling and wall, using the dimensions given by the manufacturer. Alternatively, use a length of coving as a guide, but take care always to hold it at the same angle.

PREPARING LENGTHS OF COVING

1 Measure the coving (crown molding) required for each run and cut it to length with a fine-toothed saw. Mitre the ends, using a large mitre box, where they will meet at internal and external corners.

2 Mix enough adhesive for one length of coving at a time, otherwise it may become unusable. Butter the back edges of the coving with a liberal amount of adhesive.

2 Using the point of a trowel, score the surface of the ceiling and wall between the parallel lines. This will provide a key (scuffed surface) for the adhesive, ensuring a good grip.

3 Press the coving into place, aligning it carefully with the guidelines. Support the coving with nails driven partially into the wall below its bottom edge; remove them when the adhesive has set.

4 Continue the coving on the adjacent wall, carefully aligning the mitred ends of the two lengths. Any slight gaps between them can be filled later.

5 Complete the external corner with another length of coving, butting the ends together. Fill any gaps at external and internal angles with cellulose filler and sand down once dry.

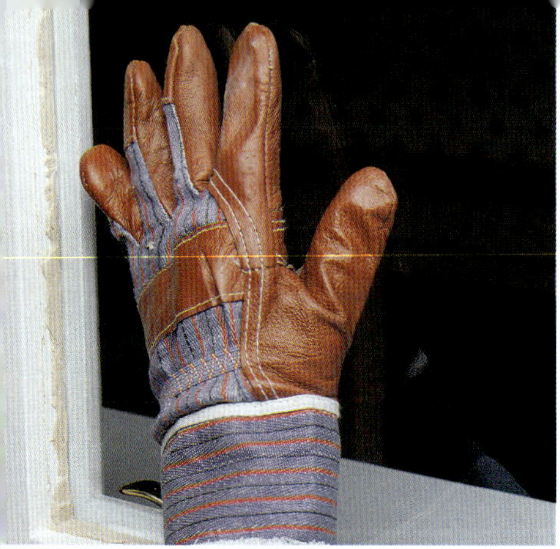

RECORD

REPAIRING WINDOWS & DOORS

Windows and doors can be subject to considerable wear and tear. Most are made of wood, which can become distorted with age and/or exposure to damp conditions. The latter can cause extensive damage to external doors and windows if they are not well maintained. Windows, and sometimes doors, also have the added weakness of glass. Being very brittle, this is easily broken, and knowing how to replace panels of glass yourself can save you a lot of money. Hinges can be a source of trouble in both windows and doors. Their screws can loosen, preventing the window or door from opening freely, and they can cause squeaks, rattles and binding. All of these problems are easily fixed.

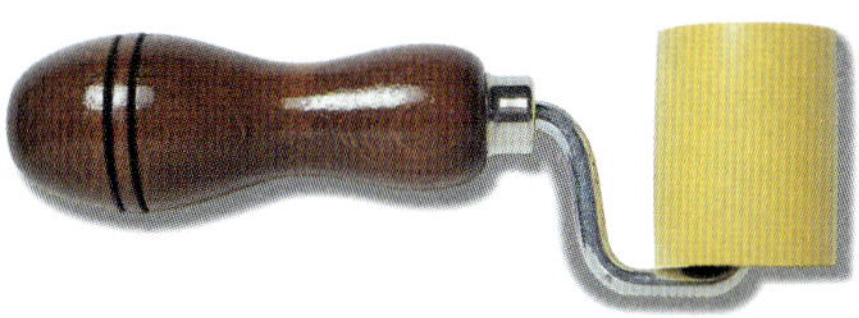

REMOVING WINDOW GLASS

Removing broken window glass is a common do-it-yourself job, and something that is worth learning how to do properly.

Make sure you wear thick gloves that cover your wrists. Lay newspapers on the ground on both sides of the window. Collect the glass in newspaper or a cardboard box and dispose of it safely; your glass supplier may accept the broken pieces for recycling.

An old chisel can be used to chop out the old putty – do not use a good one, as its blade will be damaged by the sprigs (or clips in a metal frame) that hold the glass in place. Pull out the sprigs or clips and remove all the putty from the recess.

TIP

When removing broken glass from a window, apply a criss-cross pattern of adhesive tape to the pane to prevent the glass from flying around. For extra safety, grip the broken slivers of glass with a pair of pincers or pliers and pull them from the frame. Don't knock them out with a hammer.

1 Remove the broken glass, wearing gloves to prevent cuts.

2 Use an old chisel to remove the putty from the edges of the rebate (rabbet).

3 Pull out the glazing sprigs with pincers. Then remove the remnants of glass and putty.

REPLACING LEADED LIGHTS

Replacing the glass in a leaded-light window is a little trickier than working with normal window panes. That said, it is a task well within the scope of anyone with patience and a practical frame of mind.

Many leaded-light windows will have one or more panes of coloured glass, so these will need to be replaced. The best place to look for authentic coloured replacements is in an architectural salvage yard. A glass merchant can cut a piece of old glass down to size for you.

You will also need a really sharp trimming knife to cut through the lead cames at the corners, and a soldering iron to fuse the lead together.

1 Use a sharp trimming knife to cut through the cames at the corners at 45 degrees.

2 Lever up and fold back the cames all around the pane to remove the old glass.

3 With the new glass in place, press the cames back into place with a seam roller.

4 Fuse the lead together at the corners using a small electric soldering iron.

REPLACING WINDOW PANES

The first stage in replacing a window pane is to measure the size of the glass needed and then buy the new pane. Your supplier will be able to cut the glass to fit.

1 Knead the putty in your hands until it becomes workable. Then squeeze a thin layer into the rebate (rabbet) of the frame, feeding it from your palm between finger and thumb.

MEASURING UP

Take measurements of the width and height of the recess in several places. The size of glass you need is 3mm (⅛in) less than the size of the recess. If in doubt, cut a cardboard template to fit and take this with you to the glass supplier. Reckon on buying some new glazing sprigs or clips to hold the glass in place, and buy the correct putty for either wooden or metal windows.

PUTTING IN THE NEW GLASS

Take a small amount of putty and work it in your hands until it is pliable; if it sticks to your fingers, roll it out on newspaper to remove some of the oil. When it is workable, begin pressing a layer into the window recess, squeezing it out of the palm of your hand between thumb and forefinger rather like toothpaste.

Put the glass in place, resting it on a couple of wooden matches, and press it gently into the opening until putty is squeezed out at the back – press against the sides of the glass, not the centre. Then fit the glazing sprigs to hold the glass, sliding the head of the hammer across the surface of the glass, or refit the clips. Remove putty that has been squeezed out on the inside of the window.

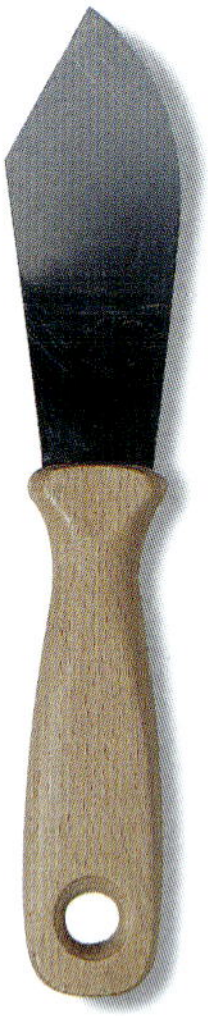

Add more putty to the outside of the window, using the same thumb-and-forefinger technique, until you have a good bead all the way around the glass. Take a putty knife and smooth off this bead at an angle of 45 degrees, pushing the putty into the edges of the frame. If the knife sticks, wet it with water.

Leave the putty for about 14 days before painting over it to disguise and seal the joints, allowing the paint to overlap on to the glass to prevent moisture from seeping down into the frame.

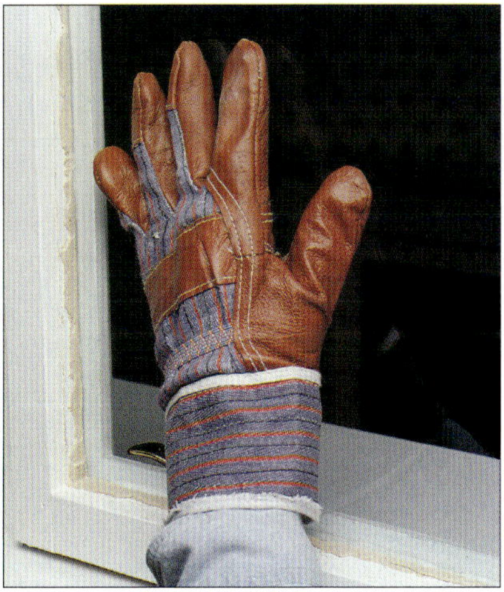

2 Support the bottom edge of the pane on a couple of wooden matches and press it into the putty, applying pressure to the sides rather than the centre.

3 Tap in the glazing sprigs at 300mm (12in) intervals. Hold the hammer so that its head slides across the face of the glass, that way, you will avoid breaking the glass.

4 Add more putty to the rebate and use the putty knife to strike it off to a 45-degree bevel. Make sure that the putty seals against the glass all round and that the sprigs are covered.

5 Trim the excess putty on the inside and outside of the frame to leave a neat finish. Allow the putty to harden before painting. Clean smears from the glass with methylated spirit.

REPAIRING WINDOWS

The most obvious signs that there is something wrong with a window are when it starts to rattle in the wind or to stick, making it difficult to open and close. Rattling is most likely to be caused by worn hinges or wear of the window itself; sticking by swelling of the wood, build-up of paint or movement of the frame joints.

REPAIRING HINGES

Loose or worn hinges are often a cause of window problems. To start with, try tightening the screws or replacing them with slightly longer screws of the same gauge. If that does not work, replace the hinges with new ones of the same size and type plus new screws. Remember that steel hinges will rust quickly, so apply suitable primer immediately, then repaint to match the window when this has dried.

Check the opening and closing of the window. If the window is sticking on the far edge, it may be necessary to deepen the recess for one or both hinges; if it binds on the closing edge, one or both recesses will be too deep and may need packing out with card. A rattling window can often be cured by fitting draught-excluder strip.

WORN WINDOWS

Sash windows are particularly prone to wear. The best answer is to remove the windows and fit brush-pile draught excluder inside the sash channel. A new catch to hold the windows together may also be necessary. Fit a new inner staff bead (window stop) around the window so that it fits more closely against the inner sash.

WARPED WINDOWS

Wooden hinged windows can sometimes warp so that they meet the frame only at the top or at the bottom. The best way to cure this is to fit some mortise window locks, which fit into holes cut in the casement, with the bolts shooting into more holes in the frame. These allow the window to be held in the correct position (get someone to push from the outside while you lock it) so that the warp will self-correct.

STICKING WINDOWS

Over time, a build-up of paint may cause windows to stick, especially when the weather is damp and the wood begins to swell. Use a plane to cut down the offending areas (this is much easier if you remove the window from its frame), then repaint before refitting the window.

Make sure that all bare wood is covered with paint, as this will prevent water from getting in, which causes the wood to swell. Also, check that the putty is in good condition.

TIP

When replacing painted steel hinges with brass versions, always use brass screws to match the new hinges.

ABOVE: A binding window may be cured simply by tightening the hinge screws or replacing them with longer ones.

ABOVE: If a window is binding on the far side, it may be that the hinge recesses need to be deepened with a chisel.

ABOVE: A sticking window may be swollen or have too much paint on it. Plane down the leading edge of the window.

ABOVE: A loose window joint can be re-glued with fresh adhesive. Clamp it up while the adhesive dries.

REHANGING DOORS

There may be occasions when the way in which a door opens is not the most convenient. Switching the hinges from one side to the other may provide a more attractive view of the room as the door is opened or allow better use of the wall space. Alternatively, making the door open outward may create more useful space. However, for safety, never have a door opening outward on to a stairway.

SWITCHING THE HINGED SIDE

When switching the hinged edge of a door from one side to the other, you will need to cut a new mortise for the latch and drill new holes for the door handle spindles. The old latch mortise and spindle holes can be filled by gluing in small blocks of wood and lengths of dowel. Leave the blocks and dowels slightly proud of the surface, then plane and sand them flush when the glue has dried. If you reverse the door, you will be able to use the old latch and door handle spindle holes, but the latch itself will need to be turned around.

You will need to cut a new slot for the striker and striking plate (keeper) on the other side of the frame, and fill the old recess with a thin block of wood stuck in place. Again, make this oversize, planing and sanding it flush once the adhesive has dried.

FILLING HINGE RECESSES

1 When switching the hinged side of a door, you will need to fill the old hinge recesses. Cut slivers of wood to the correct length and width, but slightly thicker than the recess depth.

REVERSING DOORS

When rehanging a door, it can reduce the amount of work required if you reverse the door – that is, turn it so that the side which faced inward now faces outward. This is the case when changing the hinges from left to right or the other way round. There are, however, two problems with doing this. The first is that the two sides of the door may be painted in different colours, which will mean a complete repainting job.

The second is that the door may not fit properly the other way round. Both doors and frames can move slightly over time, and while the door will operate perfectly well fitted one way,

2 Apply adhesive to each sliver of wood and tap it down into its recess. Wipe off excess adhesive with a damp cloth. Set the door aside for the adhesive to dry.

3 When the adhesive has set, use a jack plane to remove the wood that projects above the surface of the door edge. If necessary, fill any gaps around the slivers with wood filler.

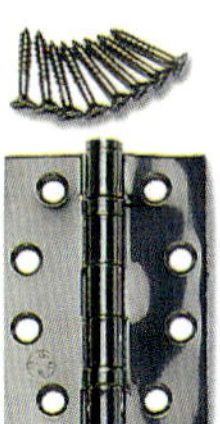

it may bind or catch when fitted the other way.

You will also need to chisel out new recesses for the hinges in both the door and the frame; if the door is reversed, you may be able to use part of the old hinge recesses in the door and need only fill the unused portions. Fill the old hinge recesses with thin blocks of wood glued into place and sanded flush.

If the door has rising butts or some other form of handed hinges, these will need to be replaced.

After rehanging the door, the light switch may be in the wrong place if it is in the room the door opens into. There are two choices here: reposition it on the other side of the door (which means running a new cable) or move it to the other side of the wall so that it is outside the room, but more or less in the same place (little or no new cable, but possible problems in securing the switch mounting box).

TIP

Modern honeycomb-cored internal doors are quite light in weight, but traditional panelled doors can be very heavy. If you are rehanging such a door, make sure you have someone on hand to help lift it in and out of the opening.

CHANGING THE LATCH POSITION

1 Remove the existing door handle and latch from the door, along with the operating spindle. Cut a block of wood to fill the latch recess and glue it in place, wiping off excess glue with a damp cloth.

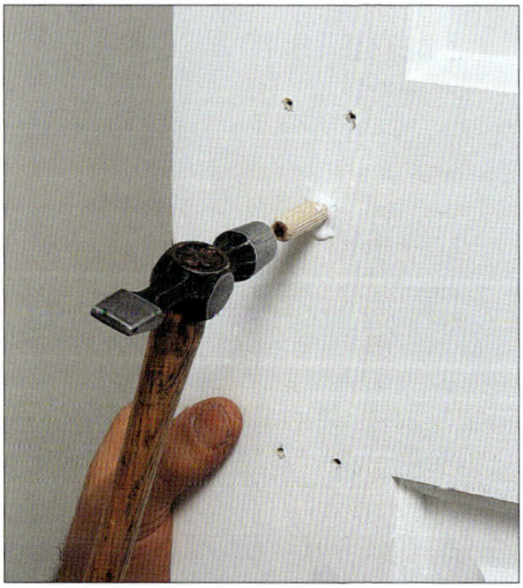

2 Plug the spindle hole on each side of the door by tapping in lengths of glued dowel. Fill all the screw holes with wood filler. When the glue and filler has dried, sand everything smooth.

OPENING IN TO OPENING OUT

When making a door open outward, you will be able to use the same latch and handle positions if the door is hung from the same side of the frame. You will have to reverse the latch, but will be able to make use of parts of the hinge recesses in the door. However, you will need to reposition the striking plate (keeper) and make new hinge recesses in the frame.

The one extra job will be to move the door stop, unless this is positioned centrally in the frame. Moving the door stop needs care to avoid splitting it – slide a chisel in behind the stop and lever it out. Remove the sides before the top, starting in the middle.

When repositioning the door stop, hang the door first, so that you can be sure that the stop fits snugly.

If you change the side of the frame from which the door is hung (as well as changing it from in to out), you can retain the existing door hinge, latch and door handle positions, although new recesses must still be cut in the frame for the hinges and striking plate.

TIP

To prevent the paint from chipping when you remove a door stop, run a trimming knife blade along the joint between door stop and frame to cut through the paint.

3 On the other side of the door, cut a recess in the edge for the latch and drill a hole for the spindle. You may need to drill another hole for a key if the latch is lockable.

4 Fit the latch and the operating spindle. Then add the handles. Fit hinges to the other side of the door and cut recesses in the frame for the hinges and striking plate (keeper).

REPOSITIONING THE DOOR STOP

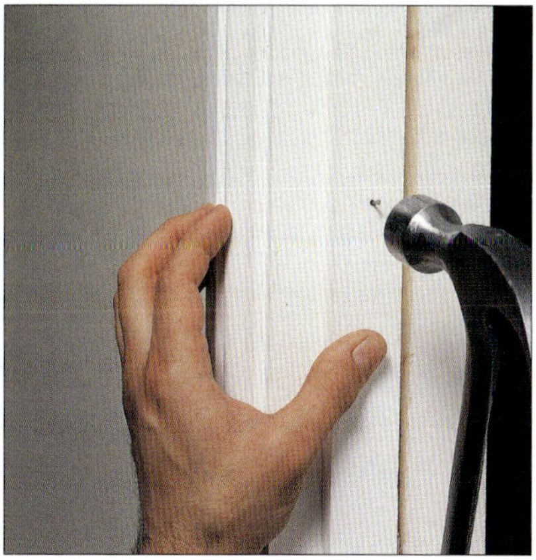

1 After cutting through the paint film, carefully slide a chisel under the door stop and gently prise it from the frame. Remove the old nails.

2 Drill new nail clearance holes in the stop and nail it to the door frame in its new position. Fill all the nail holes before repainting.

REPAIRING DOORS

Doors can develop all sorts of problems, from simple squeaks and rattles to suddenly refusing to open and shut properly. Fortunately, most of the problems are easy to solve, although for most repairs you will need to remove the door from the frame.

ABOVE: You can fix a squeaking hinge by unscrewing each half of the hinge in turn and packing the recess with cardboard.

SQUEAKS

A door normally squeaks simply because the hinges need oiling. Often you can dribble sufficient oil on to the hinges with the door in place, but if they are caked in dirt and paint, it is best to remove the door and work the hinges back and forth with oil.

A door may also squeak if the hinges are binding, usually because the recesses have been cut too deep into the door and/or frame. To cure this problem, unscrew each half of each hinge in turn, place a piece of cardboard behind the hinge, then refit the screws.

RATTLES

The simplest way to stop any door rattling is to fit a draught excluder. With an internal door, you could also try moving the door stop; with all types of door, you could try moving the latch striking plate (keeper), although this is not easy – drilling out and filling the old screw holes with glued-in dowels helps.

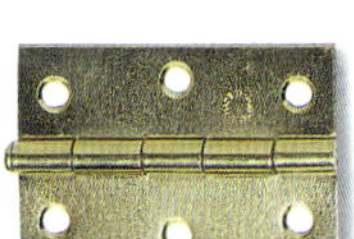

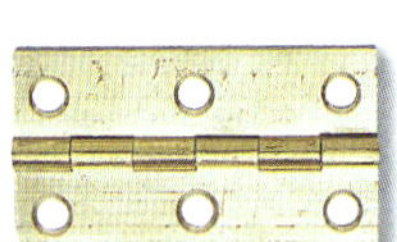

WARPED DOORS

If a door has become warped, you can straighten it with pairs of clamps, stout lengths of wood and packing blocks. Mount the door between the timbers, say lengths of 50 x 100mm (2 x 4in), and position the packing blocks to force the door in the opposite direction to the warp. Force it beyond straight by tightening up the clamps and leave for as long as you can. When the clamps are removed, the door should be straight.

BINDING

External doors often bind during cold, damp weather, becoming free again when the weather is dry and warm. This is a sign that the bottom of the door was not sealed when the door was painted, allowing moisture to get in.

Binding doors can also be caused by a build-up of paint on the leading (non-hinge) edge. The cure is to remove the door and plane down the leading edge, repainting it once the door has been fitted. Add primer to the bottom of the door to prevent more moisture from getting in.

If a door binds at the bottom, it may be because the hinges have worked loose. Try tightening the screws, fitting larger or longer screws if necessary. If this does not work, remove the door and plane down the part that is rubbing.

A door can bind seriously when you have fitted a new floor covering. In this case, remove the door and cut a strip off the bottom with a door trimming saw.

ABOVE: Take the door off its hinges and plane the leading (non-hinge) edge if it is binding.

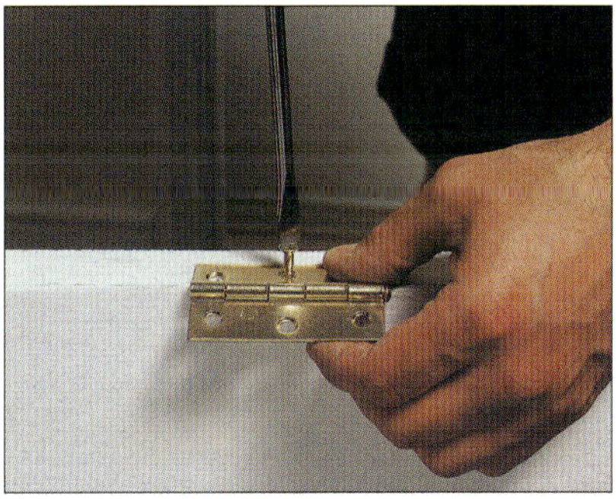

ABOVE: Fit longer screws to a hinge if the old ones have lost their grip.

ABOVE: Running the base of a door over abrasive paper may be enough to cure binding.

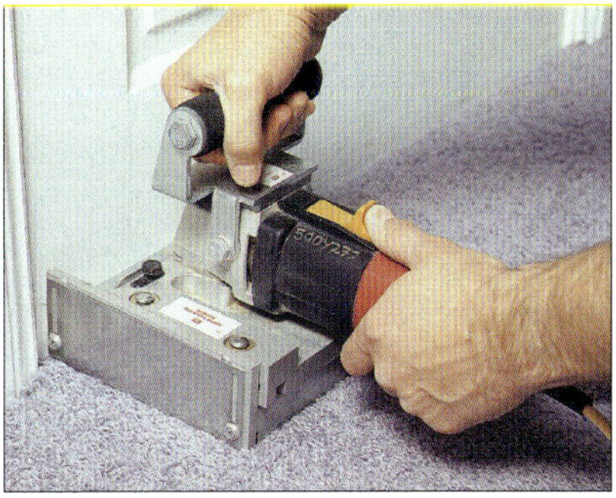

ABOVE: You can hire a door trimming saw to adjust the height after fitting a new carpet.

REPAIRING FLOORS & STAIRS

Of all the surfaces in your home, the floors take the most punishment. The continual passage of people to and fro, plus the scraping of furniture, can cause substantial damage over time. In addition to day-to-day wear, wooden floors can also be attacked by rot and insects, with damage extending to the supporting structure of joists below. Older wooden floors usually have individual boards that may warp, crack and shrink, opening up gaps that lead to draughts. Solid floors may develop cracks or be uneven, while floor coverings such as tiles and carpet can suffer from a variety of ills. Stairs are subject to heavy wear, too, as a result of which their joints can become loose and their treads broken.

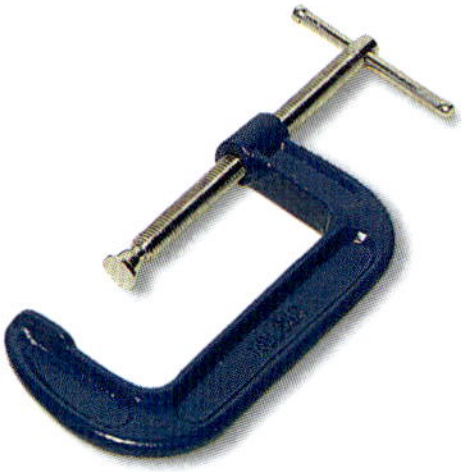

LIFTING FLOORBOARDS

The majority of floors in older homes will have individual floorboards nailed to supporting joists. In modern homes, sheets of flooring-grade chipboard (particle board) will be nailed or screwed to the joists. If a new floor covering is to be laid, it is essential that the floor is in good condition. If floorboards are to be exposed, they must be in even better condition, as any defects will be visible.

To inspect the underfloor space or fit new floorboards, you will need to lift existing floorboards. You may find some that have been cut and lifted in the past to provide access to pipes or cables. These should be easy to lever up with a bolster (stonecutter's chisel) – do not use a screwdriver as you will damage the floorboard.

To lift boards that have not been cut, check first that they are not tongued-and-grooved – a tongue along one edge of each board fitting into a groove along the adjacent edge of its neighbour. If they are, use a floorboard saw or a circular saw with its cutting depth set to 20mm (¾in) to cut through the tongues.

Lever up the floorboard with your bolster, and use a floorboard saw to make a right-angled cut across it. Make the cut exactly over a joist so that the two parts of the board will be supported when they are replaced.

Chipboard sheets are easy to unscrew, but you may need to cut through tongues in the same manner as for traditional floorboards to be able to lift them.

1 If the board is tongued-and-grooved, cut through the tongue with a circular saw. Lift the end of the floorboard by levering with a bolster (stonecutter's chisel).

2 Use wooden wedges to keep the end of the board raised. Check that there are no pipes or cables underneath and cut through it above the centre of a joist with a floorboard saw.

JOIST PROBLEMS

Most of the problems associated with floor joists are due to dampness, which may occur if airbricks (vents) have become blocked or if there are not enough airbricks to ensure adequate ventilation of the underfloor space.

Lift a few floorboards and inspect the joists with a torch and a mirror, prodding any suspect areas with a bradawl (awl). If sections of joist are damaged, you should be able to cut and lift floorboards or chipboard (particle board) sheets over the damage and bolt on a new section of joist of the same size, making sure that it is fixed to solid wood. Do not bother to remove the old joist unless it is actually rotten. If you do find signs of dry rot (typically white strands), all damaged wood must be removed by a firm of professionals. If you find signs of woodworm attack, treat the affected areas with a recommended woodworm eradicator or call in a professional firm.

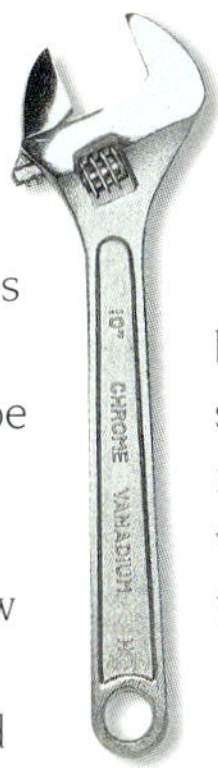

If you want to strengthen a floor so that it will support a partition wall running directly above a joist, you can sandwich the existing joist between two reinforcing joists. These should be supported at each end by metal joist hangers screwed to the wallplate or masonry and butted up to the existing joist. Cut the new joists to length, drop them into the hangers and drill holes through all three joists at 900mm (3ft) intervals. Pass 12mm (½in) bolts through the holes and tighten.

1 Cut the new joist section to length and clamp it in place while you drill holes through it and through the old joist. A right-angled drill attachment makes this easy.

2 Fit washers beneath the bolt heads, pass them through the holes and add another washer beneath each nut before tightening them with an adjustable spanner.

REPAIRING WOOD FLOORS

A wood floor should have a sound and smooth surface. Even if the wood is covered by carpet or tiles, any faults not rectified will eventually show through any floor covering and may damage it. It is therefore essential that you fill holes, cracks and gaps, as well as make the surface level and smooth.

FILLING HOLES

Nail and screw holes can easily be plugged using a flexible wood filler applied with a filling or putty knife. If the floorboards are to be left exposed and treated with a clear sealer, try to match the wood filler, or stopping, to the colour of the surrounding floorboards – so carry out the filling after any sanding.

Larger recesses can also be filled with flexible filler, but if a knot has fallen out, leaving a large round hole, plug this by gluing in a short length of dowel and planing it smooth when the glue has dried. Select a dowel that matches the colour of the floor or stain it once planed down.

FILLING CRACKS

You will find two main kinds of crack in wood floors: splits in the ends of the floorboards and gaps between the boards.

A split can often be cured by skew (toe) nailing – i.e. driving two nails through the end of the board at an angle toward the centre and down into the joist. As the nails are driven in, they should close up the split.

Gaps between floorboards are more difficult to deal with. If they are narrow, flexible wood filler will work, but for wider gaps, you must cut slivers of wood and glue them into place in the gaps. Once the glue has dried, plane or sand the slivers flush with the surrounding floor and stain to match.

If there are lots of wide gaps between floorboards, a better solution is to lift all the floorboards one by one, starting at one side of the room and working toward the other, and re-lay them tightly against one another. Floorboard clamps will help you do this, as they force a board against its neighbour while you nail or screw it down.

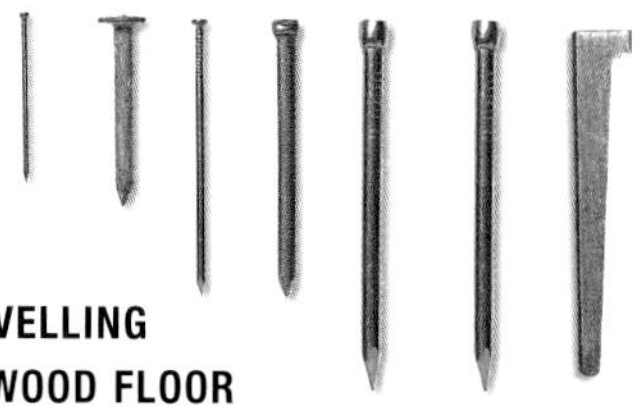

LEVELLING A WOOD FLOOR

Individual rough patches on a wood floor can be sanded down by hand, but where floorboards have become cupped or are heavily encrusted with old paint, grease and polish, the best move is to hire an industrial-type sanding machine and re-sand the floor. Begin with coarse abrasive and progress through to the fine grades, working across the floorboards at an angle. Finish off by working along the boards with fine abrasive. Hire an edging sander as well, unless you own a belt sander, because the floor sander will not sand right up to the skirtings (baseboards).

FILLING GAPS BETWEEN FLOORBOARDS

1 Drive glued slivers of wood between floorboards to fill large gaps. Leave them just proud of the surrounding boards, wipe off excess glue with a damp cloth and allow the glue to dry.

2 Plane down the wood slivers flush with the floor when the glue has dried. If the floorboards are to be left exposed, stain the slivers so that they match the colour of the boards.

FILLING HOLES AND SPLITS

ABOVE: Use flexible wood filler to cover the holes made by nail heads and screws.

ABOVE: With a split board, glue the split, then drive in nails at an angle to close it up.

FITTING NEW FLOORBOARDS

Over a period of time, floorboards can develop a number of faults. The natural flexing of the wood as it is walked on can begin to loosen nails, leading to squeaks and creaks. If sections are lifted regularly, they can be damaged, or the wood may simply warp and split with age.

LOOSE FLOORBOARDS

If floorboards are loose, the best answer is to replace the nails holding them down with screws. Do not put a screw in the middle of a board – there could be a pipe underneath. If nail heads are protruding, use a hammer and nail punch to set them below the surface of the floorboards. This is essential before attempting to use a sanding machine or laying carpet or sheet vinyl.

DAMAGED FLOORBOARDS

If floorboards are split or broken, the damaged section, at least, will need to be replaced. The most likely problem is that old floorboards will have become "cupped", or turned up at the edges. You can overcome this by hiring a floor sanding machine.

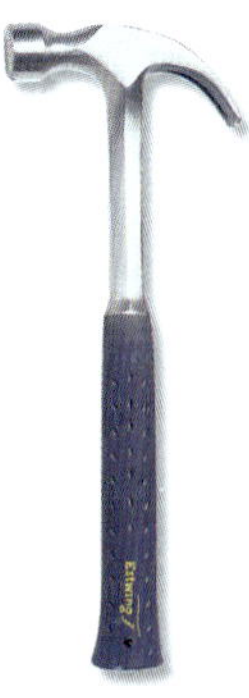

You do not need to replace a whole floorboard if only part of it is damaged; simply lift the board and cut out the damaged section, making the cuts over the centres of joists.

FITTING FLOORBOARDS

ABOVE: Plane down a floorboard if it is too wide to fill the gap.

If a replacement floorboard is too wide, plane it down to fit the gap – do not fit a narrower replacement floorboard, as this will result in draughts. If the board is slightly thicker, chisel slots out of it where it fits over the joists; if it is thinner, use packing

FIXING FLOORBOARDS

ABOVE: Drill pilot holes for floorboard nails to avoid splitting the wood.

ABOVE: Use card or plywood packing pieces over the joists if the board is too shallow.

ABOVE: Use a chisel to cut slots to fit over joists if the board is too thick.

pieces of cardboard or plywood between the joists and the board. Secure each floorboard with two floorboard nails at each joist, positioning them about 25mm (1in) from the edge of the board and exactly in the middle of the joist. It is a good idea to drill pilot holes in the board first.

TIP

When laying new floorboards, make sure that you can still gain access to pipes and cables underneath. If necessary, cut removable inspection hatches in both the floor and any new floor coverings.

ABOVE: Hammer down protruding nails to prevent them from damaging the floor covering.

ABOVE: Secure loose floorboards by replacing the nails with screws.

REPAIRING SOLID FLOORS

Provided a solid floor is basically sound and dry, you should be able to fill cracks and holes using a quick-set repair mortar. All loose material should be removed and the cracks enlarged if necessary to give the mortar something to grip.

The surface of the crack or hole should be brushed with a solution of one part PVA (white) glue and five parts water to reduce absorbency and help the mortar adhere to the floor. Use the same PVA glue and water solution to make up the mortar, then trowel it into place, building up two or more layers in a deep hole. Level the surface with a plasterer's trowel.

DEALING WITH DAMP

Concrete floors should incorporate a damp-proof membrane to prevent moisture from rising up from the ground below. However, it is possible that this may have broken down, or not have been incorporated at all. To check for rising damp, lay a piece of polythene (polyethylene) sheet on the floor and seal its edges with tape. After a couple of days, moisture should be visible on the underside of the sheet if the condition exists. To protect against rising damp, paint the floor with two or three coats of a waterproofing compound. When it has dried, floor coverings can be laid on top, or a self-levelling compound added.

1 After opening out a crack in a solid floor and brushing out all debris and dust, brush the surfaces with a solution of PVA (white) glue to help the new mortar bond to it.

2 Mix a small amount of quick-set repair mortar, again using PVA solution, and work it into the crack with a small trowel. Smooth the mortar flush with the surrounding floor and leave to harden.

LEVELLING SOLID FLOORS

Little skill is required to produce a smooth, flat, solid floor surface, as a self-levelling floor compound will do the job for you.

Before you start, clear the room, removing all skirtings (baseboards) and doors; nail battens across thresholds to prevent the compound from spreading. Fill any cracks or holes more than 6mm (¼in) deep and brush the floor with PVA (white) glue/water solution. Mix the floor levelling compound in a bucket and tip it out on to the floor, spreading it with a plasterer's trowel or a float. Leave it to settle. Once the compound has dried, you can refit the skirtings and doors, but check that the latter will clear the higher floor when opened.

1 If the floor is excessively porous, seal it by brushing on a coat of diluted PVA (white) glue. Then mix up the self-levelling floor compound according to the manufacturer's instructions.

2 Starting from the corner farthest from the door, pour the compound on to the floor. Do not pour too much on to the floor at any one time, otherwise you will not be able to reach across it.

3 Using a plasterer's trowel, smooth the compound to a thickness of approximately 3mm (⅛in). Allow at least 24 hours for the compound to dry before walking on it.

REPAIRING FLOOR TILES

Of all the types of floor covering, tiled finishes can be the easiest to repair, since individual tiles can often be lifted and replaced. The way you do it depends on whether the tile is hard or soft and on how it has been secured to the floor. Even damaged carpet can be patched effectively, but care needs to be taken to avoid further damage to surrounding areas.

Ceramic and quarry tiles are among the most difficult tiles to replace, as first you will have to chip out the old tile. Drill a few holes in the tile with the biggest masonry drill you own, then use a club (spalling) hammer and small bolster (stonecutter's chisel) to chip out the tile, making sure you do not damage the surrounding tiles. Chip out all old adhesive or mortar and grout from the hole.

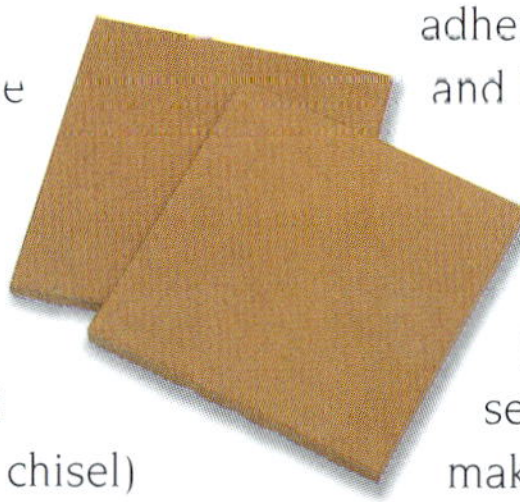

Lay some new tile adhesive (for ceramic tiles) or mortar (for quarry tiles) and push the replacement tile gently into place. If it is not flush with its neighbours, lift it quickly and add or remove adhesive or mortar as necessary. Clean any excess mortar or adhesive off the face of the tile and leave to set before making good the gaps around the tile with grout (ceramic tiles) or more mortar (quarry tiles). If re-laying several tiles, it helps if you make up some small spacers.

1 Remove any cracked quarry or ceramic tiles with a club (spalling) hammer and small bolster (stonecutter's chisel). Wear gloves to protect your hands, and safety goggles to shield your eyes.

2 Bed a new quarry tile on mortar, but use the recommended adhesive for a ceramic tile. Level the tile with its neighbours using a strip of wood; wipe off excess mortar or adhesive.

REPAIRING WOODEN MOSAIC TILES

There are two ways to replace wooden mosaic tiles. One is to lift the whole tile, which consists of four groups of timber strips, and replace it with a new one. First drill or chisel out one strip, then lever the rest of the tile from the floor. The second method is to remove just the damaged strip or strips and glue in replacements taken from a spare tile, pressing them into place with a block of wood.

If the new strip sits a little proud of its neighbours, it should be sanded down, using abrasive paper and a sanding block, until it lies flush. Then sand the entire tile and revarnish it. If the tiles are pre-finished, you will have to sand the back of the strip before gluing it.

1 First drill a sequence of closely spaced holes through the damaged mosaic strip, stopping each when you just break through the wood. Take care not to allow the drill to wander.

2 Carefully cut away the strip, working outward from the holes with a narrow-bladed chisel held bevel down. Do not let the chisel slip when you approach the edges of adjoining strips.

3 Apply a little adhesive to the new mosaic strip and place it carefully in position, taking care not to get adhesive on the adjoining strips. Using a block of wood and a hammer, tap it down.

REPLACING SOFT FLOOR TILES

Most soft floor tiles – vinyl, cork, lino and rubber – are replaced in the same way. First you have to soften the adhesive holding the tile in place, which is best done with a hot-air gun, starting at one corner and gradually peeling the tile back. This becomes easier once you can direct the hot-air gun beneath the tile. An old chisel can be used to remove any remaining adhesive. Check that the replacement tile is an exact fit.

Some soft tiles are self-adhesive, requiring only the removal of backing paper, while others require a separate adhesive. Always add the adhesive to the back of a replacement tile to avoid staining the other tiles.

With the adhesive in place, or the backing paper removed, hold the tile against the edge of one of the surrounding tiles and lower it into place. You may only get one attempt at this, so take care to get it right.

TIP

If you do not have any spare tiles and are unable to obtain a matching colour or pattern for the existing flooring, consider replacing the damaged tile with one of a contrasting colour or pattern. To disguise the repair, replace a few of the undamaged tiles with similar contrasting tiles, setting them out in a regular or random pattern. If you cannot find tiles of the correct size, buy larger ones and carefully cut them down to fit.

1 Remove a vinyl or cork tile using a hot-air gun to soften the adhesive. Work a scraper under the edge and gradually prise the tile from the floor.

2 Apply adhesive to the back of the replacement vinyl or cork tile, set one edge in place against its neighbour and lower it in place.

PATCHING CARPET

Provided you have a matching piece, you can patch most types of carpet, but it may be worth cleaning the carpet first, since the patch could be a brighter colour. First decide how large the patch should be – if the carpet is patterned, you may want to join along a pattern line – cut the patch about 25mm (1in) larger than this all round, with the same part of any pattern. Lay the patch over the carpet, lining up the pattern exactly, and secure it with adhesive tape.

Using a trimming knife fitted with a new blade and a metal straightedge, make a single cut down through both thicknesses of carpet along each edge of the patch. Remove the tape and lift both pieces of carpet – the patch should fit exactly into the hole in the carpet with the pattern matching.

With foam-backed carpet, lay double-sided tape on the floor around the edges of the hole so that each strip overlaps the joint between the old carpet and the patch. Brush the edges of the patch and the hole with latex adhesive to prevent fraying, then press the carpet patch on to the tape. Remove excess adhesive with a damp cloth.

With fabric-backed carpet, use non-adhesive carpet repair tape and latex adhesive on the back and edges of the patch and the hole. Press the patch down into the hole with a wallpaper seam roller and wipe off any excess adhesive with a damp cloth.

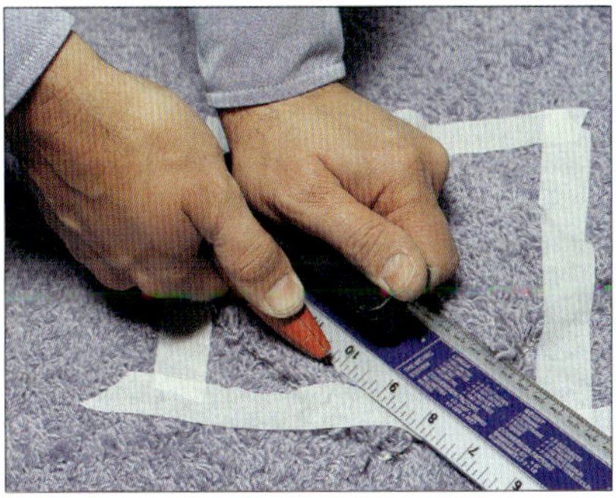

1 Use a trimming knife and straightedge to cut through both the patch and the existing carpet to ensure an exact fit.

2 Press the carpet patch on to double-sided adhesive tape. Brush the edges with latex adhesive to prevent fraying.

3 The finished patch of carpet should fit exactly into the hole and the seams should be invisible in long-pile carpet.

CURING STAIRCASE PROBLEMS

A timber staircase consists of a series of evenly spaced horizontal treads that form the flight. Most staircases also have vertical risers, which fill the space between the rear edge of one tread and the front edge of the tread above; these may be nailed in place, or may have tongued edges that slot into grooves in the treads.

The treads are supported at each side by two parallel beams called strings. A closed-string staircase has the treads and risers set into grooves cut in the inner faces of the strings, while an open-string staircase has the outer string cut in a zigzag fashion so the treads can rest on the cutouts. The inner string – the one against the wall of the stairwell – is always a closed string.

At the open side of a conventional flight, a guard is fitted to run between the top and bottom newel posts – main uprights supporting flight. This usually consists of a series of closely-spaced balusters, which are fixed between the top edge of the outer string and the underside of a handrail, but it may be a solid panelled barrier. There may also be a wall-mounted handrail at the other side of the flight; freestanding flights must obviously have a balustrade at each side.

Stairs creak because one of the components has become loose; a footfall then causes the loose part to move against an adjacent component of the flight. A cure is simple if the underside of the flight is accessible, but less straightforward if it is not.

1 If there is no access to the underside of the flight, secure loose or squeaking treads by fixing metal repair brackets to tread and riser. If the underside can be reached, check that the wedges securing the treads and risers to the strings are in place. Hammer them in firmly if they are loose.

4 Insert a crowbar (wrecking bar) between the string and the tread, and prise it up and out to free it from the risers above and below it. Mark out and cut a replacement. Plane the nosing to shape, and cut notches in one end for the balusters.

2 Glue back any of the support blocks beneath the fronts of the treads if they have fallen off. Fit extra blocks beneath troublesome treads. Drill clearance holes up through the rear edge of each tread, then drive screws up into the bottom edge of the riser above to lock the tread to it.

3 If the tread is found to be split, it must be replaced. Start by prising off the side moulding, then tap the balusters out with a mallet. Insert a knife into the joint along the back of the tread to check if it has been nailed or screwed. If it has, use a hacksaw blade to cut the fixings.

5 Glue and clamp support blocks to the rear face of the riser below, and nail another block to the closed string to provide extra support for the replacement tread.

6 Fit the new tread in place and secure it to the support blocks and to the cut-out in the open string with screws rather than nails. With the tread securely fixed in position, replace the balusters in their notches and nail the side moulding back on.

HOME INSULATION

- Insulation materials
- Insulation & draughtproofing
- Ventilation
- Overcoming damp conditions

INTRODUCTION

Insulation is a means of preventing heat from escaping from a house. Heat loss can occur through roofs, walls, floors, doors and windows, and each of these can be insulated in different ways – with loose-fill or blanket insulation, or by installing double glazing, to name a few.

Related to insulation is draughtproofing, which is also a method of reducing heat loss, particularly under doors, through letter plate openings and keyholes, and through gaps in windows.

Insulating and sealing a house totally is not the answer, however, as there always needs to be some air ventilation to prevent condensation, which can lead to mould and structural damage. So a combination of insulation, draughtproofing and ventilation is required.

This chapter shows how to insulate, draughtproof and ventilate the main areas of the home where heat loss can be a problem. Doing this will save energy and money, and will also cut down on unnecessary wastage of fossil fuels, which in turn causes the widespread environmental problems associated with the release of carbon dioxide into the atmosphere.

CAUSES OF HEAT LOSS

The primary areas of heat loss are through the roof, walls and floors – around 25 per cent of heat is lost through the roof and pipework, 35 per cent through the walls, and 15 per cent through the floors – so these are the first areas to work on.

Doors and windows are the next most likely places where heat is lost, due to draughts coming through gaps and cracks. About 15 per cent of heat loss is attributed to poor draughtproofing.

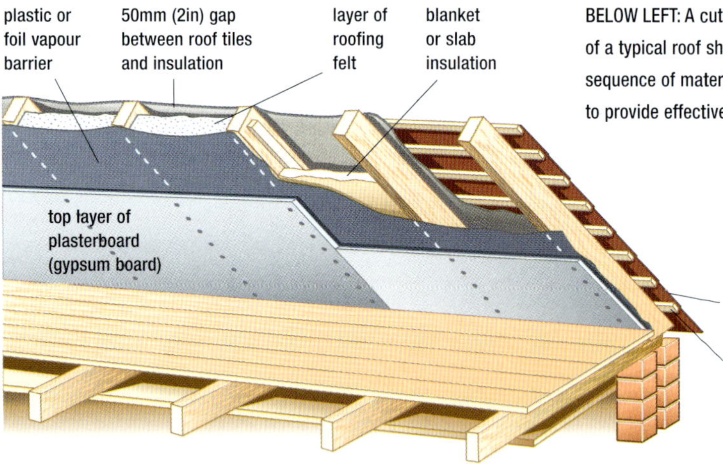

BELOW LEFT: A cutaway section of a typical roof shows the sequence of materials necessary to provide effective insulation.

ABOVE: Draughts can enter your home through the smallest of gaps. You can easily prevent draughts through keyholes by installing keyhole covers.

CAUSES OF CONDENSATION

Condensation can be caused by a lack of ventilation and over-insulation in properties not designed for it, both inside the rooms and within the building's structure. When water vapour condenses, the water runs down windows and walls, and causes mould, health problems, and even damage to the structure of the home.

People themselves are a major source of the moisture in the air inside a building. Breath is moist and sweat evaporates; one person gives off 250ml (½ pint) of water during eight hours of sleep, and three times as much during an active day.

Domestic activities create even more moisture. Cooking, washing up, bathing, washing and drying clothes can create as much as a further 10 to 12 litres (about 3 gallons) of water a day, and every litre of fuel burnt in a flueless oil or paraffin (kerosene) heater gives off roughly another litre of water vapour.

The air in the house is expected to soak up all this extra moisture invisibly. It may not be able to manage unaided. However, a combination of improved insulation and controlled ventilation will help eliminate condensation. An electric dehumidifier can also help in soaking up excess moisture.

ABOVE: A significant cause of condensation in the kitchen is cooking. Steam rises from pans and the vapour then condenses, forming droplets on walls and ceilings.

ABOVE: Constant condensation ruins paintwork and will eventually cause wooden window frames and sills to rot, unless action is taken to increase ventilation.

PROVIDING GOOD INSULATION

Good insulation reduces the rate at which expensive domestic heat escapes through the fabric of your home and helps to protect vulnerable plumbing systems from damage during cold weather. The different parts of your home can be insulated by various methods, and most jobs can be handled by a competent person.

ROOFS AND PIPEWORK

The roof is a good place to start your insulation project. This is where pipework is at greatest risk of freezing, so pipes must be tackled as well. The main options for roof insulation are loose-fill, blanket and slab insulation, and pipes are best insulated with foam taped around them.

WALLS

The best solution for cavity walls is a job that must be left to the professionals. Despite the extra outlay, the work is very cost-effective, and you can expect to see a return on your investment after a few years. The usual procedure is to pump foam, pellets or mineral fibres into the cavity through holes drilled in the outer leaf of the wall. Make sure that the work is carried out by an approved contractor.

Applying insulation to the inner faces of walls is well within the scope of most people. One possibility is to use thermal plasterboard (gypsum board) to dry-line external walls. Another is to add a framework of wood strips to the wall, infill with slab or blanket insulation and face it with plasterboard. To prevent condensation, plastic sheeting should be stapled to the insulating material.

FLOORS, DOORS AND WINDOWS

Suspended floors can be insulated by fixing sheets of rigid polystyrene (plastic foam) between the joists, and solid floors can be lined with a vapour

ABOVE: Installing cavity wall insulation is a specialist job that can take up to three days.

ABOVE: You can insulate a suspended floor by laying loft (attic) or wall insulation batts between the joists.

ABOVE: Glass is an extremely poor insulator, and double glazing can cut down on heat loss. It can also help to reduce noise penetration from outside and will give added security against burglars.

barrier of heavy-duty plastic sheeting, topped with a floating floor of tongued-and-grooved chipboard (particle board) panels. Draughty floorboards can easily be repaired by applying silicone sealant (caulking) to small cracks, or by tapping slivers of wood into larger gaps.

Doors and windows are the two main sources of draughts in the home, and many products have been designed to deal with the problem. For example, gaps under doors and around windows can be sealed with draught excluder strips. Some are self-adhesive and easy to apply, while others can be fixed with screws. Make sure you choose the correct size for your doors and windows.

Windows can also be insulated by installing double glazing, either as a thin film stuck to each window frame or by fitting sliding units on to separate tracks within the window frames.

ABOVE: To control ventilation in steamy rooms, such as kitchens and bathrooms, extractor fans can be fitted. The types linked to humidity detectors are ideal, as they activate automatically.

PROVIDING GOOD VENTILATION

A free flow of fresh air, ventilation is essential in a home, not only for humans to breathe, but also to prevent condensation occurring. There are many types of extractor fan that will help air to circulate. These can be fitted to ceilings, windows and walls, and can be installed by any competent do-it-yourselfer. For underfloor ventilation, airbricks are a good solution: ideally there should be an airbrick every 2m (6ft) along an external wall.

OVERCOMING DAMP

The best way of dealing with damp is to install a damp-proof course, but seek professional guidance before carrying out this work yourself. Other solutions include waterproofing exterior walls, installing ventilation fans and buying an electric dehumidifier.

BOSCH
PST 55-PE
380 W

INSULATION MATERIALS

There are three basic aspects involved in conserving heat in your home: insulation to prevent heat from escaping; draughtproofing to prevent cold air from seeping into your home; and ventilation to prevent condensation from forming and causing problems. Various types of insulation material are made to cope with different situations; all are easy to use. Likewise, draughtproofing materials are easy to install, although ventilation devices require a bit more effort to fit. None of this work is beyond any competent do-it-yourselfer equipped with a relatively small collection of basic tools. As with all do-it-yourself work, due regard for your own safety, and that of others who may be nearby, is essential.

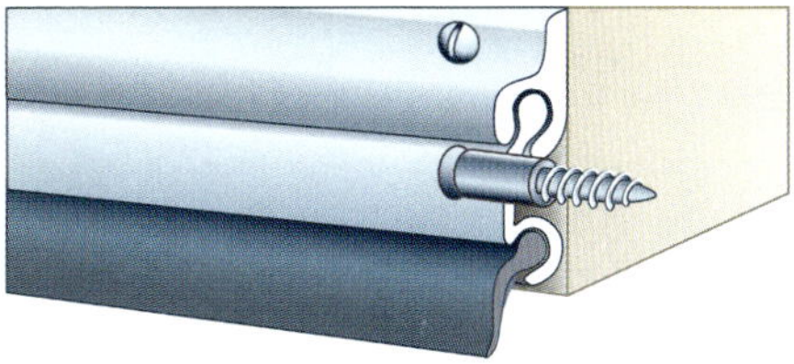

TYPES OF INSULATION

Before thinking about individual types of insulation, it is important to understand the concept of cost-effectiveness. Insulation costs money to install, and can bring benefits in two main ways.

It can reduce heating bills, since the home will waste less heat and the same internal temperatures can be maintained without burning so much fuel. The annual saving on the heating bill will therefore "pay back" the cost of the extra insulation. Also, when replacing a heating system, having better standards of insulation allows a less powerful, and less expensive, boiler to be used – an indirect saving, but valuable none the less.

ESSENTIAL BUYS

Good insulation need not mean great expenditure. The most effective items are relatively cheap and could save you a great deal in the long term. Any water storage tanks in the roof must be insulated to protect them from freezing. Padded jackets are available for the purpose. Likewise, any exposed pipework in the roof should be fitted with insulating sleeves.

ABOVE: Fix reflective foil between rafters to act as a vapour barrier over insulation.

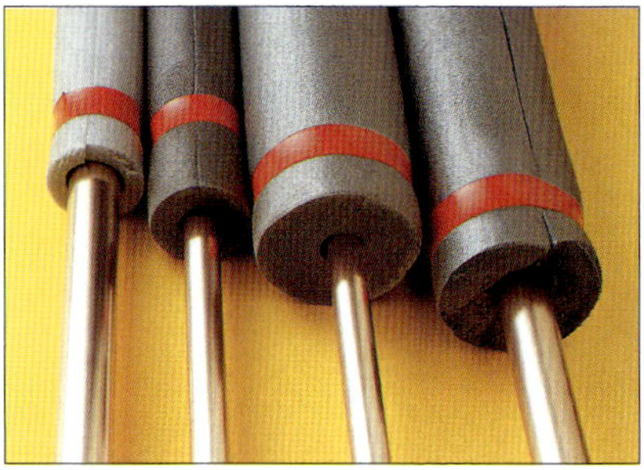

ABOVE: Split foam pipe insulation comes in sizes to match standard pipe diameters.

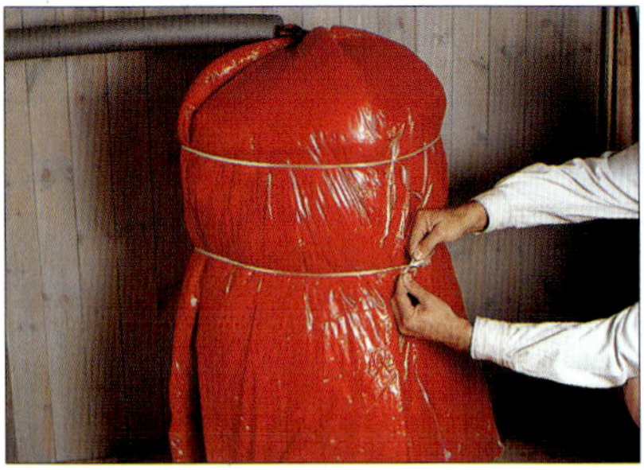

ABOVE: Secure an insulation blanket to a hot water cylinder.

ABOVE: Insulate a cold water cistern with a purpose-made jacket.

LAYING LOOSE-FILL INSULATION

Lay loose-fill insulation by pouring the material between the joists. Spread it out so that it is level with the tops of the joists to ensure a thick and effective layer.

LOOSE-FILL INSULATION

This is sold by the bag and is simply poured between the joists and levelled off with their top surfaces. The dustier varieties, such as vermiculite, can be unpleasant to work with.

BLANKET INSULATION

This consists of rolls of glass fibre, mineral fibre or rock fibre, in standard widths to unroll between the joists. A typical roll length would be 6–8m (20–26ft), but short lengths are also available, known as batts. Always wear a face mask, gloves and protective clothing when laying the insulation.

SLAB INSULATION

These products are light and easy to handle, but as with the blanket versions some types may cause skin irritation. The slab widths match common joist spacings.

LAYING BLANKET INSULATION

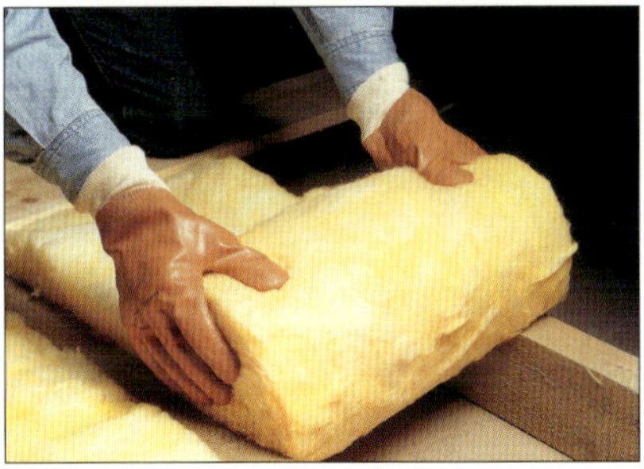

If the roof of the house is pitched (sloping), blanket insulation can be laid over the loft (attic) floor. This is one of the most cost-effective forms of insulation.

PAY-BACK PERIODS

Hot water cylinder jacket *****
Pay-back period: less than 1 year.

Loft (attic) insulation ****
Pay-back period: 1–2 years.

Reflective radiator foil ****
Pay-back period: 1–2 years.

Draught excluders ***
Pay-back period: 2–3 years.

Flat roof insulation **(*)
Pay-back period: 2–4 years.

Floor insulation **
Pay-back period: 3–5 years.

Cavity wall insulation **
Pay-back period: around 5 years.

Double glazing **(*)
Pay-back period: 5 years or more.

Solid wall insulation *
Pay-back period: over 10 years.

* Star rating indicates cost-effectiveness.

DRAUGHT EXCLUDERS

Draught excluder strips are an inexpensive method of sealing gaps around windows and doors. The strips are self-adhesive and easy to apply, although foam strips offer variable levels of success. Avoid the cheapest varieties, as they may soon become compressed and will not do the job properly. Look for products that are guaranteed for between two and five years. These will be easy to remove and replace if you wish to upgrade the draughtproofing system.

Rubber strips, commonly with E- or P-shaped profiles, are dearer, but are better in terms of performance and longevity. Normally, casement windows are easier to draughtproof than the sash variety.

The most effective way of keeping draughts out at the sides of sashes is to fix nylon-pile brush strips to the window frame. The top and bottom do not need special treatment, as any of the products recommended for casement windows can be used.

The gap between the bottom of a door and the threshold (saddle) can be draughtproofed by attaching a solid blade or brush strip to the bottom edge of the door, so that it meets the floor or sill, or by fixing a special strip across the threshold so that it is in contact with the underside of the door.

Unused chimneys can be sealed, or a temporary solution is to block off the flue with a "balloon" device which can be removed when a fire is needed.

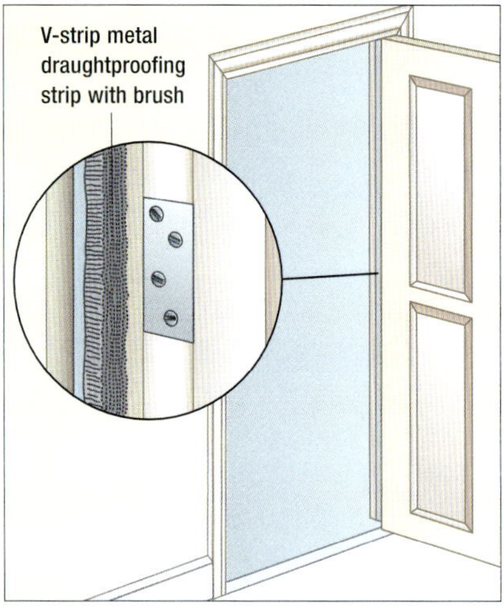

ABOVE: A metal draughtproofing strip can be fixed to a door frame, such as the example shown here, a V-strip type. The insert shows where the brush strip should be fixed.

ABOVE: A brush-type strip fitted at the base of the door works well on uneven surfaces.

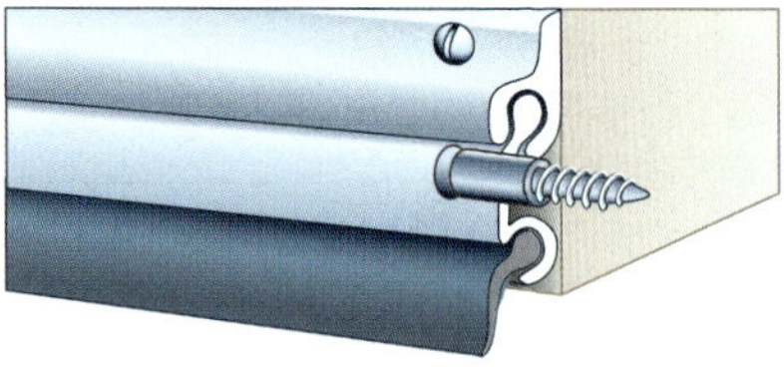

ABOVE: A flexible rubber blade held in a plastic or aluminium extrusion, secured by screws.

EXTRACTOR FANS AND AIRBRICKS

There are several options for ensuring a constant circulation of air in the home. Each works by providing ventilation, thus preventing condensation and its associated problems.

Extractor fans can be fitted in ceilings, windows or walls. Ceiling fans are particularly effective in bathrooms and kitchens, where warm water vapour rises. Window fans need care when installing; you can either cut a hole in a single-glazed window or order a new pane with the hole already cut by a glass supplier. Wall extractor fans are fixed to an outside wall. Always check for pipes before cutting into brickwork.

Airbricks are installed into external walls to ventilate the space below suspended wooden floors.

ABOVE: A ceiling-mounted extractor fan works by extracting the moist air that tends to collect just below the ceiling. A fan like this extracts this air to an outlet.

ABOVE: It is best to install a wall extractor fan as high as possible, where rising steam collects. Employ an electrician if you are unsure about how to install the wiring.

ABOVE: An airbrick contains perforated openings that allow ventilation in rooms and under wooden floors. It is important to keep them clear of earth, leaves and other debris, so clean them regularly.

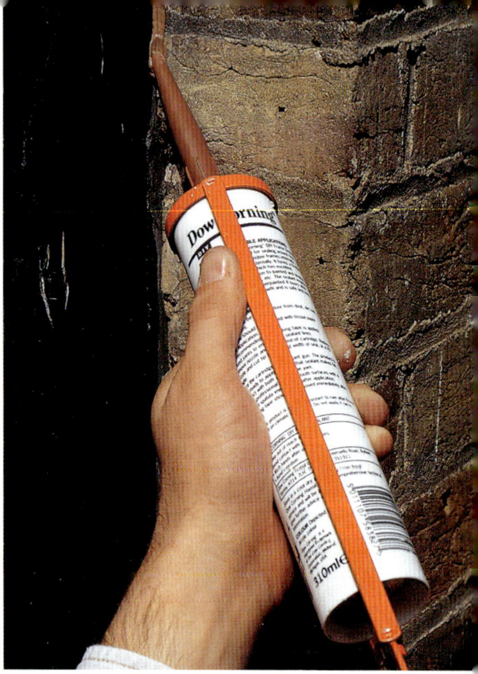
310ml

CARPET GRIPPER

INSULATION & DRAUGHTPROOFING

Heat rises, so the most important area of your home to insulate is the roof. Fortunately, this is very easy to do, although working in a small roof space can be difficult. Keeping the heat below the ceiling may have unforeseen consequences, however, in that any pipes and water tanks in the roof may freeze, so these too must be wrapped in insulating material. Once you have dealt with the roof, turn your attention to the walls and floors, since both can be insulated to provide a real bonus in energy saving. Floors not only act as heat sinks, but if boarded, they can allow in cold draughts. Sealing the gaps between boards will make your rooms feel cosy, as will draughtproofing the doors and windows. For extra comfort, opt for double glazing.

INSULATING ROOFS

In a building with a pitched (sloping) roof, where the loft (attic) space is used only for storage, it is usual to insulate the loft floor. To do this, use either blankets of glass fibre or mineral wool, sold by the roll, or else use loose-fill material (vermiculite, a lightweight expanded mineral, is the most widely used). Some kinds of loose-fill insulation, usually mineral wool or fireproofed cellulose fibres, can be blown into the loft by specialist professional contractors.

Blanket materials are generally easier to handle than loose-fill types unless the loft is awkwardly shaped, contains a lot of obstructions or has irregular joist spacings. The rolls are generally 600mm (24in) wide to match standard joist spacing, and common thicknesses are 100mm (4in) and 150mm (6in). Choose the latter unless there is already thin sonic loft insulation, and ensure that it is laid with eaves baffles to allow adequate ventilation of the loft, otherwise condensation may form and lead to rotting of the wood. It is essential to wear protective clothing when handling glass fibre insulation. Wear a face mask, gloves and cover any exposed skin with suitable clothing.

Apart from being awkward to handle, loose-fill materials have another drawback. To be as effective as blanket types, they need laying to a greater depth – usually at least an extra 25mm (1in). With few ceiling joists being deeper than about 150mm (6in), there is nothing to contain the insulation and allow for maintenance access, unless strips of wood are fixed along the top edge of every joist.

LAYING LOOSE-FILL INSULATION

1 Lay loose-fill insulation by pouring the material between the joists. Prevent it from running out at the eaves by fixing lengths of wood between the joists.

2 Level it off with a spreader, which you can make from chipboard (particle board). You may need to add strips of wood to the joists to obtain the required depth of insulation.

LAYING BLANKET ROOF INSULATION

1 Clear all stored items from the loft (attic) area, then put down a sturdy kneeling board and use a heavy-duty vacuum cleaner to remove dust and debris.

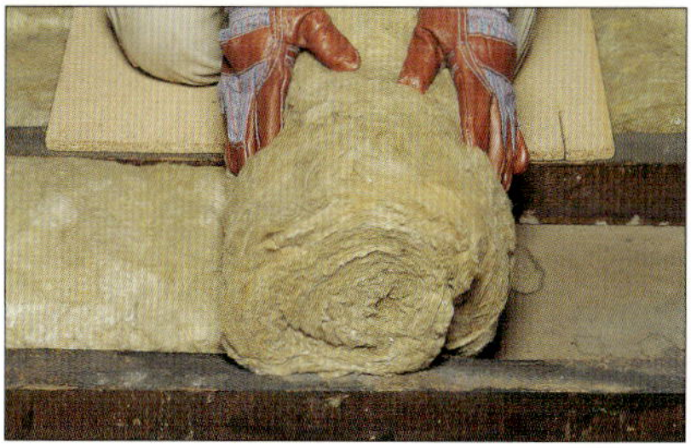

2 Always put on gloves and a face mask, and wear long sleeves, to handle the insulation. Unroll it between the joists, leaving the eaves clear for ventilation.

3 Butt-join the ends of successive lengths of blanket. To cut the material to length, either use long-bladed scissors or simply tear it.

4 While working across the loft, make sure that any electrical cables are lifted clear of the insulation so they cannot overheat.

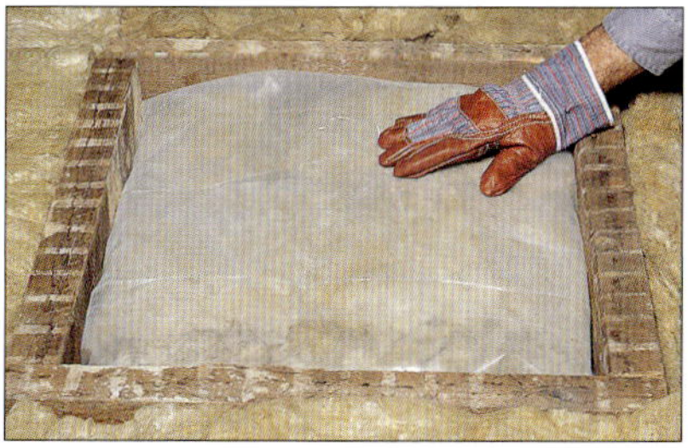

5 Insulate the upper surface of the loft hatch by wrapping a piece of blanket in plastic sheeting and stapling this to the hatch door.

6 Do not insulate under water tanks. If the tank has a lid, blanket insulation can also be wrapped around the tank and tied in place.

INSULATING PIPEWORK

When the loft (attic) floor is completely insulated, remember to insulate any water tanks and pipework within the loft, since they are now at risk of freezing. For this reason, do not lay insulation under water tanks.

FOAM PIPE INSULATION

Exposed pipework in the loft can easily be protected by covering it with proprietary foam pipe insulation. Basically, this comprises lengths of foam tubing, which have been split along the length and which come with inside diameters to match common domestic pipe sizes. All that is necessary is to open the split to allow the foam to be fitted over the pipe.

PIPE BANDAGE INSULATION

An alternative method is to use pipe bandage, but this is more labour intensive, since it must be wrapped around the pipe, although the fibrous material is useful for pipes with awkward bends. To secure it, tie each end firmly with a short length of string.

JACKETS FOR TANKS

Tanks can be insulated with proprietary jackets, or you can tie lengths of blanket insulation around them, or tape on thick rigid foam sheets. Alternatively, you can build a plywood box around the tank and fill the gap between it and the tank with loose-fill insulation material.

INSULATING PIPES WITH BANDAGE

1 Pipe bandage can be used instead of foam insulation. Wrap it around the pipe in a spiral, with successive turns just overlapping. Don't leave any pipework exposed.

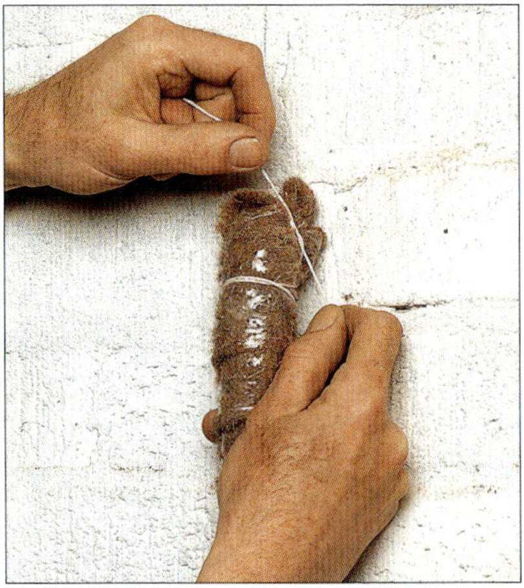

2 Tie the insulation bandage in place at the end of each length, or where the pipe passes through a wall. Simply tear the material to length as necessary.

INSULATING PIPES WITH FOAM

1 The quickest and easiest way of insulating pipework is to slip on lengths of foam pipe insulation, which is slit lengthways. Join the lengths with PVC (vinyl) tape.

2 To make neat joins in the insulation at corners, cut the ends at 45 degrees, using a mitre box and a carving knife or hacksaw blade. Tape the corner joint.

3 Make a V-shaped cut-out in the insulation at a tee joint, then cut an arrow shape to match it on the end of the insulation which will cover the branch pipe.

4 As with butt and corner joints, use PVC tape to secure the sections of insulation together and prevent them from slipping out of position. In time, you may need to renew this.

BOXING-IN PIPES

Some people regard visible pipes in the home as an eyesore. Moreover, where the pipes are in rooms that are unheated, or where they run against external walls, there is a possibility that they may freeze during a severe winter. Fortunately, with a little time and minimal woodworking skills, exposed pipes can be hidden successfully from view and protected from freezing at the same time, by building boxing around them and filling it with loose-fill insulation. If the boxing is decorated to match the room, the pipes can be concealed completely. Be sure to allow for the boxwork to be easily removed in situations where it may be necessary to gain access.

ACCESSIBILITY

Bear in mind that stopcocks, drain taps, pumps, hand-operated valves and the like will need to be readily accessible and require some form of removable box system. For this reason, the boxing around them should be assembled with screws rather than nails. If a panel needs to be regularly or quickly removed, turn buttons or magnetic catches are a good idea.

BOXING BASICS

Steel anchor plates and screws can be used to secure the sides of boxing to walls, and these will be easy to remove when necessary. Battens (furring strips), either 50 x 25mm (2 x 1in) or 25 x 25mm (1 x 1in), can be used to fix boards at skirting (baseboard) level.

Disguise the boxing by decorating it to match the rest of the room. If pipework is running along a panelled or boarded wall, construct the boxing so that it follows the general theme, using similar materials and staining and varnishing the boxes accordingly.

WALL PIPES

Measure the distance the pipes project from the wall, taking account of any joints and brackets. Cut the side panels from 25mm (1in) board slightly over this measurement and to their correct length. Fix small anchor plates flush with the back edge of each panel and spaced at about 600mm (24in) intervals.

If using plywood, you may need to drill pilot holes. Hold the panels against the wall and mark the positions of the screw holes on the wall. Drill the holes and fix the panels to the wall with rawl plugs and screws.

Cut the front panel to size from 6mm (¼in) plywood. Drill evenly spaced screw holes in the front panel and fix it in position with 19mm (¾in) No. 6 screws. Use cup washers underneath the screw heads to protect the panel if it is likely to be removed often. Trim the edges flush with a block plane.

With horizontal pipes, arrange the boxing so that you can remove the top panel to make filling with loose-fill insulation easy. For vertical pipes, leave a small access panel at the top of the box and pour the insulation through this, tapping the boxing to make sure that it fills the void completely.

BOXING-IN WALL PIPES

1 Measure how far the pipes protrude from the face of the wall.

2 With a pencil, mark the positions for the side batten fixings.

3 Attach the side battens, screwing them firmly into position.

4 Cut the front panel of the box to size with a jigsaw (saber saw). Use 6mm (¼in) plywood.

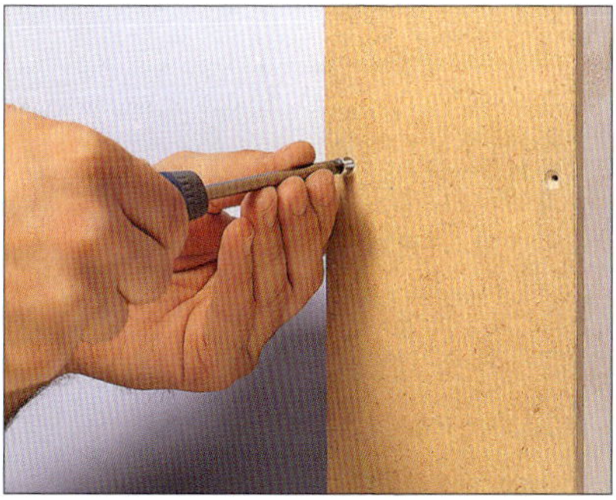

5 Drill pilot holes and screw the front panel into position, using 19mm (¾in) No. 6 screws.

6 Trim the edges of the front panel with a block plane. Add loose-fill insulation from the top.

INSULATING SOLID WALLS

House walls are the most extensive part of the whole building and absorb a lot of heat, which is why a house takes so long to warm up once it has become cold. Some of the lost heat can be retained by insulating the walls.

For solid walls, the most economical solution is to dry-line them on the inside with insulating plasterboard (gypsum board), fixed directly to the wall with panel adhesive or nailed to a supporting framework of treated wood strips. Alternatively, ordinary plasterboard sheets can be used, with insulation blanket or boards placed between the support strips and covered with a plastic vapour barrier.

INSULATING CAVITY WALLS

The cavity wall consists of two "leaves" of masonry with a gap, usually of 50mm (2in), between them. Their insulation performance can be improved by filling the cavity with insulating material. This is done by specialist installers who pump treated fibres, pellets or insulating foam into the cavity through holes drilled in the wall's outer leaf.

For wood-framed walls, the best alternative is to remove the interior finish, install insulation batts and cover these with a vapour barrier, such as plastic sheeting. Then add a new inner skin of plasterboard.

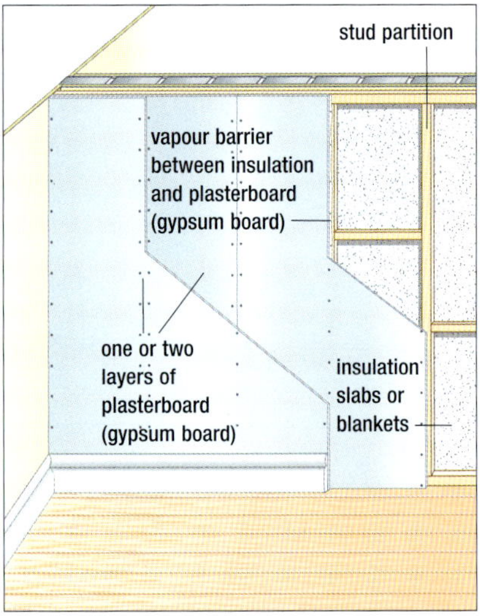

ABOVE: A wall can be insulated by erecting a stud partition wall in front of it, filling the void with blanket or slab insulation, and adding two layers of plasterboard (gypsum board) to the framework.

ABOVE: Fix a framework of 50 x 25mm (2 x 1in) softwood strips to the walls with masonry nails to support the edges and centres of the insulating boards.

ADDING THE DRY-LINING

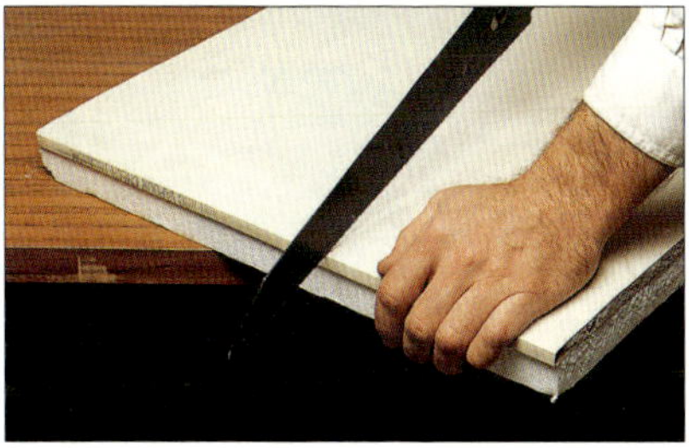

1 Mark cutting lines on the board surface in pencil, then cut along the line with the insulation facing downwards, using a fine-toothed saw.

2 Use a simple lever and fulcrum to raise the boards to touch the room ceiling as they are fixed. A skirting (baseboard) will cover the gap.

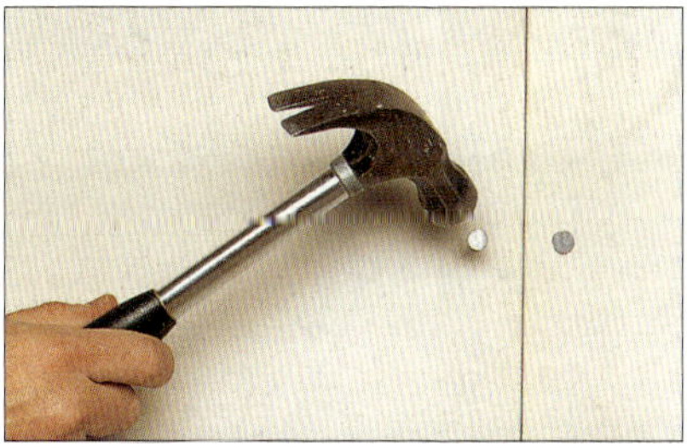

3 Fix the boards by positioning them against the supporting framework so that adjacent boards meet over a strip, and nail them in place. The nail heads should just "dimple" the surface.

4 At external corners, remove a strip of the polystyrene (plastic foam) insulation as wide as the board thickness so the edges of the plasterboard (gypsum board) can meet in a butt joint.

5 Arrange the boards at external corners so that a paper-covered board edge conceals one that has its plaster core exposed. Finish off all joints with plasterboard tape and filler.

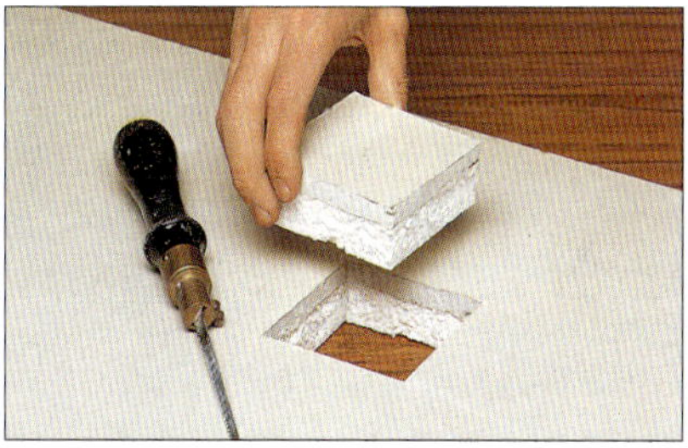

6 To make cutouts for light switch boxes, plug sockets and similar obstacles, mark their positions on the boards and cut them out with a padsaw.

INSULATING SUSPENDED FLOORS

Few people think of ground floors when considering insulation, yet a surprisingly large amount of heat can be lost through both solid and suspended wood floors. Insulating a suspended floor will involve disruptive work, since the floorboards will need lifting. However, if you are prepared to do this, the methods are very similar to laying roof insulation.

LIFTING FLOORBOARDS

Unless you have a basement that allows you to reach the underside of a suspended floor, to insulate it you will have to lift all of the floorboards.

To lift a board, tap the blade of a bolster (stonecutter's) chisel into the gap between two boards, close to the end of the board you want to lift, and lever the board upward; repeat for the other side.

Continue levering until the end of the board is clear of the floor and you can insert the claw of a hammer beneath it.

Use the hammer to lever the end high enough to insert a length of wood beneath the board to hold the end clear of the floor. Continue in this way along the board until you can lift it completely.

INSULATION METHODS

With suspended wood floors insulation can be fixed between the joists after lifting the floorboards. One method is to cut strips of rigid expanded polystyrene (plastic foam) and rest them on nails driven into the sides of the joists, or on battens nailed to the sides of the joists. Bear in mind that the material is very light and may be dislodged by severe draughts caused by windy weather; a few nails driven into the joists to "pinch" the edges of the insulation will help.

Another method of treating a suspended floor is to fill the gaps between joists with lengths of insulation blanket, supported on nylon garden netting stapled to the joists. Pull up the netting tightly before nailing down the boards so that the blanket does not sag and let cold air through. The insulation is then covered with a vapour barrier.

USING INSULATION BLANKET

1 To insulate the void beneath a wooden floor, lift all the floorboards. Then drape lengths of garden netting loosely over the joists and staple them in place.

2 Lay lengths of loft (attic) insulation blanket or wall insulation batts in the "hammocks" between the joists. If the netting sags, pull it up a little and staple it again.

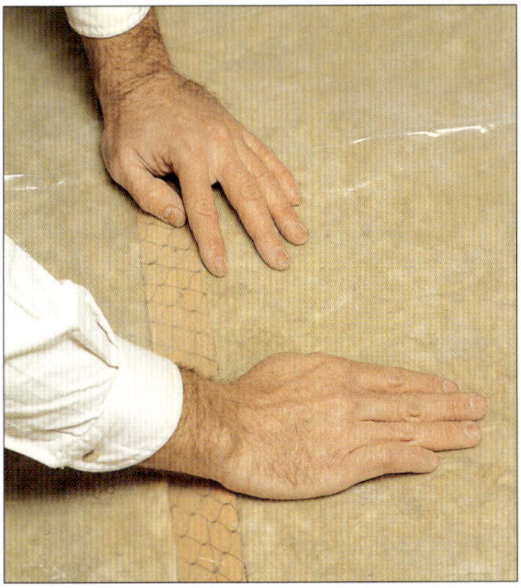

3 To prevent moisture from the house condensing within the insulation, cover the insulation with a vapour barrier of heavy-duty plastic sheeting.

4 Re-lay the floorboards by nailing them to the joists. Take this opportunity to close up any joints between the boards for a neat finish and to cut down draughts.

INSULATING SOLID FLOORS

With direct-to-ground concrete floors (slab on grade), the commonest method of insulation involves lining the floor with a vapour barrier of heavy-duty plastic sheeting, and installing a floating floor of tongued-and-grooved chipboard (particle board) panels. If additional insulation is required, place rigid polystyrene (plastic foam) insulation boards directly on top of the vapour barrier, then lay the new flooring on top of them.

Treat damp floors with one or two coats of a proprietary damp-proofing liquid and allow to dry before laying the vapour barrier. A gap of 9mm (3/8in) should be left between the chipboard and the wall to allow for expansion. This gap will not be noticeable once a new skirting (baseboard) is installed. The layer of trapped air under the floating floor will help keep the area warm.

Since the new floor will be at a raised level, any doors will need to be removed and planed down to a smaller size. Also, the flooring will either have to be cut to fit around architraves (door trim), or the architraves will have to be shortened so that the flooring fits beneath them.

LAYING A FLOATING FLOOR

1 Remove the skirtings (baseboards) and put down heavy-duty plastic sheets. Tape the sheets to the walls; they will be hidden behind the skirting later. Then butt-joint 25mm (1in) polystyrene (plastic foam) insulation boards over the floor, staggering the joints in adjacent rows.

2 Cover the polystyrene insulation board with tongued-and-grooved flooring-grade boards. Use cut pieces as necessary at the ends of rows, and add a tapered threshold (saddle) strip at the door. When finished, replace the skirtings with hammer and nails.

DRAUGHTPROOFING FLOORS

Gaps between the boards of a suspended wooden floor can allow cold draughts to enter a room. There are various methods for coping with this problem, depending on the size of the gaps and whether you want the boards exposed as a decorative feature, or are happy to conceal them beneath a floorcovering.

EXPOSED FLOORBOARDS

Large gaps in floorboards can be filled with strips of wood, carefully cut to fit tightly. Spread adhesive on the sides of each strip and tap it into the gap. Allow the glue to set, then plane down the strip so that it is flush with the surrounding floor. The strips can then be stained to match the colour of the other floorboards.

In severe cases, and if you want the boards to be exposed, you may have no option but to lift all of the boards and re-lay them, butting them tightly together as you do so. You can hire special flooring clamps for this purpose, which attach to the joists and allow you to push the boards tightly together before you nail them down. ►

TIP

A papier-mâché mix made from pieces of newspaper and a thick solution of wallpaper paste can be used to repair small holes in floorboards. Add woodstain to match the surrounding boards, then sand the repair smooth when dry.

ABOVE: Tap slivers of wood in place to cure draughts through large gaps. Leave the repair slightly proud of the surface. Once the glue has set, sand down the raised area to a smooth finish with a power sander or planer.

ABOVE: Stop draughts at skirting (baseboard) level by filling any gaps with silicone sealant (caulking) and covering with quadrant (quarter-round) moulding. Secure the quadrant moulding with pins.

COVERED FLOORS

Where there are large gaps between floorboards, and especially if the boards themselves are in poor condition, you can cover the floor with sheets of hardboard to provide a sound surface for carpeting or some other form of floorcovering. At the same time, this sub-floor will eliminate draughts.

Before laying, condition the hardboard by spraying the textured side of each sheet with 450ml (¾ pint) of water. Stack the sheets back-to-back and flat, separated by strips of wood, on the floor of the room where they are to be laid. Leave them for 48 hours, until they are completely dry.

Begin laying the hardboard sheets in the corner of the room farthest from the door, fixing each sheet in place with 19mm (¾in) annular (spiral) flooring nails. Start to nail 12mm (½in) from the skirting (baseboard) edge. To ensure the boards lie flat, work across the surface in a pyramid sequence, spacing the nails 150mm (6in) apart along the edges and 230mm (9in) apart in the middle.

Butt boards edge to edge to complete the first row, nailing the meeting edges first. Use the offcut (scrap) from the first row to start the next row, and continue in this way, staggering the joins between rows.

If boards are in really poor condition, you may be better off replacing them completely with tongued-and-grooved chipboard (particle board) panels, which will eliminate draughts.

ABOVE: Nail across a hardboard sheet in a pyramid sequence to avoid creating bulges. Nails should be 150mm (6in) apart along the edges and 230mm (9in) apart in the middle.

LAYING A HARDBOARD SUB-FLOOR

1 Condition the hardboard sheets by brushing or spraying them with water, and leave them for 48 hours before laying.

CARPET

If the gaps between boards are narrow, and you don't want the boards to be exposed, the easiest method of coping with a draughty floor is to lay fitted carpet with a good underlay.

Put down the underlay and cover with double-sided adhesive tape. Unroll the carpet and butt the edges up against the walls of the room and ensure that the carpet is lying flat. Trim the edges against the skirtings (baseboards) and tape them down.

Laying carpet will effectively block the passage of air through the floor. For added protection, you can repair any major gaps between the boards with a silicone sealant (caulking).

LAYING CARPET

When the gaps between floorboards are relatively narrow, simply laying a good-quality, thick underlay beneath the carpet will prevent draughts from being a problem.

2 To ensure a secure fixing, use annular (spiral) flooring nails. A piece of wood cut to size will allow you to space nails correctly and rapidly.

3 Use the offcut (scrap) from each row to start the next so that joins are staggered.

DRAUGHTPROOFING DOORS

Ill-fitting doors are a major source of heat loss, as well as causing cold draughts. Fitting efficient draught stripping around them will reduce the losses and cut down the draughts, and is a simple job to carry out.

Doors are best draughtproofed with pin-on (tack-on) plastic or sprung metal strips or types containing a compressible rubber seal. Special draught excluders are available for door thresholds (saddles), and can be fitted to the door bottom or across the threshold. There are even excluders designed to fit over letter plate openings.

REMEMBER VENTILATION

Don't forget that draughtproofing a home will close off many "unofficial" sources of ventilation, turning it into a well-sealed box. Fuel-burning appliances such as boilers and room heaters must have an adequate source of fresh air to burn safely, so it is wise to ask a fuel supplier to check that there is adequate ventilation in rooms containing such appliances. Often a ventilator in a window pane will solve the problem. However, you may need to take more drastic steps, such as fitting an airbrick into a wall with a vent cover that can be opened and closed.

Efficient draughtproofing may also increase condensation, especially in kitchens and bathrooms. This can be prevented by providing controlled ventilation in these rooms with an extractor fan.

ABOVE: Letter plate openings can be draught-proofed in a variety of ways. You can fit a hinged plate to the inside to provide extra protection. Alternatively, rubber and brush seals are available that will also do the job.

ABOVE: Draughts may not only pass around doors, but also through them. The problem is quite easy to solve. Keyhole covers are inexpensive. Many locks intended for external doors are provided with them as standard.

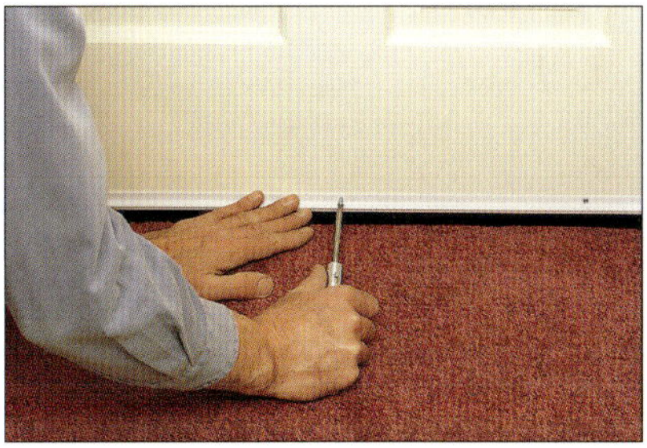

1 The simplest type of door-bottom draught excluder is a brush seal mounted in a wood or plastic strip. Simply cut it to length and screw it on to the foot of the door.

2 Alternatively, fit a threshold (saddle) strip. Cut the metal bar to length and screw it to the sill, then fit the compressible rubber sealing strip in the channel.

3 Draughtproof a letter plate opening by screwing on a special brush seal. Check beforehand that it does not foul the letter plate flap if this opens inwards.

4 Draughtproof the sides and top of the door frame by pinning (tacking) on lengths of plastic or sprung metal sealing strip. Pin the edge farthest from the door stop bead.

5 Alternatively, stick lengths of self-adhesive foam excluder to the stop bead against which the door closes. At the hinge side, stick the foam to the frame.

6 A third option is to use lengths of self-adhesive brush strip excluder. These three types can also be used for draughtproofing hinged casement windows.

DRAUGHTPROOFING WINDOWS

Windows are a major source of draughts in the home and are responsible for about ten per cent of heat loss. Many products have been designed to deal with these problems, but they vary in cost-effectiveness. The simplest are draught excluder strips, similar to those used for doors, while the most expensive remedy is to replace single-glazed units with double glazing. The latter will provide a considerable degree of comfort, as well as reducing sound transmission, but it may take up to 20 years to recoup your investment in terms of energy savings.

SEALING THE GAPS

You can choose from a variety of draught stripping products for windows, but some are more effective on certain types of window than others. For example, modern self-adhesive foams are much more efficient and longer lasting than older types, and are ideal for hinged casement windows. Simply stick strips around the rebate (rabbet) of the frame so that the opening casement compresses them when closed.

Sash windows, however, are not so easy to treat. The best solution is to use the same type of plastic or sprung metal strips that are suitable for doors. These can be pinned (tacked) around the frame to provide a seal against the sliding sashes. The job can be completed by attaching strips of self-adhesive foam to the top edge of the upper sash and bottom edge of the lower sash, so that these seal against the frame.

SASH WINDOWS

1 To fit a sprung metal strip excluder to a sliding sash window, first prise off the staff bead (window stop) that holds the inner sash in position, and swing it out.

4 Use the special wheeled springing tool provided with the draught excluder to make a small groove in the strip, causing it to spring outwards to press against the sash.

2 Measure the length of strip needed to fit the height of the window, and cut it to length with a pair of scissors. Beware of the sharp edges of the metal.

3 Pin (tack) the strip to the side of the frame so it will press against the edge of the sliding sash. Drive the pin through the edge facing towards the room.

5 Pin a length of the strip along the inner face of the top sash meeting rail (mullion), and "spring" it so it presses against the outer face of the bottom sash rail.

6 You can draughtproof the bottom edge of the lower sash and the top edge of the upper one by sticking on lengths of self-adhesive foam draught excluder.

DOUBLE GLAZING

The glass in windows is the least efficient part of the house at keeping heat in, and the only way of cutting this heat loss while still being able to see out is to add another layer of glass. Double glazing can be done in two ways: existing single panes of glass can be replaced with special double-glazed panes called sealed units, or a second pane can be installed inside the existing one – so-called secondary glazing.

SECONDARY GLAZING

This is the only practical form of double glazing for the do-it-yourselfer, and it is relatively inexpensive. There are dozens of types available, providing hinged and sliding inner panes that blend in well with most types of window; similar systems are also available from professional installers. The panes are either fixed directly to the window frame, or fitted within the window reveal on special tracks.

SLIDING UNITS

Do-it-yourself secondary glazing systems come in kit form and are easy to install. The kits provide enough materials to cover a range of window sizes; all you need do is cut the lengths of special track to fit within the window reveal and screw them in place. You do have to provide your own glass, however, and careful measurements must be taken so that you can order this from your local glass supplier. Then all you need do is fit the glazing gaskets and insert the panes in the tracks.

FITTING SLIDING UNITS

1 Measure the height and width of the window reveal at each side. If the figures differ, work from the smaller measurements for height and width. Cut the track sections to size.

4 When positioning the bottom track on the windowsill, use a straightedge and a spirit (carpenter's) level to check that it is perfectly aligned with the top track.

2 Offer up the side track sections and screw them to the window reveal. Use thin packing pieces to get them truly vertical if the walls are out of square.

3 Next, secure the top track section in place. Screw it directly to a wooden lintel or pre-drill holes in a concrete beam and insert plastic wall plugs first.

5 Measure up for the glass as directed in the kit manufacturer's instructions, and order the glass. Fit cut lengths of glazing gasket to the edges of each pane.

6 Fit the first pane into the track by inserting its top edge in the top channel, and then lowering its bottom edge. Repeat the procedure for the other pane.

CLEAR FILM

There is a particularly cheap form of secondary glazing that involves attaching a clear PVC (vinyl) film to the inside of the window with double-sided adhesive tape. This can be discarded during the summer months and fresh film applied for the winter.

A sturdier option is acrylic sheet. If you opt for this method, make sure that at least one window is easy to open in case of an emergency.

DON'T FORGET THE DOORS

Heat is lost through external doors too, and solid doors are best. If you prefer a glazed door, however, opt for a modern replacement fitted with a sealed double-glazing unit. You can reduce heat loss still further with an enclosed porch.

FITTING THIN-FILM SECONDARY GLAZING

1 Start by sticking lengths of double-sided adhesive tape to the window frame, about 12mm (½in) in from the surrounding masonry.

2 Press the film on to the tape, pulling it as taut as possible. Then play hot air from a hairdrier over it to tighten it up and pull out any wrinkles.

3 When the film is even and wrinkle-free, trim off the excess all the way around the window with a sharp knife.

APPLYING SEALANTS

Silicone sealants (caulking) are good for filling large or irregularly shaped gaps around windows and doors. They come in white, brown and clear versions. Use a caulking gun for ease of application, although products that do not require a gun are also available.

To make a repair with silicone sealant, clean the frame rebate (rabbet) and apply the sealant to the fixed frame. Brush soapy water on to the closing edge of the window or door. Close and immediately open the door. The soapy water acts as a release agent, preventing the door or window from sticking to the sealant.

Because silicone sealants are flexible, they will absorb movement in the structure of your home that otherwise would produce cracking. For particularly large gaps around frames, you can use an expanding foam filler.

TIP

For good adhesion, always clean and dry window and door frames thoroughly before applying self-adhesive sealant.

ABOVE: Fill cracks between the window frame and plasterwork with silicone sealant (caulking).

ABOVE: You can also use silicone sealant outdoors to seal gaps between frames and masonry where a rigid filler might crack.

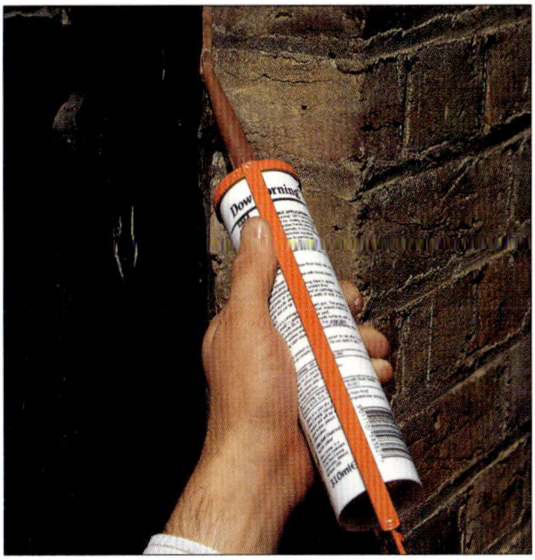

ABOVE: Coloured silicone sealants can be used to blend in with their surroundings – or you can paint over them when a skin has formed.

VENTILATION

You can go too far in draughtproofing your home; if you seal up all the sources of outside air, you will prevent moist air from being carried away. This will cause condensation to form on any cold surfaces, such as windows, tiles and exterior walls. In severe cases, this can result in mould growth and even damage to the structure of your home. Moreover, a lack of airflow can cause problems with certain types of heater. The ideal is to keep out the cold draughts, but provide a sufficient flow of air to prevent condensation and ensure the efficient operation of heaters. The judicious use of manual vents, airbricks and electric extractor fans will provide all the ventilation you need without making you feel chilly.

FITTING A CEILING EXTRACTOR FAN

An extractor fan provides positive ventilation where it is needed, in a kitchen or bathroom, removing stale or moist air before it can cause a problem. There are three places you can fit an extractor fan: in a window, in a wall or in the ceiling, where ducts carry the stale air to the outside. In a kitchen, an extracting stove hood can serve the same function, provided it is ducted to the outside; a recirculating stove hood only filters the air.

It is important that an extractor fan is positioned so that the replacement air, which normally will come through and around the door leading to the remainder of the house, is drawn through the room and across the problem area. In a kitchen, the problem areas are the stove and the sink; in a bathroom, they are the lavatory and shower unit.

Ceiling-mounted extractor fans are particularly efficient in bathrooms and kitchens, since the warm moist air will tend to collect just below the ceiling. Moreover, fitting the fan in the ceiling often makes for an easier installation, since all you need do is cut a circular hole in the ceiling with a padsaw, taking care to avoid the ceiling joists. From the fan, plastic ducting needs to be taken to an outside wall or to the eaves, where it is connected to an outlet. On no account allow it to discharge into the roof.

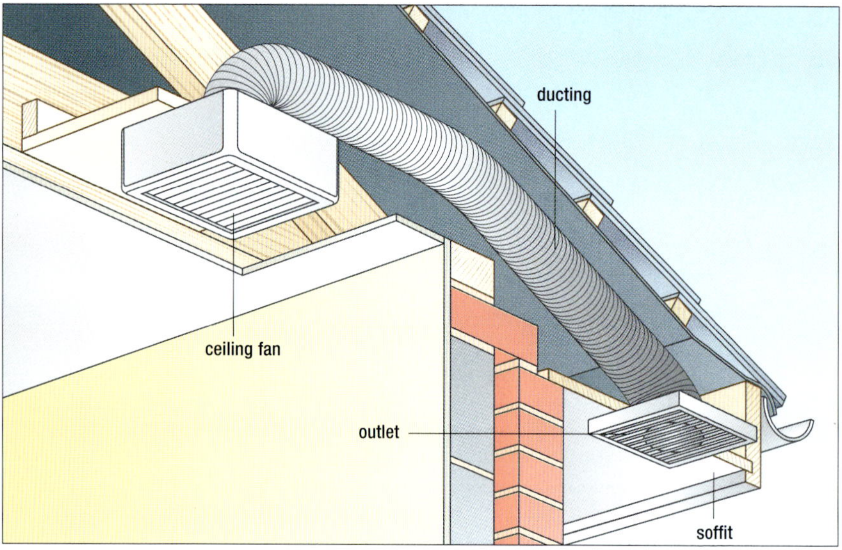

ABOVE: Fit an extractor fan in the ceiling so that it discharges via a duct to a hole with an outlet at the soffit.

FITTING A WINDOW EXTRACTOR FAN

If a simple window ventilator already exists in a fixed window, you may be able to replace it with an extractor fan. If not, you will have to cut a hole in one of the window panes. However, this will not be possible if the glass is toughened or laminated. The same applies to double-glazed units; they must be ordered with the hole pre-cut.

The only window you can cut a hole in is one made from normal glass in a single-glazed frame, and even here you may prefer to order a new pane from a glass supplier with the hole already cut. That way, the only work you will have to do is to take out the old pane and fit the new one.

Fit the extractor fan near the top of the window, since warm, moist air rises and it will do the most good at high level. Also, this will keep the fan away from inquisitive children, who may be tempted to push things into it.

To cut the hole in the glass yourself, you will need a beam circle cutter as well as a normal glass cutter. Use the beam cutter to score two circles: one the correct size for the extractor fan, and one slightly smaller inside it. Then use the normal glass cutter to make cross-hatched lines inside the inner circle, and single radial lines between the two circles. Tap out the glass from the inner circle, then use the glass breaker rack on the glass cutter to snap off the remaining margin of glass. Smooth the edge with fine abrasive paper wrapped around a circular tool handle or piece of thick dowelling rod. Once you have a hole of the correct size, fitting a window fan is simply a matter of following the instructions.

ABOVE: If the window was fitted originally with a simple ventilator unit such as this one, you may be able to remove it and fit an extractor fan in the existing hole.

ABOVE: If no ventilator is fitted, you will need to cut a hole in the glass to fit an extractor fan. For this, you will need a special tool known as a beam circle cutter.

FITTING A WALL EXTRACTOR FAN

Most designs of extractor fan will require a circular hole to be cut through the house wall. The best tool to use for this is a heavy-duty electric drill fitted with a core drill bit, both of which you can hire. These will cut a hole of exactly the right size. Make holes in both leaves of a cavity wall and fit the sleeve supplied with the extractor fan. Some fans require a rectangular hole to be cut, which may mean removing one or more whole bricks. Take care when doing this; cut through the mortar joints around the bricks with a cold chisel and club (spalling) hammer, and try to ease the bricks out in one piece. Keep as much debris as possible out of the wall cavity, since this could bridge the cavity and lead to damp problems. Once the sleeve for the fan is in place, make good the brickwork and plaster.

Fitting the fan is easy – simply drill holes for wall plugs to take the fan on the inside wall, and fit the outlet on the outer wall.

WIRING

An extractor fan needs to be wired up via a fused connection unit to the nearest power supply circuit. If you are not sure how to do this, employ a qualified electrician to do the job. In a bathroom or shower room, with no opening window, a fan is a compulsory requirement and it must be wired via the light switch so that it comes on with the light and remains on for 15 minutes afterwards.

1 The first step when fitting a wall-mounted extractor fan is to mark the exact position of the wall sleeve. Place the fan near the top of the wall for the best performance.

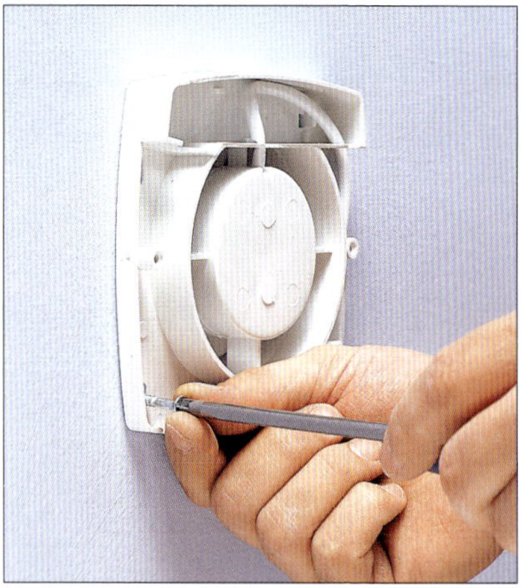

4 Offer up the extractor and mark its fixing-hole positions on the wall. Drill these and fit them with wall plugs so that you can screw the extractor to the wall surface.

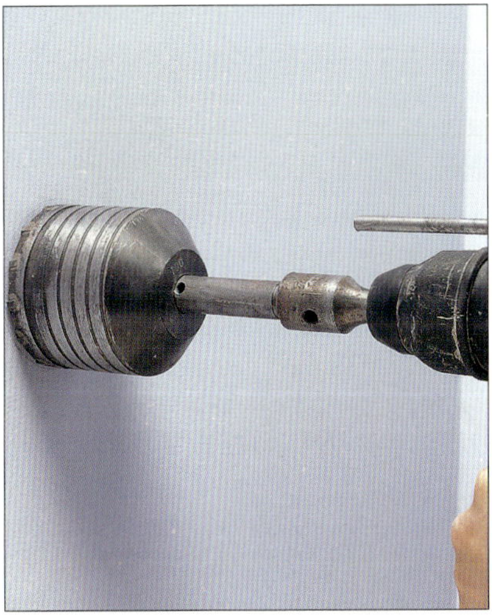

2 Use a core drill bit, fitted to a heavy-duty electric drill, to cut a hole of the correct size through both leaves of the wall (if it is of the cavity type).

3 Check the fit of the sleeve in the hole and push it through the wall. Mark it off for length, then remove it and cut it down with a hacksaw. Replace it.

5 Wiring comes next (get help with this if necessary). Make a check that the extractor functions correctly, after which the cover of the unit can be put on.

6 Finally, fit the outlet on the outside wall. Sometimes this simply pushes into the end of the sleeve. In other cases, you may need to screw it to the wall.

FITTING EXTRA AIRBRICKS

In other rooms, fitting small "trickle" ventilators at the top of window frames and putting in extra airbricks will often supply enough ventilation to allow the moist air to disperse before condensation becomes a problem.

UNDERFLOOR VENTILATION

A suspended wooden floor consists of floorboards or sheets of flooring-grade chipboard (particle board) supported on joists. To keep the joists and the flooring dry, some kind of underfloor ventilation is essential. This takes the form of airbricks in the outer walls.

The first thing to check is that all the existing airbricks are free of debris and have not been blocked up in the mistaken belief that this will save money on heating. Next, check that there are enough airbricks – there should be one airbrick for every 2m (6ft) of wall length. Inserting a new airbrick is not difficult, as most match the size of standard bricks.

Decide where you want to put it, drill out the mortar around the existing brick and remove it. With a cavity wall, you will have to continue the hole through the inner wall and fit a terracotta liner to maintain the airflow. Use the corners of the hole in the outer wall to line up and drill four holes in the inner wall, then chip out the hole with a bolster (stonecutter's) chisel and club (spalling) hammer, working from the inside. You will need to lift floorboards to do this.

Fit the airbrick from the outside, applying mortar to the bottom of the hole and the top of the brick, pushing mortar in the sides. Point the mortar joints to the same profile as the surrounding joints. Mortar the liner in place from inside the house.

VENTILATING ROOF SPACES

If your house has a gable end wall, the roof space can be ventilated by fitting airbricks in the gable. If the house is semi-detached, ask your neighbour to do the same, and fit another airbrick in the party wall to allow air to circulate.

SAFE VENTILATION

There are two very important points to remember concerning ventilation. Firstly, many fuel-burning appliances need an adequate supply of fresh air to work efficiently and safely, so rooms where they are sited must contain provision for this if they are well sealed against natural draughts. Secondly, disused flues must be ventilated at top and bottom; if they are not, condensation can occur within the flue, which may show up as damp patches on the internal chimney walls.

TIP

You may need to install more airbricks in a room where there is a solid concrete hearth (from an old cooking range, say). This can create "dead" areas which may need extra ventilation to prevent rot.

1 Airbricks are the same size as one, two or three bricks. To fit one, start by drilling a series of closely-spaced holes through the joint around a brick.

2 Then use a club (spalling) hammer and a wide bolster (stonecutter's) chisel to cut out the brickwork. With solid walls, drill holes right through and work from inside too.

3 Fit a cavity liner through to the inner wall if the wall is of cavity construction, then trowel a bed of fairly wet mortar on to the bottom of the opening.

4 Butter mortar on to the top of the airbrick and slide in place. Push more mortar into the gaps at the sides. Inside, make good the wall with plaster and cover the opening with a ventilator grille.

5 As an alternative to the traditional terracotta airbrick, fit a two-part plastic version. The sleeves interlock to line the hole as the two parts are pushed together.

6 Slide the outer section into place, and point around it. Slide the inner section into place from the inside of the house. Make good the plaster and fit its cover grille.

OVERCOMING DAMP CONDITIONS

Damp conditions can cause serious problems if allowed to persist in the home, even leading to structural decay, so it is essential to deal with damp as soon as it becomes obvious. The first task is to recognize the type of damp you are faced with: it could be condensation, caused by moisture inside the home, or penetrating or rising damp from outside. In some cases, finding a remedy is relatively straightforward; in others, solving the problem can be complex and costly, and may require the involvement of professionals. If damp conditions are not corrected, they may lead to wet rot or dry rot in structural wooden framing. Both can be a major problem if not tackled quickly, since they weaken the wood with potentially disastrous consequences.

DAMP

This can ruin decorations, destroy floorcoverings, damage walls and plaster, and cause woodwork to rot, so it is important not only to treat the symptoms, but also to track down the causes. These might be rain coming in through the roof or walls, condensation, moisture being absorbed from the ground, or a combination of any of these.

ABOVE: A patch of mould on the inner face of an external wall is usually the first sign of penetrating damp.

PENETRATING DAMP

This is caused by moisture getting in from the outside, often because of wear and tear to the structure of your home, but it may also affect solid walls that are subjected to strong driving rain. The first sign of penetrating damp appears after a heavy downpour and can occur almost anywhere, although it may be some distance from the actual leak; mould often forms directly behind where the problem lies. Pay particular attention to rainwater systems, which are common causes of penetrating damp.

RISING DAMP

This is caused by water soaking up through floors and walls, and is usually confined to a 1m (3ft) band above ground level. It is a constant problem, even during dry spells.

The main areas to check for rising damp are the damp-proof course (DPC) around the foot of walls, and damp-proof membrane (DPM) in the ground floor. Older properties were often built without either, which can lead to widespread rising damp. If existing

ABOVE: Gaps between masonry and woodwork around windows will let in rain, causing patches of damp to occur.

materials have broken down or structural movement has caused defects, there may be isolated, but spreading, patches of damp where water is penetrating. A DPC that is less than 150mm (6in) above ground level will allow rain to splash above it and penetrate the wall, which may cause damp patches at skirting (baseboard) level. If a DPC has been bridged, there will be evidence of damp just above skirting level. A wall cavity filled with rubble may also allow damp to penetrate.

DEALING WITH DAMP

Once the cause of penetrating damp has been traced and repaired, the problem will be eradicated. When the damp patches have dried out, it may be necessary to replaster those areas and make good any decorations.

Dealing with a DPC that has been bridged is quite straightforward. If the ground level is the cause, digging a 150mm (6in) trench along the house wall, then filling it with gravel will allow rainwater to drain away rapidly. When you suspect that debris in the cavity is the cause, removing a few bricks will give access to remove it.

The remedy for rising damp caused by a non-existent or defective DPC or DPM is not so easy; the only solution is to install a replacement or make repairs.

DAMP-PROOFING METHODS

Laying a new damp-proof membrane involves digging up and re-laying the floor slab, which is the most effective method of damp-proofing a concrete floor. However, a floor can also be damp-proofed by applying several coats of moisture-curing urethane, but it is essential that any leaky patches are sealed first with a hydraulic cement.

A third option is to apply two coats of rubberized bitumen emulsion to the old surface, then cover this with a cement/sand screed, which will raise the level of the floor by about 50mm (2in).

Whichever method you choose, the DPM material should be taken up the adjoining walls to meet the DPC, if there is one. The problem of damp floors caused by rising ground-water levels, which typically affects basements, is more serious and requires structural waterproofing or "tanking". This is certainly a job for the professionals.

ABOVE: A damp-proof course should be clear of soil, debris or plants growing up walls, otherwise moisture can bypass it.

INSTALLING A DAMP-PROOF COURSE

There are many ways of installing a damp-proof course, ranging from physical DPCs that are cut into the brickwork to chemical slurries, which are pumped into a series of drilled holes.

In theory, it is possible to do the job yourself, but dealing with rising damp is rarely simple; it is worth seeking the advice of professionals. If there is a mortgage on your home, the lender may require a guarantee of workmanship, which rules out tackling the job yourself. The standard of workmanship is as important as the system used, so choosing a reputable company that offers an insurance-backed guarantee is essential, and often compulsory.

If you do choose to go ahead yourself, you should be able to hire the necessary equipment to install a chemical DPC, and the same company may supply the chemical too.

After installing a DPC, walls and floors can take up to a month for each 25mm (1in) to dry out, while old plaster may be heavily contaminated with salts from rising damp, which will continue to absorb moisture from the air. Delay replastering for as long as possible to allow the walls to dry out.

1 A chemical damp-proof course is injected into a line of holes drilled in the wall about 115mm (4½in) apart.

2 Once injected into the drilled holes, the chemicals overlap to form a continuous impermeable barrier.

3 When the fluid is dry, the drilled holes are filled with mortar and then a rendered surface can be painted.

WATERPROOFING WALLS

The external walls of modern brick houses are built with a cavity between the inner and outer leaves of the wall that effectively prevents damp from reaching the inner leaf. Unless the cavity becomes bridged in some way, there should be no problems with penetrating damp. However, older properties are likely to have been built with solid walls and it is possible that, over time, the masonry may become porous, allowing damp to penetrate to the inside.

Penetrating damp in solid walls is difficult to cure, and one solution, albeit rather drastic, is to build false walls inside, complete with vapour barriers, effectively creating cavity walls. However, this solution is expensive, and it will reduce the size of rooms considerably.

Less expensive is to treat the outer faces of the walls with a water-repellent coating. This will prevent rainwater from soaking into the walls and reaching the interior.

The first job is to clean the walls and make good any structural defects. Wash them down and treat them with a fungicide to kill off any mould. Check the condition of the mortar joints and repoint any that are soft and crumbling; fill cracks in the joints or bricks with mortar or an exterior-grade filler.

When the walls have dried, brush on the water-repellent liquid, following the manufacturer's instructions; you may need to apply more than one coat.

1 Brush, clean, and remove any fungal growth from the wall. Fill any surface cracks so that the surface is sound.

2 Apply the water seal by brush, working from the bottom up, coating the whole wall. If necessary, apply a second coat.

CONDENSATION

When warm, moist air reaches a cold surface, such as a wall exposed to icy winter winds or ceramic tiles, the result is condensation. It is most likely to occur in bathrooms and kitchens where the main activities are bathing, washing and cooking.

Controlling condensation requires a fine balance between good ventilation and adequate heating, but while the modern home is warm, it is also well insulated and draughtproofed, so the level of ventilation is often poor. The key to success is to provide sufficient ventilation, without allowing expensive heat to escape.

Ventilation can be provided by a variety of passive and active means. Passive ventilation may be achieved by opening windows and/or fitting airbricks and simple vents. Active ventilation relies on powered extractor fans.

CONDENSATION OR DAMP?

If you are not sure if a moisture problem is due to condensation or damp, lay a piece of aluminium foil over the patch, seal the edges with adhesive tape and leave it for 48 hours. Condensation will cause beads of moisture to appear on the surface of the foil; penetrating or rising damp will produce beads of moisture underneath the foil.

ABOVE: Water vapour from everyday activities, such as cooking, can cause condensation.

ABOVE: Poor ventilation will make condensation problems worse.

COPING WITH CONDENSATION

Steam from cooking can be removed by a fully vented stove hood, but where a great deal of steam is produced, when you take a shower for example, the best way to remove it from the room is with an extractor fan.

To be quick and efficient, the fan must be sited properly and it should be the correct size for the room. In a kitchen, a fan must be capable of ten to 15 air changes per hour, and in bathrooms six to eight air changes per hour, which should be increased to 15 to 20 air changes for a power shower. Simply multiply the volume of the room by the number of air changes required and look for a fan that offers the same cubic metre/foot capacity per hour (m^3/hr or ft^3/hr).

An extractor fan should be installed as high as possible on the wall, and as far as possible from the main source of ventilation; usually diagonally opposite the main door is ideal.

More widespread condensation can be alleviated with an electric dehumidifier, which draws air from the room, passes it over cold coils to condense it, then collects the drips of water. The dry air is then drawn over heated coils and released back into the room as heat.

TIPS

- In bathrooms, keep the door shut when taking a bath. When running a bath, run the cold water first to minimize the amount of steam that is produced.
- Where condensation occurs in a confined space, such as a built-in wardrobe, causing mould and mildew, use silica gel crystals to absorb excess moisture from the air.
- In kitchens, make sure a tumble-drier is properly vented.

RIGHT: A stove hood removes steam from cooking at source. Beware, however, since some stove hoods merely recirculate the air, filtering out the particles from cooking, but not the moisture. For this, you must have an extractor hood. Remember, too, that kettles produce steam, as do other forms of cooking that may not be in range of a stove hood. Consequently, it may be worth adding a window vent or even an additional extractor fan.

DRY ROT

The fungus that causes dry rot loves moist, humid conditions and has a taste for resins and silicones in untreated wood. However, the grey strands are fine enough to penetrate masonry, which means that it can spread rapidly from room to room.

Untreated dry rot will destroy floors, doors and skirtings (baseboards), and infect plaster and ceilings. Initially, it manifests itself as a brownish-red dust, but within days the spores will have developed into a fungus that looks like a mushroom growing upside-down, and it also gives off a distinctive musty smell. This is the final stage of germination, by which time the fungus will be producing millions of spores to infect surrounding areas.

Dealing with dry rot is a job that should be entrusted to a specialist, as it may recur if not treated properly. Make sure you choose a reputable company that offers an insurance-backed guarantee.

PREVENTATIVE ACTION

- Make sure that a damp-proof course (DPC) has not been bridged, by looking for tell-tale signs of damp on walls above skirtings (baseboards).
- Dry rot will not flourish in well-ventilated areas, so make sure there is good ventilation in roofs and under suspended wooden floors. If necessary, fit air vents or extractor fans in soffits and gable end walls.

ABOVE: An example of severe dry rot on a destroyed wooden floor.

ABOVE: A sporophore, or dry rot fungus, on a structural roof timber. Immediate action is necessary as soon as the fungus is spotted to minimize its spread through wooden structures.

ABOVE: Inspect your loft (attic) space and check for the first signs of dry rot. Ensure there is good ventilation in the loft and under the floors to help prevent the conditions in which dry rot can flourish.

WET ROT

This thrives on wet wood and frequently appears where wood is close to the ground or near leaking plumbing, and in woodwork where the protective paint coating has broken down. Skirtings (baseboards) may also be affected where a damp-proof course is defective.

Wet rot can be due to a number of species of fungus, but the most common consist of brown or black strands that appear on the surface, causing the wood to crack and eventually disintegrate. Affected wood tends to look darker than healthy wood and feels spongy.

Once the cause of the damp conditions that have led to the problem is eliminated, wet rot fungus will die. Treat small areas, such as window frames, with proprietary wood hardener solution and insert preservative tablets into holes drilled into the wood to stop any recurrence. Where damage is extensive, the wood should be cut out and replaced.

REPAIRING WET ROT

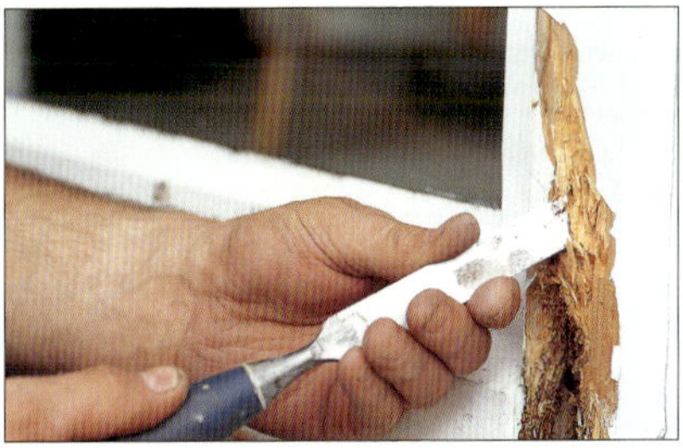

1 Chisel out all the rotten wood, making sure only sound wood is left.

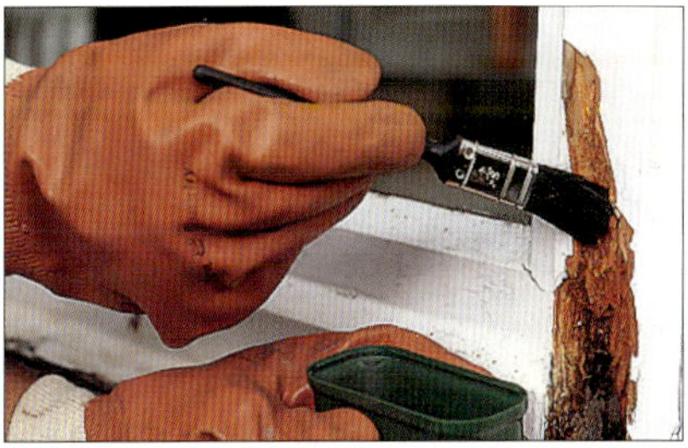

2 Brush the sound wood with hardener and leave to dry as recommended.

3 To fit wood preservative sticks, drill holes of the correct size in the sound wood. Push the preservative sticks into the drilled holes and below the surface.

4 Fill the damaged area with exterior wood filler. Leave to dry before sanding. Then apply a good paint finish.

OUTDOOR REPAIRS

- Repairing drains, gutters & roofs
- Repairing fences & walls
- Repairing paths, drives & patios

INTRODUCTION

Even in the most temperate of climates, the weather can take an incredible toll on the structure of your home. The sun can crack and blister paintwork and the coverings of flat roofs; rain can soak into woodwork, causing it to rot, or seep into brickwork or behind flashings, penetrating the walls; a moist atmosphere causes fixings to rust and fail, leading to unsightly staining of walls, sagging gutters, missing roof tiles and broken fences; the wind can carry away or wreck all manner of structures; while the action of frost and snow can cause masonry and concrete to crumble. If you are to protect your home and its surroundings from the elements, you must be prepared to carry out regular outdoor maintenance and repairs.

The secret to keeping the outside of your home looking good is not letting things get out of hand. Don't delay

ABOVE: Carry out the majority of outdoor maintenance work during the summer months. The dry, warm conditions will make the tasks much less arduous.

ABOVE: Guttering and downpipes are essential to carry away rainwater, preventing it from running down the walls and causing damage. They must be in good condition.

TIP

If you decide to make concrete yourself, consider buying a second-hand concrete mixer, and selling it again when the job is complete – it should save you money on buying or hiring costs.

when you see a problem; tackle it as soon as possible. Once a surface or finish outdoors begins to break down, the weather will quickly get in and speed up the process, turning a simple repair into a major project in no time. Fortunately, most outdoor maintenance and repair tasks require fairly basic skills, and they are not beyond the average do-it-yourselfer; structures tend to be of a rugged nature, requiring only a limited degree of finesse when it comes to finishing off.

Don't be over-confident, however. The weatherproofing and structural integrity of your home may depend on some tasks being done correctly, and some work may need to be carried out in fairly hazardous situations (on a roof for example). If you are in any doubt about completing a task successfully and safely, call in the experts.

ABOVE: The front door is often the first impression callers get of your home, so it pays to make sure that it is kept in good condition; that goes for the path, too.

RIGHT: Your home is a valuable investment, but it is under constant attack from the elements. You must carry out regular maintenance and repairs to prevent its fabric from deteriorating; once the weather gets in, it can cause untold damage. Fortunately, you don't need a lot of skill to carry out many outdoor tasks.

REPAIRING DRAINS, GUTTERS & ROOFS

Making sure that the drains, downpipes and guttering around your home are well maintained is essential to ensure that rainwater and waste water from indoors are carried away without having an opportunity to damage the structure. From time to time, however, pipes or gutters may become blocked, leading to an overflow. When that happens, you must be able to deal with the situation immediately, otherwise the results could be disastrous. Roofs are exposed to the full force of the weather and may, in time, become damaged: tiles may become dislodged, felt coverings may crack or blister, and flashings may deteriorate. Fortunately, all can be fixed with relative ease.

CLEARING DRAINS AND PIPES

A large auger can be used to clear blocked underground drains. It should be passed down through an open gully and along the drain until you reach the blockage.

The main soil pipe will run vertically either inside or outside the house. If it is blocked, your best chance of clearing it will be to unscrew an inspection hatch and then to use either an auger or drain rods to dislodge the blockage.

USING DRAIN RODS

These are used for clearing drains when there is a blockage between one (full) inspection chamber and the next (empty) one. When you discover the empty chamber, go back to the last full one and rod from there. Drain rod sets come with a choice of heads – plungers to push the blockage along the pipe, scrapers to pull it back and wormscrews or cleaning wheels to dislodge it.

Start with a wormscrew connected to two rods, lowering it to the bottom of the chamber. Feel for the half-round channel at the bottom of the chamber and push the wormscrew along this until it enters the drain at the end.

INSPECTING A SOIL PIPE

1 If you suspect that the blockage is in the vertical soil pipe, or at its base, begin by unscrewing an inspection hatch. Wear gloves and protective clothing.

Push it along the drain, adding more rods to the free end, and only turn the rods clockwise, otherwise they may become unscrewed. Keep working at the obstruction until water flows into the empty chamber, then use the scraper and plunger to clear the underground drain section.

wormscrew

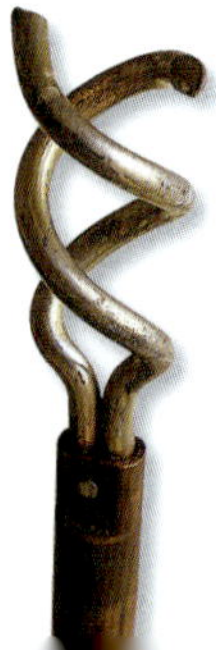

cleaning wheel

scraper

plunger

2 Then remove the inner cover – make sure you are standing well out of the way, as the contents of the pipe will be discharged through the opening.

3 Use an auger or drain rods to clear the blockage before replacing the cover. Make sure it is tight, then flush the system through by turning on taps and flushing lavatory cisterns.

ABOVE: Use drain rods in an inspection chamber to remove a blockage. You can hire a set from a local tool-hire company; they will come with all the necessary fittings.

ABOVE: Use an auger in a waste gully at the foot of a drainpipe to clear a blockage. Alternatively, you may be able to shift it with the aid of a bent wire coat hanger.

CLEARING GUTTERS

The gutters and downpipes of your home are essential to remove rainwater. Nevertheless, they are exposed to the elements and are likely to become blocked, so regular maintenance is necessary to keep them clear and also to keep them in good condition.

Autumn is the ideal time to clear out gutters, removing leaves, birds' nests and general dirt and debris so that the winter rains can drain away freely. Use a garden trowel or gutter clearing tool to scoop out blockages from the gutters into a bucket, which should be secured to your ladder.

If there is a blockage near to the top of a downpipe, use something like a bent metal coat hanger to pull it out. Blockages farther down can be removed by using drain rods fitted with a wormscrew head.

LEFT: You can use a garden trowel to clean sediment and the remains of dead leaves from gutters. Protect downpipes temporarily with balls of screwed-up newspaper.

ABOVE: Alternatively, use a gutter cleaning tool specially designed for the job. You could even make your own from a length of broom handle with a piece of plywood screwed to the end. Cut the plywood so that it approximates the shape of the gutter profile and will clear the overhang of the roof covering.

REPAIRING GUTTERS

If a gutter is sagging, the most likely cause is failure of the screws that hold a bracket in place. First, remove the section of gutter above the offending bracket.

If the screws have worked loose, it may be possible to retighten them, perhaps replacing them with longer or larger screws; if the holes have become too large, move the bracket slightly to one side, making new holes in the fascia board for the bracket screws. Make sure it aligns with its neighbour. A rise-and-fall bracket is adjustable in height and so corrects sagging gutters without the need to remove them.

CAST-IRON GUTTERS

Traditional cast-iron gutters may look attractive, but they can give no end of trouble. To start with, they rust, so need regular painting to keep them looking good.

UNBLOCKING DOWNPIPES

You could fit a wire balloon into the top of a downpipe to prevent birds from nesting and to keep leaves and other debris out. If a downpipe gets blocked, clear it with drain rods fitted with a wormscrew.

PAINTING CAST-IRON GUTTERS

ABOVE: Prior to painting a cast-iron gutter, clear it out using a wire brush.

ABOVE: Treat cast-iron guttering with black bituminous paint to seal leaks.

REPAIRING CAST-IRON GUTTERS

ABOVE: If a cast-iron gutter bolt has rusted in place, you will not be able to unscrew it. Remove it by cutting through the bolt with a hacksaw.

ABOVE: Wearing gloves, use glass fibre to repair a crack in a cast-iron gutter. Remove the gutter from the brackets to make it easier.

A more serious problem, however, is that the putty used to seal the joints can dry out, causing leaks.

You may be able to overcome minor joint leaks by cleaning the gutter out and brushing the inside with bituminous paint, but a proper repair will mean unscrewing the joint and replacing the old putty with non-setting mastic (caulking). Use a hacksaw to cut through the securing bolt if it has rusted in place. Then remove the screws holding the gutter to the fascia board and lift it clear. It will be very heavy – do not drop it, as it will shatter. Clean the joint faces, apply a layer of mastic and replace the gutter, using a new nut and bolt to connect the sections.

A crack or hole in a cast-iron gutter can be repaired with a glass fibre repair kit sold for use on car bodywork. Clean the damaged area thoroughly, then apply the glass fibre sheets over the damage and fill to the level of the surrounding metal with the resin filler provided with the kit. Glass fibre bandage can also be used in the same way for repairing cast-iron downpipes. Once it has cured, you can paint it as normal.

PLASTIC GUTTERS

Plastic guttering has largely replaced cast iron and is easier to repair. It is also much easier to replace because it is much lighter in weight and the joints simply clip together.

Leaks at the joints between lengths of plastic gutter are prevented by rubber seals, and if these fail it is usually quite easy to replace them. Take the old seal to the shop as a guide when buying a replacement. Otherwise, try cleaning them with some liquid soap to make them more efficient. If an end stop is leaking, replace the rubber seal in this in the same way.

The alternative is to use a gutter repair sealant, available in a cartridge for use with a caulking gun, forcing this into the joint to make a seal. Self-adhesive gutter repair tape is also available for sealing splits in plastic gutters and for covering small holes in gutters and downpipes.

When separating and reconnecting lengths of plastic guttering, note that some types simply snap into their securing brackets, while others have notches cut near the ends to take the clips. When fitting a new length, you will have to cut the notches with a hacksaw.

REPAIRING END STOPS

Rubber seals in the end stop of plastic guttering can be replaced if they fail.

REPAIRING PLASTIC GUTTERS

ABOVE: Gutter repair sealant can be used to fix a leaking joint between gutters.

ABOVE: Repair a crack in a gutter with gutter repair tape applied to the inside.

REPLACING ROOF SLATES

Slates that cover a pitched house roof can sometimes fail and work loose; you can repair small areas of damage yourself, but large-scale repairs may mean wholesale replacement of the roof covering, which should be entrusted to a professional roof contractor. Never walk directly on a roof covering; use a proper ladder that hooks over the ridge.

The most common cause of roof slates slipping is "nail sickness", that is one or both of the nails holding a slate has rusted through and snapped. The slate itself may be undamaged and still be on the roof somewhere.

If only one nail has failed, use a slate ripper to cut through the other one. This tool is slid under the slate, hooked around the nail and given a sharp tug to break the nail off or wrench it free of the batten (furring strip).

With the slate removed, you will be able to see, between the two exposed slates, one of the wooden battens to which the slates are attached. Cut a strip of zinc or lead sheet, about 150 x 25mm (6 x 1in), and nail one end of it to the exposed batten so that the strip runs down the roof.

Slide the slate back into its original position and secure it by bending the end of the zinc or lead strip over the bottom edge. Note that slates at the edges of the roof have mortar fillets beneath them to prevent the wind from blowing debris into the roof space. The mortar also prevents the edges from lifting in strong winds.

1 Use a slate ripper to cut through a slate nail that is still holding the slate.

slate ripper

slater's axe for cutting slates

REPLACING A DISLODGED TILE

Most concrete and many clay tiles are held in place by hooks, or nibs, on the top edge, which fit over the roof battens. If these are still intact, a dislodged tile can simply be replaced by gently lifting the surrounding tiles, supporting them on wooden wedges and slipping the tile back into position. If the nibs have broken off, the tile can be replaced in the same way as a slate. Edge tiles also have a fillet of mortar beneath them.

2 Slide out the damaged slate by lifting it with the blade of a trowel, taking care not to let it fall to the ground. Look for the batten (furring strip) between the exposed slates.

3 Fil a narrow strip of lead or zinc sheet in place by nailing one end of it to the batten under the slates. Use a galvanized nail and leave the strip running down the roof.

4 Slide the old (or replacement) slate into place over the lead or zinc strip. It may help to lift the slates in the course above by inserting wooden wedges beneath them.

5 Align the bottom edge of the slate with its neighbours, then bend the end of the strip over the bottom edge of the slate to hold it securely in place.

RIDGE TILES AND VALLEYS

On a pitched roof, ridge tiles and valleys seal the junctions between the faces of the roof.

RIDGE TILES

The curved tiles that run along the top of a tile or slate roof are mortared into place. With age and weathering, one or two may have become loose.

To replace ridge tiles, you need a roof ladder with hooks that fit over the ridge and wheels that allow you to run it up the roof from the top of a conventional ladder.

Once you have reached the ridge, remove the loose tiles, then use a small trowel to scrape away crumbling mortar until you reach sound mortar. Dampen the tiles and trowel on a bed of fresh mortar. Place each ridge tile gently into position, tapping it down with the handle of the trowel. Add mortar to the ends of each ridge tile to fill the joints with its neighbours.

VALLEYS

If you have a dual-pitch roof – different parts of the roof pointing in different directions – there will be a lead-lined valley between them to allow rainwater to escape and provide a junction between the tiles.

A severely damaged roof valley will need to be replaced completely – a job for professionals. But simple cracks can be repaired with self-adhesive flashing tape. Once the area around the crack has been cleaned, the tape is applied and rolled out flat using a seam roller.

REPLACING RIDGE TILES

1 If a ridge tile is loose, carefully lever it free and place it safely to one side. Clean away debris and apply a fresh bed of mortar.

REPAIRING VALLEYS

1 Clear out any leaves and debris from a leaking roof valley using a stiff brush. Wash off the lead and allow to dry completely.

2 Soak the old (or replacement) ridge tile in water, then place it in position, pushing it firmly down into the mortar.

3 With the ridge tile firmly in place and level with its neighbours, fill the joints with mortar and trowel them off to a neat finish.

2 Roll out self-adhesive flashing tape to repair the roof valley. In some cases, you may need to apply a special primer first.

ABOVE: Lead flashing is used to seal between a pitched roof and a parapet wall. It should be secured in a mortar joint.

REPAIRING FELTED FLAT ROOFS

Unless expensive materials have been used, the average life of a felted flat roof is about 10 to 15 years. If a felted flat roof fails, it is not worth trying to repair it and you should re-cover it. However, there are things you can do to repair minor faults and to extend the roof's life.

REPAIRING CRACKS AND BLISTERS

You will need bituminous mastic (caulking) to repair a crack or blister in a felted flat roof. Although quite messy, the job is straightforward.

First remove any loose chippings from around the damaged area with a brush. Using a hot-air gun, soften the felt first if necessary, and brush or scrape away dirt, moss and any other debris. With a crack or split in the roofing felt, pull back the edges; with a blister, make a cross-shaped pattern of cuts in the centre of the blister and peel back the four sections. If any seams are lifting, clean the area below them.

When the underlying surface has dried out, apply mastic to the exposed area and press down the edges of the crack, blister or lifted seam, using a wallpaper seam roller. If a crack cannot be closed up, use polyester reinforcing tape or flashing tape to strengthen the repair.

Some emergency roof repair compounds can be used to seal a leaking roof even if it is wet or under water. Instant repair aerosols can be used on damp roofs; check the manufacturer's instructions.

PATCHING A BLISTER

1 When tackling a damaged flat roof, brush all solar-reflective chippings, and dirt and debris away from the area to be repaired. This will show the extent of the damage.

SOLAR SEAL

A solar-reflective roof seal will absorb less heat and will remain more flexible, preventing the formation of blisters.

2 If necessary, use a hot-air gun to soften the damaged roofing felt before lifting the edges with a scraper. Clean the area beneath the damage and allow to dry out.

3 If the roofing felt has formed a blister, cut a cross shape in it with a sharp knife. Carefully fold back the triangular flaps of felt to expose the structure below.

4 When the damaged area is dry, apply the repair mastic (caulking) with a small brush, working it under the flaps of felt. Be generous to ensure a waterproof seal.

5 Self-adhesive flashing tape can be applied to cover up a crack that will not close up. Make sure it is pressed down firmly, particularly around the edges.

REPROOFING FELTED FLAT ROOFS

If a felted flat roof has several cracks or blisters, or is in bad condition generally, it is possible to waterproof it with either a bituminous emulsion or a longer-lasting elastomeric liquid rubber.

The whole roof should be swept clean before treating the surface with fungicide to kill any mould. Carry out any local repairs, then apply emulsion or liquid rubber.

Some bituminous emulsions require a priming coat before applying the main coat; all liquid rubber compounds are one-coat treatments.

When the emulsion or liquid rubber has dried, reapply stone chippings. Use new chippings if the old ones are dirty or have lost their shine – their purpose on a flat roof is to keep it cool by reflecting sunlight.

1 Sweep the whole roof clear and treat the surface with fungicide. Slit open blisters, allow the interior to dry and stick the flaps down with a layer of mastic (caulking).

2 Apply liquid rubber compound over the entire roof surface, spreading it evenly with a soft brush or broom.

3 Clean up splashes before they dry, and re-cover the roof with a good layer of loose stone chippings once the rubber compound has dried.

REPAIRING ROOF JUNCTIONS

The junction between a flat roof and the house wall is particularly prone to damage, allowing water to seep through. The correct way to seal this joint is with lead flashing, inserted into one of the mortar courses of the wall.

If a mortar fillet has been used to seal the junction, or if lead flashing has split, the simplest way to effect a repair is with self-adhesive flashing tape.

Clean the surfaces that are to be covered and apply any necessary primer before removing the backing paper and pressing down the flashing tape, first with your fingers, then a seam roller. Wear heavy gloves when doing this. The tape can be cut with scissors if required. Make good the mortar joints where any lead flashing meets the house wall, using fresh mortar.

1 You can use self-adhesive flashing tape to seal porous felt or metal flashings. In some cases, you may need to brush on a coat of special primer first.

2 Unroll the flashing tape, peel off the release paper and press the tape into position. Try to keep it as smooth and straight as possible.

3 Run a wallpaper seam roller firmly along both edges of the flashing tape to ensure that it bonds well.

PAINTING PIPES AND GUTTERS

New plastic pipes and gutters do not generally need to be painted. Older systems may be discoloured, however, in which case a coat of paint will rejuvenate them.

Clear away any rubbish that has built up and pour one or two buckets of water into the gutter to clean the system. Modern plastic gutters should require little additional preparation, but older cast-iron systems are prone to rusting, which can leave ugly deposits on brickwork and render. Remove the rust with a wire brush, clean the surface with turpentine, then lightly sand and remove all dust. Metal pipes and gutters should be primed, then a suitable undercoat and top coat applied. Begin at the top of the work area and work downward.

If the pipework and guttering have an existing bituminous paint finish, you will need to apply an aluminium primer before over-painting to prevent the old finish from bleeding through. When it comes to repainting the walls, any rust stains should be treated with a metal primer, otherwise they will show through the new finish. When the primer has dried, apply your decorative finish.

PAINTING PIPES

1 Start painting pipework from the top and work downward. This will prevent any dust or dirt you may disturb from dropping on to the newly painted surface and spoiling it.

2 Use card to protect the wall behind when painting downpipes. This will also prevent the brush from picking up bits of dust from the wall, which would mar the finish.

PAINTING BARGEBOARDS

A wealth of products has been developed for painting exterior woodwork. Never try to economize by using interior gloss paints outside; they will not cope with temperature extremes and will soon flake and split. Do not be afraid to experiment with bright colours on woodwork, but choose a finish that complements, rather than clashes with, other houses in the neighbourhood.

Choose a dry, calm day to paint and avoid working in direct sunlight, as the glare will prevent you from obtaining good, even coverage. Furthermore, if you are using a water-based (latex) paint, it will dry too rapidly, leaving hard edges.

Start by priming any bare areas, then apply an undercoat and finally one or two coats of gloss. With a standard gloss paint, begin by applying the paint vertically, and then use sideways strokes to blend it well. Work in the direction of the grain, blending in the wet edges for a uniform finish. If you are using a one-coat paint, apply the finish quite thickly in close, parallel strips and do not over-brush, as this will leave noticeable marks.

LEFT: Paint bargeboards early on in your work schedule. By starting from the top and working down you ensure that any dislodged dirt or paint droplets only fall on unpainted surfaces.

REPAIRING FENCES & WALLS

Making sure the fences and walls around your property are kept in good condition is essential. Not only do they provide a physical marker of the boundary, but also they prevent your children or pets from straying, ensure privacy and help keep out the uninvited. Most fences are made completely of wood, which can suffer considerably when exposed to the elements. A regular programme of maintenance and repair is essential if a wooden fence is to do its job properly. Even a masonry wall can deteriorate through the effects of weathering: bricks and mortar joints can crumble, while ground movement can lead to serious damage.

ERECTING PANEL FENCES

One of the most popular choices for marking boundaries, fences offer instant privacy and security. They are less expensive to construct than walls and need less maintenance than hedges.

DESIGNING WITH FENCES

There is a huge selection of fencing styles in a range of different materials, including various woods, metals and plastic, so you should have no problem finding a style that will enhance your garden. In the front garden, fences with a more open structure are often used. Examples include picket or post-and-rail fences, ranch-style fences and post-and-chain fences. They do not provide privacy or much security, but they are an attractive way of marking the boundary.

In most back gardens, a boundary fence should recede from view, so choose something robust enough to support climbers and wall shrubs that will help disguise it. However, in certain circumstances you might want to make a feature of a fence. Painting with a wood stain used elsewhere in the garden or to co-ordinate with a planting scheme will emphasize its presence.

PLANNING PERMISSION

Check with your local planning (zoning) authority before erecting a new wall or fence. Normally, you require planning consent for any fence more than 1.8m (6ft) high and for a fence more than 1m (3ft) high that abuts a highway.

1 Post spikes are an easier option than excavating holes and concreting posts in position. Use a special tool to protect the spike top, then drive it in with a sledge-hammer. Check with a spirit (carpenter's) level to ensure it is vertical.

4 Lift the panel into place, supporting its free end with a scrap of wood, and fix it in position by driving galvanized nails through the holes in the brackets. Insert the post at the other end, add more clips and nail the panel to it.

2 Insert the post in the spike, checking that it is vertical again, then lay the panel in position on the ground and mark the position of the next post. Drive in the next spike so that it abuts the panel, testing for the vertical again.

3 There are various ways to fix the panels to the posts, but panel brackets are the simplest. Simply nail a pair of these galvanized U-shaped brackets to each post, either aligning them with one edge or the centre.

5 Always check that each panel is level before making the final fixings, using a spirit level. Check too that the tops of the panels are in line, unless you are working on a sloping site and are stepping them.

6 Finish off by nailing a cap to the top of each post. This will keep water out of the end grain of the timber and extend its life. Wooden and plastic caps are available, some incorporating decorative finials.

REPAIRING FENCE POSTS

A fence relies on its posts to provide much of its strength and to keep it upright – but because the posts are set in the ground and can get wet, they are prone to rotting, leading to the collapse of the fence.

The most vulnerable part of a fence post is the portion underground. Either this will be completely rotten, making the post unstable, or the post will have snapped off at ground level. In both cases, there are ways to effect a repair using the remaining sound piece of post.

If the fence post is still standing or is attached to a closeboard fence – overlapping vertical boards nailed to triangular-section horizontal (arris) rails – the best way to repair it is with a fence-post spur. This is a short concrete post that you set into the ground next to the broken post. Then you bolt the two together. Start by digging a hole roughly 30cm (1ft) square and 50cm (20in) deep in front of the broken post, that is on your side of the fence; you may need a long cold chisel and a club (spalling) hammer if you encounter concrete.

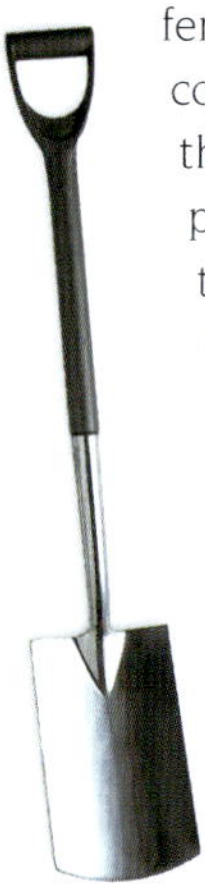

Place the spur in the hole so that it lines up with the post, then insert coach bolts in the holes in the spur, giving them a tap with a hammer to transfer their positions to the post. Drill holes in the post to take the bolts. Secure the spur to the fence post with the coach bolts and fill the hole around it, first with a layer of hardcore (rubble), ramming it down well so that there are no voids, then with a concrete collar. Trowel this off neatly. If necessary, prop the main post upright while the concrete sets.

With a panel fence, release the adjacent panels from the post and saw through it at ground level. Then hammer a repair spike – a shorter version of the normal fence-post spike – over the rotten wood in the ground. Fit the sound portion of the post into the socket of the spike and secure it with galvanized nails or rustproof screws. Finally, refit the fence panels to the posts.

POST LEVELS

A post level is a useful tool that can be strapped to a fence post to ensure that it is vertical in both directions when it is being installed.

FITTING A FENCE SPUR

1 With the fence still standing, dig a large hole – around 30cm (1ft) square – alongside the damaged post. Dig the hole to a depth of about 50cm (20in).

2 Place the concrete fence spur in the hole, setting it up against the post so that you can mark the positions of the coach-bolt holes ready for drilling.

3 Drill the holes in the damaged fence post, insert the coach bolts from the other side and secure the spur. Fit washers and nuts, and tighten the bolts with a spanner (wrench).

4 Fill the large hole first with hardcore (rubble) and then with concrete. Smooth down the surface and leave to set completely, supporting the post temporarily while it does so.

FITTING A REPAIR SPIKE

1 Remove the fence panels on each side of the damaged post. Then use a large saw, such as a bow saw or cross-cut saw, to cut off the post stump at ground level.

2 Position the repair spike carefully so that it is aligned with the remains of the old post. Using the spike driver and a sledgehammer, hammer in the repair spike over the rotten post.

3 Insert the end of the new post into the spike socket, check that it is upright and secure it with galvanized nails or rustproof screws. Replace the fence panels.

POST SPIKES

Four different types of post spike. From the left: a normal post spike for new posts; a repair spike for rotten posts; a spike for mounting in fresh concrete; a spike for bolting down to a hard surface.

REPLACING FENCE PANELS

A panel fence has posts regularly spaced at 1.83m (6ft) intervals. The panels come in a variety of designs – interwoven, overlapping and imitation closeboard are the most popular. They are all fixed between the posts in the same way: with either U-shaped metal clips or nails holding the panels to the posts.

If clips have been used, replacing a broken panel with a new one will be easy, since the panel is usually secured to the clips with screws. If the panel has been nailed in place, you may destroy it as you lever it out.

The new fence panel should fit exactly between the posts and can be secured in the same way. If the new panel is a tight fit at any point, use a planer-file or rasp to trim it; if it is loose, trim a section of the timber from the old panel to fill the gap.

1 To remove a fencing panel, start by levering out the nails holding it in place.

2 You may need to use a crowbar (wrecking bar) to lever out the panel.

3 If using clips to secure the new fence panel, nail these in place before sliding the panel through.

4 If using nails, drive them through the end section of the panel into the supporting post.

REPAIRING CLOSEBOARD FENCES

Timber fences are constantly exposed to the effects of rain, sun and wind. Sooner or later, parts of a fence will rot, split, break or simply fall off. Regular treatment with preservative or stain will prolong the life of a fence, but when repairs are necessary, do not delay, otherwise the fence will no longer do its job.

CLOSEBOARD FENCES

A closeboard fence consists of two or three horizontal triangular (arris) rails fitted between posts and supporting overlapping vertical lengths of tapered (feather edge) boarding (pales). The result is an extremely durable and strong fence. Even so, arris rails can split and sag, while individual boards can become damaged.

A horizontal gravel board will run along the bottom of the fence to protect the end grain of the vertical boards from ground moisture. Normally, this is easy to replace, as it is held with just a couple of nails or screws.

Usually, a single broken board can be levered off with a claw hammer and the nails securing it prised out. If they will not budge, hammer them into the arris rail with a nail punch. Cut the replacement board to the same length and slide its thin edge under the thick edge of the adjacent board, having levered this clear of the arris rails slightly and removed the nails from it. Then nail through both boards – each nail holds two boards. If you are replacing several boards, use a short piece of wood as a gauge to ensure even overlapping.

Make sure you treat the end grain at the foot of any new boards with preservative before they are nailed in place, as this will be very difficult to do once they are in position. You may want to treat the overlapping edges of the boards, too, as you won't be able to reach these either. Finish the job when the boards have been fitted.

Ideally, a closeboard fence should have capping strips nailed along the top to protect the end grain at the top of the boards from the weather. This is worth doing if your existing fence does not have them. Make sure the posts have caps that will shed water, too.

REPAIRING ARRIS RAILS

If an arris rail has split in the middle, you can buy a galvanized repair bracket that simply fits over the rail and is screwed or nailed in place. If necessary, have a helper lever the fence up, using a crowbar (wrecking bar) over a block of wood, while you fit the repair bracket.

A repair bracket that is similar, but with a flanged end, is available for reconnecting an arris rail that has broken where it is fixed to the fence post. This is screwed or nailed to both the rail and the post. You can use two of these brackets to replace a complete length of arris rail after sawing through the old rail at the ends and levering it from the fence.

REPAIRING CLOSEBOARD FENCING

1 Use an old chisel to lever out a damaged board in a closeboard fence. Prise out any nails that pull through the board, or drive them down into the arris rails.

2 Slide the replacement board into place, fitting its narrow edge beneath the adjacent board. Make sure the overlap is even, then nail the board to the horizontal arris rails.

3 You can reinforce a broken arris rail by nailing a galvanized steel repair bracket over the broken section. Use galvanized nails, as these will resist rusting.

4 Arris rails are tapered at their ends to fit slots cut in the posts, but this can weaken a rail. If an end breaks, nail a flanged galvanized repair bracket between the rail and the post.

REPAIRING GATES

If a wooden gate is sagging and dragging on the ground, check first that the posts are upright, using a level and paying particular attention to the hinged side. If a post has rotted, replace it with a new one.

If it is leaning slightly, it may be possible to force it back, with the gate removed, and ram some hardcore (rubble) or more concrete into the ground to hold it in place.

Wooden gates may also sag if the joints have become loose. You can fit a variety of metal brackets to support the framework of a wooden gate: flat L-shaped or T-shaped brackets at the corners where the vertical stiles meet the cross-rails or the diagonal brace, a right-angled bracket on the inside of the frame between stile and cross-rail, and straight flat brackets to repair simple splits. All will look better if they are recessed into the wood. Alternatively, you could try replacing the main diagonal support brace or fitting longer hinges.

REPAIRING METAL GATES

First, check that the posts are vertical, then that you can move the adjusting nuts – often these will be rusted or clogged with paint. If this is the case, wire brush off the worst of the rust and paint, and apply a silicone spray or penetrating oil until you can turn the nuts freely. Finally, adjust the hinges so that the gate no longer rubs on the ground and swings freely, but closes properly.

REPAIRING A SAGGING GATE

ABOVE: Fit a replacement diagonal brace to support a wooden gate.

ABOVE: Using longer hinges is one way to secure a sagging wooden gate.

REPAIRING GARDEN WALLS

A common problem with garden walls is that bricks suffer from spalling, that is the surface breaks up. This results from water getting into the brick and expanding as it freezes.

Depending on how well the wall has been built, it may be possible to remove the damaged brick and turn it around, using a masonry drill and a thin-bladed plugging chisel to remove the mortar from the joints. However, it is likely that mortar on the back of the brick will prevent its removal. Therefore, the only solution will be to break it up with a bolster (stonecutter s) chisel and club (spalling) hammer, then insert a new brick. Remove all the old mortar from the hole, then lay a bed of fresh mortar on the bottom of the hole. Add mortar to the top and sides of the new brick and push it into place, forcing more mortar into the gaps. Finally, finish off the joints to the same profile as the remainder of the wall.

A garden wall can crack along mortar lines, and this often indicates a problem with the foundations. There is little alternative to demolishing at least the split section, investigating the problem and making good the foundations before rebuilding it.

REMOVING A DAMAGED BRICK

1 Remove the mortar around the old brick by drilling and chiselling it out.

2 Insert a new mortared brick, pushing it in until it is flush with its neighbours.

3 Repoint the mortar around the replaced brick to the correct profile.

BUILDING BRICK WALLS

Although walls are mainly thought of as structures to provide security and privacy along the boundary, they are also useful within a garden for building terracing on a sloping plot as well as a range of other features, including raised beds, barbecues, garden screens, seats and plinths for containers and ornaments.

RETAINING WALLS

Solid retaining walls are made from bricks or blocks mortared together. The wall will have to be strong enough to hold back the weight of the soil behind it. For this reason, always use the double-brick construction method, but this time lay the foundations and build the wall so that it slopes back slightly. Leave weep-holes (vertical joints free of mortar) every metre (yard) or so along the base of the wall to allow water to drain out from the soil. Pack in rubble behind the weep-holes and cover with coarse gravel to prevent soil washing out and to stop the weep-holes from becoming blocked with soil.

Dry-stone walls also make good retaining walls up to 1m (3ft) high. Again, the wall needs to be built so that it leans back slightly. The blocks should be selected so that they interlock as much as possible, leaving few gaps. Pack rubble behind the wall as you go to help secure each layer. Large crevices can be filled with suitable plants.

Retaining walls provide an excellent opportunity to experiment with climbers and wall shrubs.

1 All walls require a footing. For a low wall this is one brick wide; for larger, thicker walls the dimensions are increased. Dig a trench 30cm (12in) deep and put 13cm (5in) of rammed hardcore (rubble) in the bottom. Drive pegs in so that the tops are at the final height of the foundation. Use a spirit (carpenter's) level to check they are level.

4 For subsequent courses, lay a ribbon of mortar on top of the previous row, then "butter" one end of the brick to be laid.

2 To form the foundations, fill the trench with a concrete mix of 2 parts cement, 5 parts sharp sand and 7 parts 2cm (¾in) aggregate, and level it off with the top of the pegs. Use a straight-edged board to tamp the concrete down and remove any air pockets. Leave the concrete foundation to harden for a few days.

3 Lay the bricks on a bed of mortar, adding a wedge of mortar at one end of each brick as you lay them for the vertical joints. For a single brick wall with supporting piers, the piers should be positioned at each end and at 1.8–2.4m (6–8ft) intervals, and can be made by laying two bricks crossways.

5 Tap level, checking constantly with a spirit level to make sure that the wall remains level and vertical as it grows.

6 The top of the wall is best finished off with a coping of suitable bricks or with special coping stones sold for the purpose.

REPOINTING BRICKWORK

Failed mortar joints between bricks are not only unsightly, but they also allow water into the wall, damaging the bricks when it freezes. The solution is to repoint the joints with fresh mortar.

First, use a thin-bladed plugging chisel to remove all the loose mortar until you reach sound material. Brush all the dust from the joints and dampen them with a paintbrush dipped in water or a hand-held garden sprayer.

Use a pointing trowel to push fresh mortar into the joints, working on the verticals first, then the horizontals. To do this, put a batch of mortar on a hawk – a flat metal plate or wooden board on a handle – then hold this against the wall directly beneath the joint you want to fill. Use the pointing trowel to slice off a thin strip of mortar and press it into the joint.

When you have used one batch of mortar, go back over all the joints, shaping the surface of the mortar to the required profile:

- Weatherstruck – using the edge of the pointing trowel to create a sloping profile that sheds rainwater from the wall. Start with the vertical joints and slope them all in the same direction.
- Recessed – using a square-shaped stick, or special tool.
- Flush – using sacking to rub the surface and expose the sand aggregate in the mortar.
- Concave (or rubbed) – using a rounded stick or a piece of hosepipe to make the profile.

A weatherstruck profile is often used on house walls for its rain-shedding properties, while recessed joints are only appropriate to wall surfaces inside. A concave profile is a good choice for garden walls.

ABOVE: The causes of cracked pointing should be investigated immediately and repaired. In some cases, it may be an indicator of serious problems with the foundations of the wall.

TIPS

- The secret of good repointing is to keep the mortar off the face of the brickwork. Take great care when forcing mortar into the joints, removing any excess immediately before it dries; clean off small splashes with a stiff brush.
- Let the joints harden a little before you give them a profile.
- Clean all bricklaying tools immediately after use with clean water. They will be much more difficult to clean if the mortar is allowed to dry.

1 Use a thin-bladed plugging chisel, or a small cold chisel, with a club (spalling) hammer to chop out all the loose mortar from the joints. Take care not to damage the edges of the bricks.

2 Brush any dust and debris from the joints and dampen the existing mortar with water. This will prevent the new mortar from drying too quickly, which would weaken it.

3 Load the hawk with a small amount of mortar and hold it tightly against the wall. Push narrow strips of mortar into the joints using a small pointing trowel.

4 Allow the mortar to "go off" slightly, then shape the pointing to the profile you want; in this case a concave profile is being obtained with a length of hosepipe.

FIXING TRELLISES TO WALLS

Climbing and rambling plants can provide an interesting vertical element to the garden and are useful for disguising or concealing less attractive features. There are many different types to choose from, and lots of them produce beautiful, often fragrant, blooms; others are evergreen, offering year-round pleasure.

When choosing a support for a climbing plant, it is important to take into consideration the method by which it climbs. Some climbers, such as ivy, can be grown on a bare brick wall, but most will need a trellis to support them as they grow. For example, climbers such as climbing and rambler roses are not self-clinging and need to be tied in to their supports.

1 The trellis should be sturdy and in good condition. Ensure it has been treated with wood preservative. Take the trellis panel to the wall and mark its position. The bottom of the trellis should be about 30cm (12in) from the ground. Drill holes for fixing the spacers and insert plastic or wooden plugs.

2 Drill matching holes in a wooden batten and secure it to the wall, checking with a spirit (carpenter's) level that it is horizontal. Use wood that will hold the trellis at least 2.5cm (1in) from the wall. Fix another batten at the base, and one halfway up for trellis more than 1.2m (4ft) high.

3 Drill and screw the trellis to the battens, first fixing the top and then working downwards. Check that the trellis is straight using a spirit level. The finished trellis should be secure, so that the weight of the climber and any wind that blows on it will not pull it away from its fixings.

WIRES TO SUPPORT CLIMBERS

Where plants are to be trained up walls or solid fences, stretching horizontal wires across the surface can provide an effective means of supporting them, particularly if they need to be tied in to the supports. On a fence, the wires can be secured with galvanized staples driven into the posts, provided the plant is not a vigorous grower likely to produce heavy stems, which might pull them out.

To support trees against walls, use wires held by vine eyes. Depending on the type of vine eye, either knock them into the wall or drill and plug before screwing them in. Pass heavy-duty galvanized wire through the holes in the eyes and fasten to the end ones, keeping the wire as tight as possible.

1 Drill holes in the wall and insert vine eyes to support the wires. If you use vine eyes with a screw fixing, insert wall plugs first. Vine eyes are available in several lengths, the long ones being necessary for vigorous climbers, such as wisteria, that need wires further from the wall.

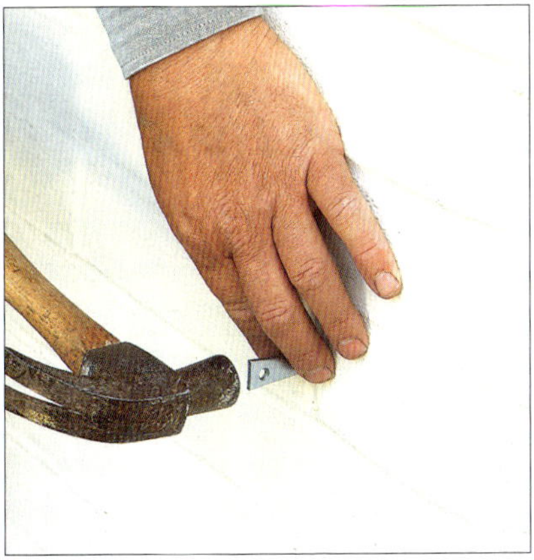

2 The simplest vine eyes are wedge-shaped. Hammer them at 2m (6ft) intervals, or closer for heavy climbers, directly into the mortar. Although wedge-shaped eyes are suitable for brick and stone walls, the screw type are better for wooden fences and posts.

3 Thread a length of galvanized wire through the hole in the first vine eye and wrap it around itself to form a firm fixing. Thread the other end of the wire through the intermediate eyes, then fasten the wire around the end eye, keeping it as taut as possible.

PAINTING EXTERIOR WALLS

The best time to tackle exterior decorating is in early summer or autumn, when the weather is fine, but not too hot. Remember that this work will be on a much larger scale than an interior decorating project, so allow plenty of time to complete it. You may have to spread it over several weekends or perhaps take a week or two off work.

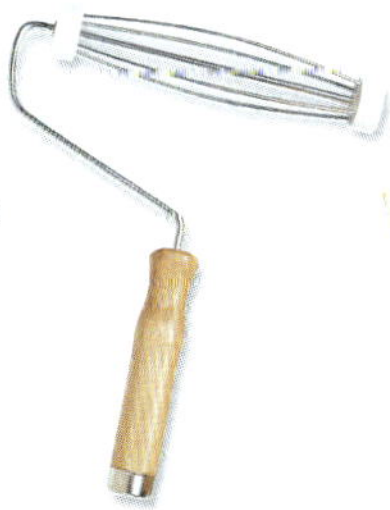

There is a wide range of paints available for painting exterior walls. Choose from cement paints, supplied as a dry powder for mixing with water, rough- and smooth-textured masonry paints, exterior-grade emulsion (latex) paints and exterior-grade oil-based paints for weatherboarding (siding). Masonry paints can typically be used straight from the can, but if you are painting a porous surface with a water-based product, it is advisable to dilute the first coat. Use a ratio of four parts paint to one part water.

Exterior paints come in a wide choice of colours, but exercise caution with some of the more flamboyant shades. White, cream, yellow, blue, green, soft pink and terracotta finishes, which are easy on the eye and blend into the background, are generally favoured by house buyers.

ABOVE: A typical example of pebbledash rendering. A coat of masonry paint can greatly improve its appearance. Use a brush with long bristles to get into all the cavities.

ABOVE: Avoid painting brickwork, if possible. Simply protect the face of the wall with a clear waterproofer. This will seal the surface and prevent water penetration.

PAINTING TECHNIQUES

ABOVE: Apply smooth masonry paint using a brush with coarse bristles.

ABOVE: You should apply textured masonry paint in the same way.

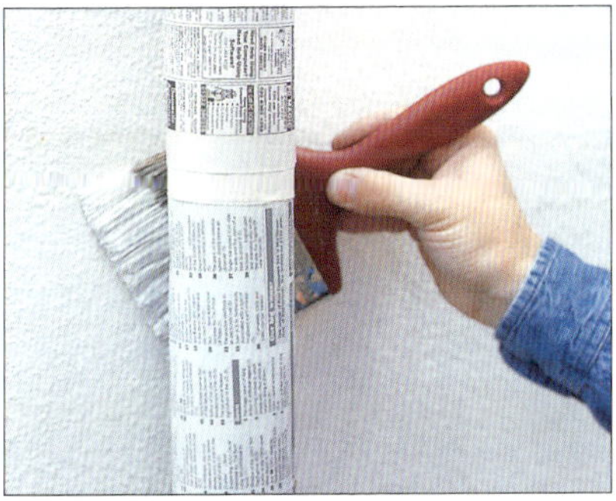

ABOVE: To protect downpipes from paint splashes, tape newspaper around them.

ABOVE: Use a banister brush to paint coarse exterior wall finishes such as pebbledash.

ABOVE: Choose a deep-pile roller for coarse surfaces and a medium one for others.

ABOVE: For speed, use a spray gun. Mask off surfaces you do not want painting.

PAINTING EXTERIOR WOODWORK

Exterior painted woodwork includes features such as fascias, soffits and bargeboards, as well as entire surfaces such as weatherboarding (siding). New woodwork should be sanded lightly, working with the grain. Remove any dust, then wipe with a cloth moistened with white spirit (paint thinner). Seal any knots with knotting solution (shellac), and fill holes or cracks. Existing paintwork should be washed down with a solution of sugar soap (all-purpose cleaner) and water, sanded and wiped off with a cloth moistened in white spirit. Scrape off flaking paint; any bare areas should be primed and undercoated in the normal way.

WINDOWS AND DOORS

Exterior windows and doors can be treated in much the same manner as other outdoor wood. Start by filling and

PAINTING A DOOR

1 Remove flaking paintwork, then smooth the surface with a palm sander.

2 Apply a suitable primer and allow to dry completely before over-painting.

3 Apply one or two undercoats and lightly rub down with abrasive paper between coats.

4 Apply topcoat to mouldings and panelled areas first, then move on to cross rails.

sanding any cracks or holes in the wood. Bare wood should be primed and undercoated, while old or defective paintwork will need sanding before over-painting. If the existing paintwork is badly cracked or blistered, it should be stripped off completely and a new primer, undercoat and top coat applied.

FENCES

For fences and outbuildings, there is a wide selection of exterior wood stains and paints in all shades. Many are water-based and plant-friendly, while being tough enough to withstand the rigours of quite harsh climates. Special paints and stains have also been developed for decking with a greater resistance to scuffing and cracking.

The best time to paint fencing is on a dry day in the late autumn, when many plants will have died back, making access easier. Brush off dirt and dust, and scrape soil away from the foot.

PAINTING A FENCE

ABOVE: Fences and gates can be painted in all shades of bright colours.

WEATHERBOARDS

For weatherboard (siding) surfaces, wash down with a solution of sugar soap. Leave to dry for a week. Replace any severely damaged sections and fill smaller cracks with a sealant (caulking). Punch in any protruding nails and cover with metal primer. Then prepare as for other woodwork.

PAINTING WEATHERBOARDS

1 It is easy to miss sections of weatherboarding (siding), so paint the undersides first.

2 Paint the facing boards next, and finish off with the end grain.